A TRACE OF PRIDE

CW01496370

A BIOGRAPHY OF)HAMA

横浜にて最初の
造船業者の伝記

YOKOHAMA NITE SAISHO NO ZŌSEN-GYŌSHA NO DENKI

VERONICA HOSKING

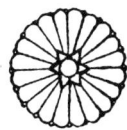

A Trace of Pride

Published by P. & A. Cutforth, Peterborough

Printed in Great Britain by
Cambs Printcentre Ltd.
Bound by Dickens

ACKNOWLEDGEMENTS

The preparation of this book, involving lengthy research into contemporary records of life in Yokohama following the opening of the treaty port in 1859, has been shared with my devoted husband, Ronald. In fact, without his help and encouragement this book would never have been written.

My grateful thanks also to Miss Hisako Ito and Mr. Takio Saito of the Yokohama Archives of History for their interest and help. Research for their Exhibition in 1988 on "Yokohama Firsts" produced additional information on Henry Cook from Japanese sources which would have been incomprehensible to us.

Japanese sub-title and calligraphy
by Kazuko Sizer.

Cover design by Ron Hosking.

A TRACE OF PRIDE

EXPLANATION

The fascinating history and social life of Japan were recorded in minute detail during the nineteenth century by diplomats, travellers, historians and other specialists in particular fields. These sources of information have been regurgitated and rearranged in hundreds of permutations by would-be historians, confident that the material can still hold the interest of readers. In general, these writers have looked at Japanese history in the round, following developments in a logical sequence, giving retrospective opinions, adding information not available at the time.

This biography deals with that history as seen and felt by Henry Cook, a man of humble origin, more concerned with survival in the early years of the Yokohama settlement. Through character and an outstanding talent, he helped to shape the history of shipbuilding in Yokohama and, as a pioneer settler, initiated many "firsts". His unusual progress from boyhood to manhood, leading to his first landing on Japanese soil with Commodore Perry's squadron at Shimoda, form an essential element of the first part of his biography.

I have written in narrative form to make the book more acceptable for readers not particularly interested in Japanese history, but have retained a high degree of accuracy according to our research and family records. Sufficient formal history has been included to place incidents into context for readers who are unfamiliar with Japan in the nineteenth century.

Initially, the main source of information about Henry Cook's life has been his granddaughter, Beatrice Mary Wright. Her mother, Beatrice Marion was Henry Cook's youngest child; she would never talk about her life in Japan and confirmed this determined silence by destroying historic documents sent to her in England during the early part of 1940. The documents were hand-written on vellum and were probably the official court records, or judge's notes, of a long legal battle involving her father, the shame of which she attempted to conceal.

Fortunately, Henry's first child, Emily, was more forthcoming and passed on many revealing aspects of her father's life to her niece, known as Mary to distinguish her from her mother; she had joined her aunt Emily in San Francisco for a period and learned a great deal about her notable grandfather. Although merely committed to memory, these details have been confirmed as remarkably accurate when compared with documentation of the time and must be given reasonable credence.

The public and consular records have been of considerable help but most information has been gleaned from the newspapers published in Yokohama for the growing number of British pioneers entering this area of Japan. "The Japan Herald", " The Japan Mail" and "The Japan Weekly Mail" contain a treasure chest of detail about the business and private life of Henry Cook, and give graphic day-by-day accounts of the dangers and difficulties experienced by him. Even so, there are many gaps in the collections of these papers both at The British Newspaper Library at Colindale and at the Japan Society in London.

When visiting Yokohama in 1988 to trace Henry Cook's grave and follow in his footsteps where possible, we were invited to meet the official researchers at The Archives of History in Yokohama (Yokohama Kaikō Shiryōkan). They had been researching his life for an exhibition of "Yokohama Firsts" and were delighted to meet a living member of his family. They were most generous in supplying documents and information that we could not otherwise have obtained. Fortunately we could reciprocate with photographs and family details unknown to them. They highly approved our intention to write this biography and have requested a copy. They have sent further documentation since our return. Their generosity will be hard to repay.

CONTENTS

CONTENTS

1
Exodus

The year was 1845 and the Irish people were suffering. The families of labourers were no strangers to privation and hardship. Regular employment was rare and unless a man could acquire a patch of land on which to grow potatoes, the family often starved. There was no Poor Law to provide outdoor relief and many people lived in dire poverty even before the disastrous failure of crops through disease.

Potato blight was the chief scourge; a fungal disease which was particularly bad in warm, humid conditions, and can be a problem even today when copper-based fungicides are available. At that time, no such treatment existed and spores washed into the soil affected crop after crop until eventually the situation became desperate. Some districts produced little food but potatoes. Wheat, oats and barley were never grown for home consumption, but only for sale as a means of paying the rent. Bread was scarcely ever seen and ovens were unknown; boiled potatoes were the staple diet of the working class.

According to the census of 1841, nearly half the families of the rural population of Ireland lived in windowless mud cabins consisting of a single room. Pigs slept with their owners, making conditions even more insanitary, and furniture was a luxury that few could afford. Those unfortunate enough to be evicted or unemployed, often put roofs over ditches or existed in hollows in bogs or river banks. Unwisely, Irish landlords hard pressed for money as a result of the economic situation, were not only applying for eviction orders against penniless tenants who owed rent, they were getting judgement orders which put the man in prison for non-payment. This left his wife and children to fend for themselves.

Typhus was accepted as inevitable at that time among the Irish people. Thousands of cases annually were treated in Dublin alone and living conditions contributed to the epidemic which escalated as a result of the potato famine. Every penny was needed to buy foodstuffs - clothes and bedding were sold. There was no money for fuel to heat water either to wash or cook food, which was mainly eaten raw. Lice were prevalent and multiplied rapidly in such filthy conditions, spreading typhus fever widely through the under-nourished population, forced to huddle together for warmth in the severe winter.

Life was intolerable and the only answer to many seemed to be emigration. Those who could afford the passage escaped to America to start a new life. For the great majority, this was out of the question but England offered an attractive alternative. The English Poor Law permitted outdoor relief in most districts and starving people were given food. The cost for a deck passage on a steamer across the Irish Channel was about five shillings, but on small coastal sailing ships it could be arranged for half that amount, although the journey took longer.

Hostility was growing in some British ports to captains bringing in Irish paupers. Liverpool was hardest hit where thousands were landed each week, but in South Wales vast numbers were arriving at Swansea, Cardiff and Newport, stretching the resources of those areas to breaking point.

The large export trade of coal from Cardiff to Cork enabled vessels to carry passengers for nothing at all. Normally, lime or shingle had to be carried as ballast for the return journey but this 'living ballast' was cheaper and mobile. This encouraged a vast influx of Irish immigrants from Cork and Waterford to ports in South Wales where there existed many small harbours frequently visited by trading vessels.

My family at this time was living near Waterford in the county of Kilkenny. As they were not totally dependent on potatoes for the bulk of their food, they were in a more fortunate position than many of the Irish peasants. William Carrol, their father, was engaged in shipping coal from South Wales to Waterford and knew intimately the coastline between Cardiff and Newport. Although not affected directly by the failure of the potato crop, the spread of disease and general atmosphere of panic among the community made him decide to uproot his family, soon to have another addition, and take them aboard on his next trip to South Wales.

His eldest daughter, aged nineteen, was already in service in a prosperous household in Kilkenny, but William decided that the other five children should go with their parents. Bridget was thirteen and helped with the children; Jeremiah, who was nine, had not long been apprenticed to a shipwright in Waterford. The other children were much younger; the twins were three and there was a toddler of two. Fears for their health and that of his wife, Julia, had finally decided the issue.

10

It was a cold, miserable, January evening when the little sailing coaster nosed into a small harbour a few miles west of Cardiff. The hold was crammed with Irish refugees, some were friends and neighbours of the Carrols who had begged a free passage. All were suffering from exhaustion and malnutrition and some from fever. Word had reached the captain that Newport was refusing to accept any more destitute Irish, so he decided to disembark small groups of passengers at intervals along the coast. There were many small villages inland where it was hoped that work or help might be found.

William Carrol himself knew the docks and shipyard area at Newport well and had friends living nearby, so he hoped to find temporary accommodation for his family there while he carried on his coal-shipping business. His family had been quartered in his cabin and an adjoining one, rather a squeeze but in comparative comfort considering the state of the other passengers.

It was morning before all the others had been quietly smuggled ashore. Most of the children aboard had been asleep and this had made it safer to slip into secret harbours undetected.

The wind had abated during the night and dawn brought a rosy glow which suffused the shore, showing the distant Black Mountains just visible on the horizon. Only William Carrol's family and the crew remained on board as he expertly steered the vessel north-eastwards into the estuary of the River Usk leading to Newport docks. The air was fresh and crisp and the golden light augured well for the future and their new venture.

2
NEWPORT - A New Home.

The comforting golden glow, softening their arrival on that bitterly cold morning, shone on the lucky and unlucky alike. A typical Irish family, the Carrols leaned instinctively on their Catholic faith to the limits of their understanding. Prayer, sometimes spoken, more often just breathed, sustained their mother, Julia, while William went ashore to find somewhere for them to stay. The children, awake now, roamed around the ship with a noisy indifference denying responsibilities. Bridget kept an eye on the twins Ann and Anthony, but mother hugged little Sarah to herself. In a strange, irrational, mystic way she willed that the soft warm pressure of Sarah would comfort the restless unborn infant within her. With a trusting confidence, underlaid with suppressed panic, she waited, and waited.

After some hours, William returned looking rather pleased with himself and hailed them with a piercing whistle from the dockside. The shipping company who employed him owned a terrace of tightly packed, narrow-fronted cottages along Commercial Wharf. The manager was willing to let them move into number sixteen at a reasonable rent. William had talked over this possibility with his supervisor before bringing his family to Newport, but dared say nothing before certainty. Unashamed relief was expressed in prayers of honest tears. A new life could begin.

Commercial Wharf led into Dock Parade and together they followed the curve of the waterfront. Some essential pieces of furniture still remained in No.16 but a few extras had to be found. Luckily, William had crammed as many of their simple but treasured possessions into his cabin as space would permit. The rooms were small and some astute organisation was needed to avoid overcrowding. It was sad, but at present very necessary, that their first-born, nineteen year old Ann, had remained behind in Kilkenny. Perhaps she could find suitable work in Wales in the not too distant future and be close to her family once again.

Rather unexpectedly, the new situation was not so very different from their old home in Ireland. At least they had escaped the fear of typhus and the distressing sight of hapless poverty suffered in the surrounding areas. There were just thirty-eight cottages along Commercial Wharf and many of the resident families lived in circumstances similar to the Carrols, with father often away at sea and mother left to manage the house, the children and all their individual needs and problems. Shipping coal kept William away from his family for short voyages only but they were frequent. The coal depot for storage and distribution was conveniently located round a bend in the road behind Dock Parade, where houses continued the number sequence from 39 to 102.

Julia was anxious to settle the children into a regular routine as quickly as possible before the birth of her seventh child, expected towards the end of April. Bridget, although only thirteen, was the eldest daughter at home and was expected to help her mother run the house with marriage being the only means of escape unless some suitable employment could be found. Deprived of opportunities for schooling, she was still unable to write and could not even sign her name.

At nine and a half years of age, Jeremiah presented more of a problem. He had the good fortune, while at Waterford, to attend a small school for a few years and could boast some basic education. On reaching the age of nine he was apprenticed for training as shipwright and carpenter to a skilled tradesman who was friendly with his father. After only a few months of feeling very much a man of the world, he was forced to leave to come to Newport. His father was anxious about Jeremiah's break in training and, before going to sea again, he arranged a hurried apprenticeship agreement with a firm operating near the dry docks about half a mile from Dock Parade. They specialised in all aspects of ship repairs and had a good reputation for small boat construction. Timber was still the chief constructional material and was ideal for trainees to learn about engineering strengths and weaknesses, and to exercise visual judgements when shaping with hand tools.

The prospects were good but from the first day Jeremiah was not happy there. After the friendly, even affectionate relationships in the Waterford shipyard, this new regime was tough. The men worked him hard, making use of him rather than intending to teach. Fortunately, he was an intelligent boy and had a natural aptitude for absorbing practical detail, so time was not wasted. After a few weeks he confided his boyish misery to his sister, Bridget, and felt better having halved the load. They always got on well together and enjoyed sharing secrets.

Mother held the ultimate secret; would they have a brother or a sister? Her pregnancy had progressed normally according to her fairly regular experience. Several of her new neighbours had promised to help and they contacted the nurse, who was kept busy looking after each of them in turn supervising the births at home. On the 27th April 1845, Julia gave birth to a baby boy. Her husband had recently returned from a voyage; he was delighted and felt that this was the time to indulge the traditional desire of a father to have a son bearing his own name. So, regardless of any future confusion in identity, the Carrol family had another William. After some persuasion he agreed to include a second name of "Henry" after an uncle - a link with Julia's family of McDonnells in Buckie in northern Scotland. In accordance with their Catholic background, arrangements were made for an early baptism. The only Catholic church in Newport, apart from the small one in St. Woollas's cemetery, was St. Mary's, about one mile from home towards the centre of the town. On the 4th May William was baptised and registered in that parish. A good friend, Mary Murray, was godmother and Cornelius Collins stood as godfather.

Life continued much as before, although Bridget had to take on more of the work and responsibility; available space in the house was considerably reduced. Jeremiah had to come to terms with the unfriendly atmosphere at work and this positive attitude matured him rapidly. The foreman began to trust him with many little jobs requiring skill and a degree of judgement. Inevitably this aroused some jealousy among one or two of the older workmen and some of the less able boys. On a few cherished occasions the foreman gave Jeremiah permission to join his father on short coastal trips. William noticed how quickly his son adapted to the language and routine of ship life and, under supervision, could take over at the wheel quite unselfconsciously.

The pattern of events changed but little, as did the relationship of Julia with her husband. On the 29th October 1848 they further decreased the living space at No.16 by increasing the family size with their eighth child, another boy. He was baptised "Henry" at St. Mary's on the 9th November and this time Bridget was allowed to be godmother. By then she was fully sixteen, very practised in motherly skills, and with a sincere natural faith. The godfather was Timothy, husband of Mary Murray who was godmother to William. The twins, Anthony and Ann, had for the past year been going to a small school not far from the church. Sarah was rather young but the headmistress agreed to find room for her next to her brother and sister. This brought some welcome relief for Bridget and her mother.

One afternoon, towards the end of 1851, a well-dressed man called at the house, it seemed without any warning. He had already called at numbers 1 to 15 along the Wharf and had a piece of paper to show the visit was official. He said he was taking details for the first national census to be made since 1841. A book of special forms was produced and he had to fill in information about every person in the house at that time, including the visiting seaman that father had brought home, John Dolan. An Irish friend, Catherine Moiris, was also there for inclusion. The man wanted to know all their names, ages and the work they did. He seemed to have some difficulty understanding their rich Irish brogue and kept asking them to speak more slowly and to repeat things they had already said. It was so awkward trying to work out all the ages, and William began to get rather impatient and sarcastically queried if his wife's next baby had to go on the list. Then he looked uncomfortable, remembering that only Bridget had known that particular secret. The official ignored the remark and went next door to No.17.

The news that another baby was on the way came as quite a shock to Jeremiah. There just was not any more room in the house. Mother disagreed. By moving things closer together in Jeremiah's room, already shared with brother Anthony, she was sure that young William could be squeezed in somehow. This idea did not appeal to Jeremiah who, now almost sixteen, resented a further encroachment of his limited privacy. He still had a further year to go before completing his apprenticeship and that time began to seem a long way off. The new baby was due in a few months, about the middle of April, and for the first time he did not welcome an extra intrusion into the family circle. But on the 19th April 1852, Julia presented her husband with yet another son and the problem of finding a new name. The whole family liked John Dolan, the seaman who was visiting during the census, so it was decided to call the new baby after him. On the 24th April, St. Mary's once again witnessed the baptism of a Carrol.

Shortly after this, something happened which possibly began the pattern of strange coincidence that was to shape the whole of Jeremiah's improbable future. His mother, ignoring his protests, moved young William into his room. Her Scottish firmness, so essential to the organisation of her family, began to feed a latent Irish temper in Jeremiah. Bridget was full of sympathy and understanding for her brother as usual but felt duty bound to support her mother.

Jeremiah relied more heavily on finding release from this frustration through the satisfaction he enjoyed using his skills in the shipyard. Even this release was denied him when something was done to him, so distressing that he could never bring himself to reveal the full nature of the hurt. He was so disturbed that, on impulse, he fled from the shipyard to gain as much distance from it as possible.

Rushing along the waterfront, Jeremiah was halted by the walls of the south docks. Berthed alongside the first pier was a fairly large ship which he could see had completed its loading and was almost ready for departure. Without going home, without thinking clearly, he walked along an unguarded auxiliary gang plank into the hold of the vessel. Trembling with mixed emotions beyond his experience to bear, he hid among the tightly roped packing cases below decks.

By chance, a crew member had been sent below to extinguish all lamps as the final gangway was being hauled aboard. He spotted Jeremiah crouched in a corner, seized him roughly and steered him up to the captain who failed to obtain a sufficiently coherent story. The captain, anxious to make use of the outgoing tide, had no wish to search beyond the immediate problem of an unwanted stowaway. He ordered that Jeremiah be given a stern warning with a rope's end and be put ashore at once. As he stumbled ashore, a couple of dock workers nodded to each other. They had seen it all before and knew better than to press their curiosity too far. The stinging pain left by the rope had the beneficial effect of clarifying Jeremiah's muddled feelings and he attempted to laugh off the whole incident with them, not very convincingly.

He arrived home at much the usual time and was determined to say nothing about the day's events. He was young and strong and the walk back had given him sufficient time in which to control the signs of his distress. Covering up at home was comparatively easy, but he dreaded going back to work on the next day. Strangely, the foreman seemed unaware of his absence, perhaps because he had given Jeremiah the task of preparing some rough timbers in the store away from the main working areas. That was fortunate, and yet unfortunate as the store was also the scene of his nightmare experience. He became more watchful than diligent.

Quite naturally the fiasco of his unpremeditated flight was at the forefront of Jeremiah's thoughts. It had sown very viable seeds of opportunity for ridding himself of all the personal problems engulfing him. Always quick to learn from experience, Jeremiah began to plan an escape with more calculated precision. He was still bound as an apprentice and could offer no papers for legitimate employment in a ship's crew. He still had to resort to stowing away.

Timing was important. He must not be missed from home or work until he was well out to sea. An ample supply of food and water would eliminate the need to break cover too early. He took to walking regularly towards the south dock at the wider reach of the river where many of the larger vessels berthed. In a busy port there was plenty of choice.

This time it was easy. Purposeful and calm, Jeremiah joined the other seamen boarding the ship, his usual working clothes blending quite naturally. Once on board he descended into the hold and made sure that this time he was well covered with some old sail cloth. It was well timed. The ship was soon under way. He could hear the rattle of the sails being manoeuvred and felt that unmistakable roll induced by the sea. He had made it! Jeremiah could relax at last and he eased himself into a more comfortable position.

He was never to know why the old sailcloth was needed by that seaman. As it was dragged across his body he felt naked and vulnerable. He had never seen such genuine surprise as he saw in that seaman's face, in spite of the dingy light. Disappointment was stronger than fear at that moment. Perhaps they would put him to work on board now that the ship was heading out to sea. It was too late to be put ashore, a large ship under sail could not turn about that easily. Hope returned. This time Jeremiah was able to give a confident and clear explanation but the captain was far from sympathetic. On the contrary, he was extremely angry. The situation demanded a quick decision. Not being familiar with the navigational channel out of Newport, the captain had taken a pilot on board. He ordered that Jeremiah be suitably flogged and he requested that the pilot should return him to the shore and hand him over to the authorities.

Escorted back to Commercial Wharf by port officials, Jeremiah had to face his parents this time. His father was due back the following day, but the outrage and disbelief of his mother destroyed any possibility of secrecy. He could never have found the courage to tell Bridget all the sordid details but, at last, he managed to unburden himself completely to Julia, his mother. The rest of the children sensed something fearful and were unnaturally silent, speaking with their eyes. In later life, Jeremiah would never discuss the full nature of the outrage he experienced; he would only admit to being "sorely abused".

He did not go to work the next day. When his father returned it was Julia who shouldered the burden and embarrassment of revealing the sorry tale.

Julia and William talked through their bewilderment well into the night; they reached the only sensible conclusion - that Jeremiah should be allowed to go to sea as soon as possible. It seemed the best way out of his dilemma. William was well acquainted with the captain of an American trading vessel berthed at one of the piers further up the estuary and it was decided to approach him for help. If Julia went with him it might strengthen their plea.

Captain Austen Cook was impressed by their sincerity. They talked for a long time in his cabin. He felt he could trust William's assessment of Jeremiah's character and skills he had developed during his apprenticeship. It was possible that Jeremiah could become a useful member of his crew but he was still untrained in seamanship. The captain was sensitive to Julia's fears for her son and, having no son of his own, he felt moved to help in a more personal way. He offered to keep a fatherly eye on the boy and supervise his education in seamanship. It was agreed that Julia and William should bring Jeremiah to meet the captain before he could consider finalising such a decision. Julia's Scottish reserve crumbled with this sudden relief from worry and tension. She was disturbed too by the guilty elation she felt that the home would be more peaceful without his restless presence. She could not restrain her tears.

Captain Cook liked what he saw in Jeremiah. The boy was intelligent and he appreciated the way Jeremiah was able to talk frankly and honestly with him. For his part, the boy was surprised how easy he found it to open his heart to the captain. Captain Cook's next suggestion was totally unexpected. He pointed out the desirability of preventing Jeremiah's present problems from ever surfacing again. It would be a useful ploy to change his identity to coincide with his change of work. This idea took them by surprise, but the common sense of it soon became obvious and they agreed. Still pressing the point, would they perhaps allow him to adopt Jeremiah and give him his own name? ... How could they have rejected such a reassuring offer!

William was reluctant for Jeremiah to lose all identity with the family and suggested that his first name should be "Henry". Jeremiah was rather pleased to keep a family name. Back at Commercial Wharf, Bridget was at last taken into their confidence. She was heartbroken for her favourite brother, but had guessed that something momentous was happening. The other children were not told of the change, only that Jeremiah was going to sea. No doubt they would discover the truth in a time suited to each of them.

Only sixteen years of age, and with all his family remaining in Newport

- from baby John whom he hardly knew to his dear Bridget - the boy destined to become my great grandfather left home with a new identity, Henry Cook.

3
Into The Unknown

It was mid-August 1852 when Jeremiah had to say goodbye. The family agreed to bid him farewell at home; a young man's image could suffer if escorted to a new job by his parents. One exception he could not deny himself was to let faithful Bridget accompany him all the way to the ship. He was quite embarrassed at the fierce hug she gave him but responded to the honesty of her emotion. The seamen on deck noticed nothing unusual, they had seen it so often and were not to know that Bridget was his sister.

A voice bellowed from the top of the gangway and demanded of the hesitant figure on the quay if he were called "Cook". The tone was more than persuasive and with sudden comprehension Jeremiah rushed on board. It was the bosun. He led him to the seamen's quarters where a narrow bunk was allotted for his use, together with a small locker at its head for his kit. Quarters were very cramped but he was relieved to see they were clean and had some natural light filtering in.

That unfamiliar name "Cook!" was called again, this time from the top of the companion-way. Jeremiah's brain and instinct still had to make a quick transition from Cook to Carrol and back to Cook. He realised that from now on he must renounce his former name and become Henry Cook to the world. The call had come from the Second Mate this time and he wanted to take him to the Captain. Left alone, Henry was unsure how to greet the captain. The cool formality of this first meeting confused him. He learned he was to continue his apprenticeship as carpenter and shipwright under the supervision of the ship's carpenter, although immediately responsible to the Second Mate. During his working hours he was to have no extra privileges and would be subject to all the disciplines and traditions of the ship. At no time might he approach the Captain directly, but only through the Second Mate.

After the Captain had established his professional relationship and given Henry a clear picture of the conduct expected from him, his attitude relaxed.

They shook hands and Henry was invited to sit down. It was made quite clear that for the first few weeks Henry was to make no contact with the Captain unless his presence was requested. He had to become an integral part of the crew, pull his weight one hundred per cent, and earn the respect and confidence of his fellow seamen. Once he had proved his capacity to adapt to new situations and had established a firm rapport with the crew, then the Captain would be able to arrange extra training in other aspects of seamanship without arousing jealousy among the men. The Captain considered it prudent not to let Henry know that he had taken the Second Mate into his confidence. A working friendship had developed between them during several difficult voyages and it was too valuable to jeopardise.

They set sail for North America via Madeira with a mixed cargo, consigned by the captain who had a shrewd knowledge where to find suitable buyers for the goods on arrival. Henry soon found that working at sea was quite different from the regular pace of shipyard life. Most of the work now had an exciting immediacy. Even the chore of containing a splitting timber became important. The natural scepticism of the ship's carpenter gradually decreased as he found himself leaving Henry to complete jobs unsupervised.

Common to many American vessels, some members of the crew were coloured. Henry had rarely seen such black men before, and certainly never worked with them. Some of them demonstrated an awesome physique and sweated profusely. He could follow very little of their humour and was not quite sure how to mix with them. It was a problem only because of ignorance and it resolved itself without any conscious effort from Henry. Working together, often combining their strength with his skill, helped to dispel any inhibitions, as did living together in a confined space and exchanging seamen's banter. Henry began to understand their rough humour and felt easy in their company. The crew in general had accepted him without question and appreciated his willingness to find time for small personal repairs for them. Through this intimacy Henry began to realise that the crew considered themselves fortunate to have a captain they found to be firm but very fair. Quite naturally Henry could not quell a hint of pride fed by the crew's opinion of his Captain.

The ship kept on a southerly course for Madeira. There was a small shipment of hand tools to unload. Henry was to learn the economy of using prevailing trade winds, when possible, to maximise trading opportunities between one port and another. In this voyage, by first sailing mainly on a reach to Madeira, the captain planned to take advantage of the south-east trade winds to America. After eighteen days of good sailing weather, Madeira was sighted at noon on the 7th September. The ship remained in port for just three days while the tools were delivered and fresh provisions taken on board. Henry could get ashore for only a very brief period. He was required for minor repairs in the wheel-house.

On September 10th, Captain Austen J. Cook set sail for Baltimore. He had a large consignment of British textiles to dispose of, but he was confident of a market with American wholesalers specialising in fabrics and spun cotton. The second day out from Madeira, Henry had his first taste of mid-Atlantic storms. The towering waves looked invincible but the ship, responding to expert helmsmanship, was successfully defiant. Her timbers shivered as each wave tested her, but she remained steadfast. Deep in Henry's heart she became his ship and he loved his ship. Thirty-nine days after leaving Madeira, they sailed up Chesapeake Bay, on the east coast of North America, to Baltimore where they dropped anchor on the 19th October.

Almost to a man, the crew had become restless as land was sighted. Most were American and this was home country. Henry noticed the change but was not affected by it. He was new to the life and had but recently become so attached to his ship. After the first day in port, most of the crew were allowed ashore and they insisted Henry should go with them. The earth was solid and resisted the rolling gait he now used so naturally to keep his balance. He was taken to three different hostelries around the port and was exhilarated by the increasingly boisterous merriment. It became impossible to quench a non-existent thirst so constantly. The crew seemed to be enjoying his discomfort and the inevitable rush for the street outside. Henry was returned to his ship with the earth now unsteady and himself staggering within the supporting arms of his mates. The ship was rolling at anchor and he fell into a restless sleep. In the morning, the rolling mysteriously ceased as he eased his aching head into an upright position.

Two of the larger wholesale companies had approved the textile samples presented by the captain. The ship was manoeuvred to a convenient pier; the precious packing cases took a full two days to unload. Henry was surprised that such a simple derrick system could hoist and swing the heavy crates into the waiting carts. The task completed, a rota was drawn up to sanction shore leave for four crew members at a time. The remainder were required for painting, varnishing and general cleaning of the ship's interior.

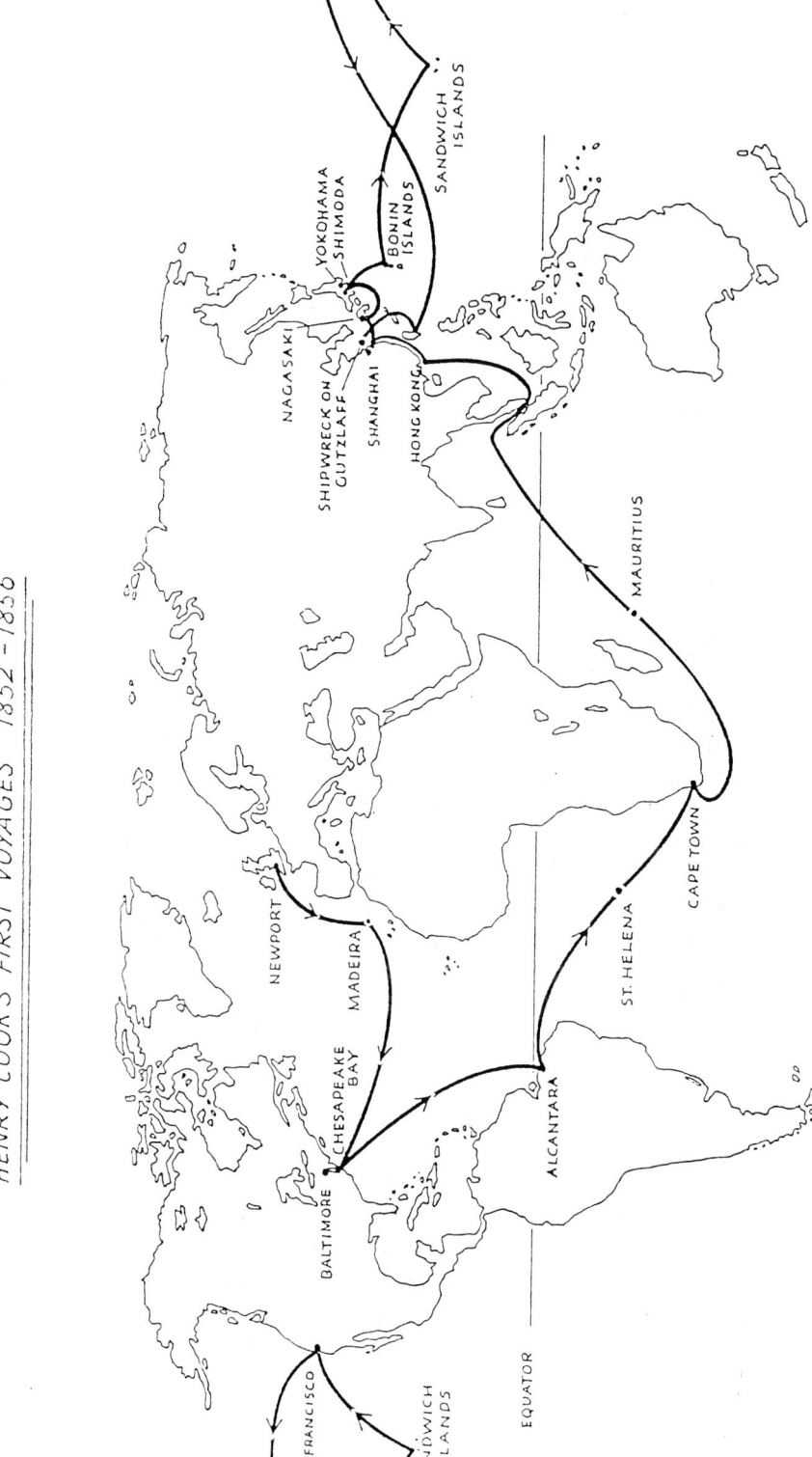

HENRY COOK'S FIRST VOYAGES 1852 – 1856

A trading vessel must earn its keep. Captain Austen was determined not to sail in ballast unless he could be sure of a very profitable pick-up at his next port of call. He relaxed his firm training policy for Henry who was allowed, on this occasion, to accompany him in the search for a suitable contract. After drawing a blank at several regular sources of trade, the Captain was put in touch with an engineering company, specialising in cutting and haulage equipment. Recommendation was essential for obtaining new contracts of this sort. A quantity of their equipment had been ordered by a timber firm in Alcantara on the north-east coast of South America, and a similar amount by a company in Cape Town. Henry was intrigued by the complications of such consignments, with some of the payment to be received at the port of call on safe delivery.

The machinery needed careful packing, balanced distribution below decks and secure lashing to avoid any shift during rough weather. While loading was in progress, knowledge of their voyage brought on board a man seeking passage to the island of St. Helena. The captain must have been satisfied with the man's credentials and agreed to let him use the small cabin next to his own. The crew never did discover why their passenger should choose a vessel so unsuited to passenger comfort but they had cause for conjecture later in the voyage. Calling in at St. Helena was an ideal break en route for Cape Town. On the 2nd November they weighed anchor and set sail for Alcantara, happy to be leaving the winter of Baltimore for the tropical warmth ahead.

As they progressed southwards the heat below decks became oppressive, particularly when winds eased down to the faintest breeze. About a day and a half's sailing from Alcantara, Henry was summoned to the main deck. The entire ship's crew, with the exception of the helmsman, were assembled in a rough semi-circle with the captain and his passenger hovering in the background. Henry was trying to respond amiably to the collective, malicious grin sweeping round the gathering. Standing awkwardly, he was seized from behind by firm hands and a quick glance revealed two of the crew dressed in outrageous clothes with faces gaudily painted.

The second mate strode forward. He was dressed as a parody of King Neptune with shaggy hemp tied round his chin for a beard, a mock crown on his head and he was holding a trident hurriedly fashioned by the carpenter earlier that day. Looking most serious, he demanded to know if Henry had ever 'crossed the Line' before. Alarmed recognition of the situation suddenly registered on Henry's face as he coaxed his voice to admit the truth. Neptune then solemnly ordered a suitable baptism of initiation into "The Honourable Company of Seamen". A large canvas tub of sea water was dragged into the centre. Henry's grotesque tormentors lifted him high above their heads and plunged him deep into the water. The gleeful cheers of the crew, silenced as water closed his ears, resounded again as he was lifted clear. After the third plunge, Henry was hauled away from the tub and placed feet first on the deck, gasping for breath. His tormentors made mock obeisance to him, a signal for the crew to close round, eager to shake his hand and enjoy the ration of spirits granted by the Captain. Naivety was steadily losing ground to experience.

After his initiation, Henry felt very much a member of the crew as their sympathetic banter was aimed at him. It was an experience he would have loved to share with Bridget. He still tried to picture his family back home but the intense reality of his life dimmed Newport to a recurring dream.

In contrast to Baltimore, facilities for berthing at Alcantara were quite inadequate. It was the 10th December when they finally began to haul in canvas and the captain decided to anchor away from the overcrowded pier. A boat was lowered and two of the crew rowed the captain and his passenger to a makeshift Customs House. Some of the machinery to be unloaded was heavy and too cumbersome to stow safely in the ship's boat. The captain arranged for a port lighter to transfer the bulk of it during the next couple of days. The passenger remained on shore.

Henry, stationed in the hold, was ordered to assist with the secure lashing of each piece of machinery to the twin derricks employed for this heavy lifting. The next morning his duties were changed to helping on the deck of the lighter and with transferring the machinery to the timber-firm's carts on the quayside across the narrow bay. After four days heavy work the crew were allowed to sample life ashore, an area none had visited before. Ship's stores were replenished and included some fresh fruit which would last for only a few days' indulgence. The captain was unsuccessful in his efforts to gain any consignment for delivery to St. Helena or Cape Town. Unwilling to resort to ballast, he made a speculative purchase of timber suitably sectioned for use in building construction.

Racking the timber securely below decks, allowing maximum flow of air to pass through its bulk, was a skilled task and one already familiar to Henry from his Newport experience. This became his first solo responsibility and the crew followed his instructions good-humouredly, ignoring his youth. By the evening of the 16th December, hatches were battened down and the ship made ready to sail.

Promptly at dawn the next morning, the passenger was rowed across from the shore and he climbed aboard with a professional competence and authority arousing fresh speculation among the crew. Within the hour the captain gave orders to weigh anchor and set course for St. Helena, with a new sense of urgency communicated only through the purposeful manner of the Second Mate. Maximum use was made of every slight change of wind direction so that a full day had been gained over schedule by the halfway point.

Christmas Day arrived during this fast run when little time could be spared for devotions or sentiment. The whole crew was living with exhilaration and pride, and this conquered the natural fatigue from sustained physical work and concentration. No special Mass or family feast for Henry this year. A few tasty extras were conjured by the cook from his normal store of sailor's fare. The captain read some standard prayers suited to the occasion and the second mate rather haltingly read the Christmas story from the captain's bible. Henry had his own small treasured bible kept safely in his locker. There were times when he enjoyed dipping into its mysteries, remembering some of his very early lessons in Ireland.

Progress was hampered eventually by a giant swell such as Henry had never seen before. The sea was a ploughed field of water with furrows of gigantic proportions, moving in unison from starboard to port. No local disturbance could account for the height above each deep, smooth trough of dark water. The slower pace of activity, dictated by the ever-masterful sea, gave an unexpected opportunity for a little New Year's merriment as 1852 drifted into 1853. The captain was noticeably worried by the reduced rate of progress.

Once this hazard had been navigated, the ship was again coaxed to its limit and St. Helena, a tiny speck in a vast ocean, appeared on the horizon, a full two days ahead of normal expectation. It was almost noon on the 10th January as they headed for Jamestown, the anchorage for St. Helena. Some four miles to the north, on their port side, the dark shape of a steamship was approaching quite rapidly. It entered the anchorage ahead of them but remained in deep water, obviously intending a brief stay. Ships often included St. Helena in their itinerary purely as a precaution in case of need. As it crossed their bow, Henry was impressed by its size and sensed a feeling of unease within himself; the black iron-clad sides of the vessel looked menacing and gave it an aura of total self-sufficiency. This feeling was reinforced when the ship's engines were used in reverse for a spectacular stop and anchors lowered with proficient arrogance. His crew mates let out an excited cheer. They eagerly pointed out the American ensign fluttering at the stern and stretched their hands across the gunwale, giving vent to their pride. It was one of their country's steam-driven warships, the *Mississippi*.

The Captain, himself American, ordered Henry and the rest of the crew to line up along the deck in salute as they passed the great iron ship to an anchorage nearer to the main quay. The passenger stood alongside the Captain, both unable to suppress a private satisfaction. A boat was lowered immediately and the passenger and his luggage were rowed ashore. The boat's two-man crew saw him make his way to a boat moored by a guardhouse. Shortly after their return to the ship, some of the crew saw this boat being rowed out to the *Mississippi*, further deepening the mystery.

There was no question of shore leave as the captain planned to sail on the morrow. Henry was included in a small party sent ashore to procure provisions and water for the next stage in this voyage seemingly without end.

On his return to the ship, Henry was summoned to the captain's cabin; also in attendance were the ship's carpenter and the second mate. Coming straight to the point, the Captain spoke approvingly of Henry's conduct and efficiency and, with the recommendation of the others present, he proposed to release Henry from some of his duties with the ship's carpenter. He was to be instructed and given practical experience in other aspects of seamanship with the second mate as his chief instructor. He would still be expected to assist with any major work requiring carpentry. Henry now realised that the Captain truly intended to be a father to him and he could find no words to express his feelings as these new opportunities opened up before him. Since starting at only nine years of age, he had been apprenticed to one trade for almost eight years and it had become for him a permanent way of life. He had fortunately matured beyond his years without the youthful smugness of early achievement so, although his seventeenth birthday was not due until April, he should be able to meet these fresh demands. He thanked them in a slightly unnatural voice, promoting a wide grin from the ship's carpenter.

4
Not All Plain Sailing

A favourable westerly wind was blowing next morning and Captain Austen Cook decided to leave St. Helena by 6 p.m., after final preparations had been completed. The crew weighed anchor that evening, a steady breeze filled the sails and the helmsman brought the ship round in line with the harbour entrance. Henry had been in the chart room while the course for Cape Town was being decided and was eagerly looking forward to seeing how the dictates of wind and weather would alter the proposed course. As he climbed to the upper deck, Henry just glimpsed the dark shape of the *Mississippi* nosing its way out ahead of them. He watched as she gradually increased the speed of her engines and finally disappeared over the horizon on a similar bearing to their own.

Good progress was maintained during the next three days. Henry was learning to take soundings and to record information accurately for the ship's log. The second mate allowed him to take over on the bridge and the ordered routine of shipboard life suited him well. Nearly a year had passed since the distressing episode in Newport which had led to his adoption by the captain. Jeremiah Carrol had died on that day and was only a memory, but he wondered at times how his family was faring and if he would ever see them again.

How often it happens that when everything seems to be going along smoothly and one feels on top of the world - - it is then that fate seems to intervene to upset the applecart. So it was for Henry at this time. His mind was full of exciting new skills to be mastered and he was seldom engaged on the odd jobs he had previously carried out for the ship's carpenter. As he came off watch early that morning, however, the latter had asked him to secure a loose rung on the companionway leading to the galley.

Henry was very tired and cold; he thought he would just return to his quarters for a hot drink before seeing to this minor repair. He sat down with a steaming mug of cocoa and relaxed. The warmth returned to his numb limbs and, in spite of himself, weariness overcame him and he drifted into a deep slumber.

It must have been an hour or so later when Henry awoke to a noise of shouting and bustle below decks. He was too bemused even to conjecture the cause. Then he realised he was still sitting on his bunk fully dressed; suddenly he remembered why he had not prepared for his rest period. He had been going to fix that ladder rung. Oh well! an hour or two wouldn't make much difference. Then he recognised his name being called and angry voices followed. He jumped up quickly and poked his head out of the small door enclosing the men's quarters. Still he did not connect the incident with any feeling of guilt.

Two crew members were carrying the cook's boy into the sick bay. He was moaning and his white face was twisted with pain. Henry emerged and before he could say a word, his arm was grabbed by the second mate. Apparently, the boy had fallen awkwardly when the rung of the companionway had slipped out of its socket and he had fractured his leg. The carpenter had reported that the rung was dangerous and that Henry Cook had been assigned the task of repair.

Henry was full of remorse. His sense of guilt was aggravated by concern for Danny, the boy who was his own age and who had befriended him from the start. He would have given anything to turn the clock back. Oh, why hadn't he seen to it straightaway? Just because he had indulged his own whim ... now he had caused trouble to Danny, the cook, and indirectly to all the crew.

A black cloud hung over Henry and he knew he would have to fact the captain. Above all, he wanted this father- figure to think well of him and to consider him worthy of the trust he had shown him a short time ago. Perhaps the captain was deliberately delaying his reprimand ...? perhaps he was not going to call him ...? after all, the second mate had imposed a punishment by ordering him to spend all his spare time in the galley until the boy was able to help the cook again.

Time dragged on. Henry had no appetite when they sat down to dinner and he felt unable to join in the conversation which seemed more subdued than usual. He left the table and went to his cabin. He was glad to be alone, glad that the hot tears in his eyes were unseen as they threatened to spill over. He felt ashamed; he had no-one to blame but himself. With all the extreme emotion of the young, he felt he would never regain the trust of his superiors or the easy comradeship with the crew. In his despair, he prayed. He opened his bible at random and read the words of Christ himself when he was near despair in the Garden of Gethsemane. He felt comforted - Christ was innocent and suffered - why should he not suffer when he was guilty? He knew as well as anybody that ship's orders had to be obeyed. Lives could be at risk if slackness were allowed to creep in.

He stopped feeling sorry for himself and thought in what way could he help to make amends. One of his treasured possessions was a large whale's tooth which a sailor friend of his father had given him on his twelfth birthday. He opened his locker and unwrapped it carefully - it was magnificent. Then he made his way to the sick bay where a makeshift splint had been improvised for the boy's lower leg by the barber. He knocked gently and went in. There was nobody in attendance so Henry went to his friend's side. Danny was looking better now and greeted Henry cheerfully. He did not want to take the gift - he knew how much Henry valued the tooth which was admired by all the crew. But Henry insisted and Danny realised the spirit in which it was given and thanked Henry warmly for his generosity. Danny stroked its smooth surface and imagined the enormous jaw from which it had come. It was like ivory; some sailors carved patterns on them or made them into small figures or animals. It was comforting to hold, but he resolved to find a way to give it back to Henry when he was better.

At last the call came for Henry to go at once to the captain's cabin. With trepidation, but also with a sincere acceptance of his guilt, he hastened to obey the summons. The voice telling him to enter sounded stern. In reply to the captain's questions, Henry answered honestly and did not spare himself. He made no plea that he was cold and tired - sailors should be able to overcome such weakness - duty came first always. His brevity impressed the captain. He had expected excuses, but there were none.

The captain remained silent and thoughtful, and Henry stood with lowered head waiting for the interview to terminate. Finally, Captain Cook said he was sorry that Henry had spoilt his good record. He realised that it was unfortunate that his lapse had had such far-reaching consequences. If nothing had happened, no doubt the repair would have been completed later and no-one the wiser. However, the accident underlined the need for prompt action at all times and negligence could not be overlooked. An entry would have to be made on his personal record and a further period of three months would be added to his apprenticeship. This was to be independent of the punishment imposed by the second mate.

Henry looked up, thanked the captain and saluted smartly. He sensed a softening of the captain's severe expression as he turned to go - or was it just his imagination? He resolved never to warrant a repetition of this interview.

The next day things gradually returned to normal and Henry accepted the ribbing of the crew and the extra work he had to undertake. He proved quite useful to the cook because he had helped to kill and draw chickens in Ireland and was not at all squeamish about preparing meat or fish for food. Much of the fresh meat on a long voyage had to be kept alive on board and killed as required. No cold storage facilities were available, especially in warm weather, and chickens were a useful cargo both for eggs and meat.

Henry's usual high spirits soon returned and he kept Danny amused with tales of his disasters in the galley, or the latest yarns from the bosun. The leg was healing well and Danny was able to get about on crutches when the sea was calm, as it had been for the last day or two. The winds had dropped considerably and progress had been slowed during this time. The canvas sagged; the ship entered a period of total calm and the still, hot air wrapped oppressively around the crew. The captain was irritable at the delay, and no activity was evident on the usually bustling deck. The crew responded listlessly to the few essential duties but sailing and navigational skills were no longer required. The ship was completely becalmed. Most of the crew had passed through the Doldrums before and knew what to expect. It was explained to Henry that the Doldrums is a zone near the Equator where the meeting of the trade-winds causes an area of rising hot air with low atmospheric pressure, high temperatures and humidity and either light variable winds or complete calm, often interrupted by violent thunderstorms. Sailing ships sought to avoid this area and the captain was not expecting to meet this phenomenon so far south. The second mate encouraged the crew by suggesting it would be of short duration.

The ship was dead; there was no life creaking in its timbers no whistle through the rigging or slap of canvas in the wind. The silence was unaccustomed and disturbing. It was important to keep the crew alert and occupied and the resourceful bosun seemed to have an endless list of moderately urgent tasks for them. Henry was allowed in the wheelhouse after completing his allotted share of work. Here, the helmsman was constantly on the alert easing the bows of the ship almost by will-power into every variable direction, seeking the slightest breath. He was pleased to hand over to Henry, after giving him careful instructions, and enjoy the consequent relief from the monotony of unrewarded concentration.

The wind was in no hurry to return. First a heartening gust from the south-east coaxed a short-lived cheer from the crew, but it died in moments. Then a longer thrust of wind from the south-west seemed more promising. After some hours of uncertainty, the south-west wind prevailed and the crew glanced appreciatively at the full canvas, so long lifeless, now primed with energy. It was impossible to make up for lost time, but the captain had not displayed the anxiety he had failed to conceal en route for St. Helena. Four days late, but only twelve hours sailing from Cape Town; Table Mountain was just revealing its permanence on the horizon. Henry had been sent aloft to check some of the rigging and noticed the tell-tale black smoke curling from a steamer which was moving on a westerly course out of Table Bay. Before it turned southward away from him, Henry recognised the *Mississippi*. He shouted down to the deck and one of the crew reported his observation to the captain, who confirmed it through his glass. They anchored in Table Bay the following morning, twenty-four days after leaving St. Helena.

Nothing could disguise the air of anticipation coupled with the certainty of shore leave. Even Captain Cook was looking more relaxed, eager to test his luck in business once again. Henry was one of the crew to row him ashore. While the captain went off to track down the company who had ordered the cargo of machinery, Henry wandered about chatting to equally idle hands on the quayside. He learned that the *Mississippi* had arrived in Table Bay on the evening of 24th January, eleven days before his own ship. The advantage of steam was obvious but, even in later years, it never challenged his biased love for timber design and sail. Table Bay was a busy port and, as all shore berths were occupied, the captain decided not to unload his cargo until a suitable berth became available. Routine shore leave was organised while the ship remained at anchor.

During the few days when their ship had been locked in the Doldrums, the crew had found time to talk and exchange confidences in a manner they would normally have avoided. Henry had disclosed something of his story and his arranged relationship with the captain. The crew had guessed there was a special reason for Henry's presence on board, so the news had not upset them and they approved of his attitude to the ship, to his work and to themselves. This lack of resentment was a great relief to Henry but he was unsure of the captain's reaction to his indiscretion and made no mention of it. Whilst on duty watch at the anchorage in Table Bay, he seized the opportunity to explain what had happened. Without revealing that he already knew about it from the second mate, the captain said that he was pleased their relationship was now common knowledge, and pointed out the greater freedom of contact it could allow. At the end of Henry's watch, they went ashore together, sharing the unspoken warmth between a father and son perhaps for the first time.

Their anchorage in Table Bay had become far from idyllic. Violent winds had sprung up which made holding to anchorage quite difficult. Each watch had been doubled and a reserve anchor made ready for instant use. Dust storms swept across the bay at irregular intervals causing great annoyance to the crew. Sometimes, after all hands had washed down the ship and swept out their lockers, another cloud of dust would descend, searching out every crack and peppering their food. It was a relief to all when a berth alongside a sheltered pier was finally cleared for them. To manoeuvre the ship into the berth tested Captain Cook's seamanship to the full and the lead-ropes were heaved expertly to the waiting shoremen who quickly hauled in the mooring ropes and secured the ship to the pier. Unshipping the machinery was quite straightforward and loading it directly into the horse-drawn wagons halved the transfer time.

There remained the problem of the stack of building timber still lashed in the hold. The captain had been unable to find a market for it in Cape Town, but a small construction firm from Mauritius, who had just completed a contract in South Africa, made an attractive offer. The manager was returning to their island headquarters and agreed to accept the timber if the bulk of their equipment could be shipped with it back to Port St. Louis. It was not an offer to refuse. When the equipment arrived at the berth its variation in size, weight and shape posed considerable stowage problems. The second mate took charge of distribution in the hold, with Henry moving the timber in stages as directed. Securing such a complex cargo against movement in high seas was so vital that the captain made detailed inspections on several occasions during the operation. When hatches finally were battened down, the ship was towed to an anchorage in the bay where preparations for departure continued for two more days. The ship's boat returned from its last trip ashore with a wired crate of excited hens, unaware of the key role they were to play in the cook's repertoire.

The voyage to the island of Mauritius was calculated to take at least thirty days. The crew were pleased to leave behind the dust of Table Bay as they headed out to sea on the morning of 15th February. Henry had now come to accept the vagaries of wind and weather as a natural part of a sailor's life. Wind was the only source of power and he was developing that sailor's instinct to gain maximum advantage from any available wind strength and direction. So, for Henry, the voyage to Mauritius was comparatively uneventful. Helping the cook to dispatch and gut a couple of the hens figured more prominently in his sea-conditioned mind. The voyage may not have been memorable but arrival at Port St. Louis most certainly was.

Pilots' instructions for the area warned against anchoring in the port unaided. With numerous hands to assist them, pilots approached each vessel entering the port and secured them by frigate chains to mooring anchors. Captain Cook had been there once before and knew the drill. His ship, in common with all the others, was moored head and stern with bows to the south-east. This was the direction from which hurricanes usually came and without such precautions the shores could, and often had, become strewn with wrecked ships. Henry was to remember Port St. Louis as the most restless anchorage he ever used. As every vessel wishing to leave the port was allowed to move only under pilot supervision, there was a constant bustle of boats rushing from one ship to another as they arrived or departed.

For some years Captain Cook had nurtured an ambition to expand his enterprise into the lucrative trade of the Far East. This would not only involve him in following most of the regular trade routes but also in crossing the Pacific Ocean to the west coast of America. Whilst at Mauritius he explained his intentions to the crew; one or two members who wished to return to their homes in America decided to leave the ship and seek a more direct passage home. Finding suitable replacements was not easy and departure was delayed for over a week. Finally, all business was completed, the ship had its full complement, so at first light on 4th April the second mate signalled for a pilot to release the ship from its moorings. As the chains dropped away and the pilot's boat eased the ship into a favourable direction for leaving the harbour, it seemed to symbolise the freeing of Henry from the past and to guide him into the most formative years of his life.

Course was set for Singapore.

5
A Cocoon In The Making

From the exotic aroma of carefully-packed spices to the fumes of rough-hewn coal, the great variety of trade in the Far East was highly competitive. Many of the ships sailing between the Chinese ports and the numerous islands to the east of the mainland were owned by large influential trading companies. After leaving Mauritius and negotiating the difficult Strait of Malacca to Singapore, Henry's ship became part of this constant search for profit.

Every sailor was aware that sailing in the China Seas and neighbouring Pacific Ocean could invite dangers to test even the most experienced crews. Wrecks were commonplace. Apart from the natural hazards of hurricane, typhoon and uncharted rocks, there was the ever-present fear of pirates operating from lonely stretches of the mainland. Less tangible and fed by rumour was the particular fear of being stranded anywhere on the coast of Japan. This mystery, which would intrigue Henry for the next few years, was fostered particularly by American seamen, some of whom had survived that misfortune.

Although European crews were equally at risk, it had become of significant concern to American sailors. The Gold Rush of 1849 had accelerated the development of California, which inevitably made trading with China from the Pacific coast of America an attractive proposition. The advent of steam-assisted navigation made it possible to sail the shortest route from San Francisco to Canton which could take ships within sight of Japanese shores. The rapid growth of the American whaling industry in the Pacific also brought many vessels close to Japanese waters. This increase in sea traffic naturally multiplied incidents of shipwreck.

Anxiety was well founded. Although there is little evidence of deliberate torture, any captured foreigners were immediately subjected to detailed and rigorous interrogation by the Japanese. Their eventual expulsion was no less painful. They were transported to Nagasaki, from any distance, in closed palanquins designed to accommodate the smaller stature of the average

Japanese. These journeys could take many days, even weeks, and the tall muscular American sailor was prone to severe cramps and, at best, extreme discomfort in this primitive form of transport. The prisoners were kept at Nagasaki until a ship suitable for their repatriation called in at Deshima, the small island linked to Nagasaki by a narrow causeway where the Dutch, under very strict Japanese control, had been allowed to maintain a small settlement since the middle of the seventeenth century.

Through talking with his captain and absorbing gossip at various ports, Henry had become aware of this strange anachronistic determination of Japan's rulers to keep their country totally isolated from the outside world - secure in a cocoon of their own culture, industry and primitive technology. He had yet to learn the history behind this vigorously protected regime and that he was to become one of the first pioneers to penetrate this cocoon and inject his own particular skills and knowledge into its metamorphic change.

The Japanese had always considered themselves to be a superior race and legends abound to support their belief.

The ancient history of Japan is shrouded in mystery, richly embroidered with details concerning the divine origin of her emperor, once believed to be an earthly descendant of the Sun Goddess, Amaterasu Omikami. It was held that Amaterasu was sent down from Heaven to establish order in the universe. She had three precious symbols - the curved jewel, the sword and the mirror - which still remain part of the Imperial regalia. Her grandson, also a god, was commanded to rule the 'Central Land of Reed Plains' which was Japan. Accompanied by other deities and equipped with the jewel, sword and mirror, he landed in Kyushu in the south. His great-grandson was the first earthly emperor, posthumously known as Jimmu Tenno. After considerable fighting in Central Japan, he successfully established his capital to the south of modern Kyoto. His conquest was celebrated by honouring his ancestress, Amaterasu, in 600 B.C. according to tradition, and this event continued to be celebrated up to A.D. 1940.

As with many primitive peoples, dependent on growing crops, the gods were personifications of Nature and sun worship occupied a central place. The return of the sun in spring and the subsequent rebirth of nature was ensured by ritual enticements in Japanese religious ceremonies. After a thousand years of civilisation in China, the islands of Japan were still inhabited by primitive tribes who lived by fishing and gathering. Archaeological evidence suggests that they bore little racial resemblance to the Japanese who are predominantly mongoloid in appearance. Another tribal group, the Ainu, were a Stone Age people who lived chiefly by hunting and fishing and worshipped the bear. They were pale-skinned, very hairy, round-eyed and different in stature from the other races. It is thought they may have come from Siberia and were primitive members of ancient Caucasian stock. They were probably fairly widespread until forced northwards by a more advanced people from the south. Now only a few remain on the northern island of Hokkaido.

It was not until the second and first centuries B.C. that considerable numbers of mongoloid invaders from mainland Asia crossed the Korean straits, bringing to Japan a new culture and knowledge. Rice began to be cultivated in flooded paddies, the skills of weaving and metal work were learned and customs and language gradually became amalgamated.

In the fifth century A.D., the Yamato clan established its power in the region around Kyoto, and its leader claimed to be descended from the first legendary emperor, Jimmu Tenno. The Yamato dynasty has reigned over Japan ever since. At that time, Shintoism was the principal religion; its origin and founder are unknown and it is indigenous to Japan. It features the worship of nature, ancestors and national heroes and belief in the divinity of the emperor used to be its major tenet.

In the next century, Buddhism was brought from India, via Korea and China, and many of the sculptures and early paintings reflect Indian and Chinese influence. Buddhism was taken up by the Court and, as it adapted to Japanese ways, its popularity grew with the ordinary people, creating a unique Japanese culture.

Prior to 710 AD., the site of the capital was changed every time a new emperor came to the throne. Then a permanent seat for the Court was established at Nara; this lasted for eighty-four years and seven successive emperors held their court there. Buddhism flourished and thousands of temples were constructed throughout the country, often reflecting the style of the Chinese pagoda. The capital was removed from Nara to the present Kyoto (Heian-kyo) and the Heian period began a long era of prosperity. A new city was laid out and the arts of painting, sculpture and architecture flourished.

Until the sixth century A.D., Japan possessed no writing system of any kind. After this they began to use Chinese characters for writing, a system of enormous complexity based on a language of monosyllables and quite unsuited to the variations of Japanese speech. It was considered too difficult for women to learn and only high-ranking nobles and scholars studied the thousands of intricate characters that represent words, not sounds. In the ninth century, a new syllabic system of writing called *kana* was invented. This brought about the first flowering of Japanese literature and poetry, mostly written by gentlewomen of the Heian period who were not inhibited by the idea that writing in *kana* was beneath their dignity, as were the gentlemen of their society. The Imperial Court gained great power; elegant courtiers devoted to poetry and the arts dominated the culture.

By the twelfth century, the Yamato emperor was ruler in name only and the real power had passed from the courtiers to the *samurai* warriors. The Zen principle of Buddhism had its influence on art and literature and the elegance of the Heian period gave way to more masculine forms of expression. Zen appealed especially to the *samurai* as it was simple, vigorous and stressed self-discipline. The emperor was still highly respected but the most powerful *samurai* took the title of *Shogun,* or generalissimo, and ruled as military dictators in the emperor's name. The *daimyo*, or feudal lords, controlled each region of Japan, regulated by the central authority of the *shoguns.* Castles were built as headquarters for the *daimyo* and towns grew up round them.

The first shogunate government was at Kamakura and was the forerunner of a long line of military governments which lasted until the Meiji Restoration in 1868. Later the seat was moved to near Kyoto, where its prosperity is reflected by the Gold and Silver Pavilions, built as villas for the *shoguns.* The latter part of the fifteenth century was marked by internal wars. Japan was a country of political chaos but economic growth advanced as trade and commerce grew. Japanese seafarers went overseas to trade as far as the Philippines, Cambodia and Siam.

The first Westerners to visit Japan were Portuguese merchants who came in 1543. St. Francis Xavier and other missionaries soon followed and the spread of Christianity was extremely rapid. Princes and leaders embraced the Faith and by 1580 there were three hundred thousand Christian converts in Japan. As civil strife was widespread at this time, there was no strong leader to check outside influences. Wars ended when Tokugawa Ieyasu beat all his rivals and made himself *Shogun* in 1603. He established the tokugawa system of administration which was to last until the overthrow of the shogunate government in 1867. Ieyasu made his headquarters at Yedo, then just a fishing village, and built a massive castle there, surrounded by a moat. When the emperor left Kyoto in 1868, Yedo castle became the Imperial Palace and the

38

city was renamed Tokyo or 'eastern capital'. The Tokugawa family kept control of the main cities and highways, silver-mines and ports, and even of the emperor himself. The *shogun* kept the *daimyo* under control by a network of spies and secret police and by a permanent hostage system involving their families.

The conflict which led to the persecution of the Christians and the ultimate expulsion of all westerners is a complex amalgam of political ambition, fear and greed. The port of Nagasaki was a centre of trade, especially silk from China. The people were overwhelmingly Christian and the town's Japanese governors were influenced by the Jesuit Fathers. Their knowledge of the language and high personal conduct made them useful as interpreters and intermediaries to both Japanese traders and Portuguese merchants.

When the Dutch and English traders came on the scene in the early part of the seventeenth century, relationships between European traders were influenced by religious bigotry, and the Japanese realised that Spain and Portugal were regarded as enemies by some European countries. Also, where a considerable section of the population had become Christian, the government was alarmed and feared another civil war in which Christian *daimyo* might get support from Christian foreigners. Ieyasu realised that trade with Holland and England was independent of religious propagation and offered a potential alternative. Edicts prohibiting Christianity were made by Ieyasu and the expulsion of priests from Nagasaki began, but it was his successor who pursued a settled plan of extermination. He was aided by the selfish policy of the Dutch, who assisted him in putting down a revolt of the Christians of a large area east of Nagasaki, who were driven to despair by the oppressive measures of two *daimyo*.

The government at Yedo decided to end all intercourse with the countries of western Europe and reinstated harsh and repressive feudal controls over Japan. It was decreed that no Japanese should leave the country under pain of death and a policy of national seclusion was enforced. The building of ocean-going ships was banned and those Japanese who had been living abroad for a certain time were forbidden to come home. The only Westerners allowed to trade with Japan were the Protestant Dutch, who were confined to a small island, Deshima, in Nagasaki harbour. Some trade with China was also allowed at Nagasaki. The entry of Dutch ships was strictly rationed but the restrictions were accepted because the trade brought them a satisfactory profit. A trickle of scientific knowledge filtered through Deshima to the

Japanese but this was insufficient to keep abreast of developments in contemporary Europe and the evolution of the Industrial Revolution.

However, the isolationist policy of the Tokugawa government and the rigid rules laid down for all classes of society, each with its own occupations, style of dress and laws, brought about a period of lasting peace and domestic prosperity. This was particularly beneficial to the townsmen and merchants, who were previously looked down upon as lower in the social scale than peasants and artisans. They were not dependent on income from agriculture, as were peasants who had to produce rice and other crops to support the *samurai*. They speculated in rice, whose price fluctuated widely, and lent money to profligate *samurai* who were uneducated in the ways of commerce. Soon a large proportion of the nation's wealth was in the hands of the merchants and bankers, which gave them power to disregard the old rules of social class and feudal superiority.

There is no doubt that the seclusion policy of Japan limited her economic growth by cutting off foreign trade and the flow of influences and technology from overseas at a time when scientific developments were rapidly changing the western world. Towards the end of the Tokugawa period, although Japan had a higher rate of literacy than much of Europe, certain scholars realised the need for modernising Japan and were aware of the material superiority of the West.

This was the situation which faced the first tentative approaches aimed to end two centuries of Japan's isolation.

PRINCIPAL AREA
OF HENRY COOK'S
ADVENTURES ~

KURIL ISLANDS

INT

SEA OF
JAPAN

HAKODATE

•PEKING

NIGATA

TOKYO
YOKOHAMA
Mt FUJI
SHIMODA

KYOTO•
KOBE•

SHIMONOSEKI

NAGASAKI

SHANGHAI• •GUTZLAFF

EAST
CHINA SEA

BONIN ISLAND

NAHA

LEW CHEW ISLANDS

•STEEP I.

AMOY•

TAIWANFOO

FORMOSA

PACIFIC

OCEAN

HONG KONG

SOUTH
CHINA
SEA

N

PHILIPPINES

6
The Cocoon Is Pierced

As the nineteenth century dawned, the Dutch were still at Deshima. To secure this privilege and the monopoly of Western trade, minimal though it was, they were paying the degrading and humiliating price of total submission to every Japanese whim and scrutiny. Nevertheless they were the chief source of Western ideas and news, and by sowing calculated seeds of distrust they were able to persuade the Japanese to reject all British and Russian initiatives in diplomacy and trade.

In 1803, the *Frederick*, an English merchantman, was sent from Calcutta to Japan with a cargo, but on arrival she was refused admittance to the harbour and ordered to depart within twenty-four hours.

Five years later, an armed British warship, HMS.*Phaeton*, sailed into Deshima hoping to achieve some surprise by flying the Dutch flag. The ruse failed. The Japanese made plans to avenge certain infringements of their law by destroying the *Phaeton*. Before anything could be accomplished, a favourable wind sprang up and the ship escaped to open sea. This incident, which caused the honourable suicides of the Japanese governor of Nagasaki and several of his officials, left embittered feelings against the British.

After the Dutch lost sovereignty of Java to the British, two attempts were made by Britain, in 1813 and again in 1814, to supplant the Director of Deshima with a Dutchman of its own choice. Both expeditions failed.

Captain Gordon of the British Navy entered the Bay of Yedo in 1818 with his little vessel of sixty-five tons. It was surrounded immediately by the usual line of guard boats, its rudder unshipped and all arms and ammunition confiscated and taken ashore. The Japanese were civil but refused all gifts and attempts to trade.

Some thirty-one years later, in 1849, HMS. *Mariner* under Commander Matheson went to Uraga, about twenty-five miles from Yedo, but still nothing of importance to Britain resulted from the encounter.

The Russians employed different tactics from the British in their overtures to Japan but met with similar rebuffs. Russian persistence and British mercantile success in the East, coupled with their acknowledged maritime supremacy, made them odds-on favourites finally to break through the historic Japanese intransigence.

Meanwhile, American interest in resolving the dilemma was gaining momentum. Safe conduct for stranded seamen was a growing concern. Coal supplies were needed at convenient refuelling ports and commercial advisers predicted opportunities for trade with Japan. The first attempt to negotiate was doomed to failure through ignorance of traditional Japanese procedure and philosophy.

It was in 1846 that the United States despatched a squadron of two ships under the command of Commodore Biddle, who was instructed to act with caution. On reaching the Bay of Yedo, the squadron was quickly surrounded by four hundred Japanese guard boats, and no American was allowed to leave his ship during a ten-day vigil at anchor. Biddle's conciliatory approach was interpreted as weakness and the emperor's answer to the application for licence to trade was very short:

"No trade can be allowed with any foreign nation except Holland."

Commander Glynn of the United States ship *Preble*, part of the American squadron in the China seas, had more success in 1849 when sent to demand the release of sixteen American seamen who had been shipwrecked on one of the Japanese islands and subsequently subjected to considerable cruelty. The undiplomatic bluntness of this experienced officer, and threats of force, secured the prisoners' release and repatriation within two days.

Gaining confidence from this incident, Washington decided to break through this wall of Japanese insularity, and in 1852 had the wisdom to commission Commodore Matthew Perry for this historic diplomatic mission. He was even granted the privilege of writing his own instructions. From the start, Perry was determined to negotiate with the blunt assertiveness which was a hallmark of his own character, and he planned accordingly. Fortunately, he would also take care to respect the sovereignty of Japan and the dignity of individual Japanese officials, though never compromising American dignity by submitting to restrictions tolerated by the Dutch.

Washington promised twelve ships in support - a promise never kept. Commodore Perry left Chesapeake Bay on the 24th November 1852 aboard the steam battleship *Mississippi*. He was aiming to arrive at Hong Kong by the first week in April to rendezvous with other ships of the American fleet. It was along the route for this journey that Henry Cook had his first memorable sightings of the *Mississippi*, not then realising the historical significance.

Two sloops of war *Plymouth* and *Saratoga* and the storeship *Supply* were already at Hong Kong anticipating the Commodore's arrival, but his intended flagship *Susquehanna* had moved on to Shanghai. The gathering squadron set sail to join it. To reach the anchorage at Shanghai, ships had to navigate through hidden obstacles of terrain at the mouth of the Yangtse Kiang. The river had a rise and fall of tide averaging ten feet, and the Chinese ignored all requests for a system of navigation markers to be installed. Vessels were obliged to find their way haphazardly into the channel. Henry later heard, with a hint of mischievous satisfaction, that the *Susquehanna*, *Plymouth* and *Supply* all grounded on going in, and Perry's *Mississippi* hit a sandbank but fortunately her engines were able to pull her off.

On the 23rd May, the *Susquehanna* with Commodore Perry and the *Saratoga* got under way for Naha, the principal port of Great Lew Chew Island (Okinawa) where the complete squadron was to meet within a month. The Commodore then busied himself among the Lew Chew Islands (Ryukyus) for the next month, except for a brief exploration of the Bonin Islands, to make sure the Japanese would receive advance news of his impending arrival. Although some thought the islands belonged to China, Perry was inclined to the general belief that they were a Dependency of the Prince of Satsuma, with dress, language and customs confirming his opinion. News was bound to travel fast back to mainland Japan. Perry returned to Naha on the 23rd June to the frustrating news that only five ships had assembled for the expedition. Washington had failed him, in spite of repeated promises to provide a complement of twelve for the squadron.

The Commodore need not have worried. Leaving *Supply* behind, the *Susquehanna* and *Mississippi*, with *Plymouth* and *Saratoga* in tow, were sufficiently impressive to astound the Japanese people. The authorities were well-prepared, but the hundreds of Japanese watching from the shore could never have imagined such a sight as these huge black ships actually moving forward against the wind and tide! The squadron slowed to an anchorage off Uraga, at the entrance to Yedo Bay, on Friday, 8th July 1853.

Hundreds of Japanese guard boats arrived with customary speed but were ordered away with the alternative threat of force. Determined to dominate the situation, Commodore Perry persistently refused to deal with any of the minor officials sent to him and matched the high-ranking Japanese officials with an equal degree of exclusiveness. When finally all his terms were met, he agreed to go ashore where he delivered his President's letter to suitably senior representatives, with a warning that he would return for a reply early in the following year with a much larger squadron.

To add more forceful persuasion, he defied Japanese expectations of his immediate departure by sailing further into the Bay of Yedo taking careful soundings for two days. He continued until in sight of the city suburbs. Then, satisfied with this display of power, Perry moved the squadron to a bay about five miles above Uraga. The following day, 17th July, they left the anchorage and set course for the return to Naha.

7
The Far East - A New Slant

Ever since leaving Mauritius, Captain Austen Cook had worked his crew to the limit. He had been trading with a rapid turnover on short-haul routes along the South China coast. Direct trade with other vessels in port had been a regular source of profit, but he had failed to secure any contract of major importance.

From the beginning of June, conflicting news and speculation was spreading from port to port with one central certainty, an American squadron was going to Japan. Captain Cook's crew were always ready to inflate the importance of their sightings of the *Mississippi* in a vain attempt to boost a flagging morale.

Henry was tired. He was intelligent and willing, but his limited education was being extended at such an alarming rate, through multiple instruction and experience, that he yearned for a change. The change came through necessity. The ship sustained some minor damage in heavy weather off the west coast of Formosa (Taiwan) and the captain made the caring, yet wholly professional decision that his vessel had earned a refit. Any weakness in structure or equipment was certain to be revealed by the ferocious gales common to the region. They returned to an anchorage in Hong Kong harbour during late August to stay for an indefinite period. At last, Henry was able to relax in the more familiar routine of construction and repair as part of the refit programme. Never before had shore leave seemed so essential to sanity, even though the climate inland was unpleasantly humid during that time of year.

Hong Kong was full of fascinating activity for any seaman of Henry's age. The waterfront had all the sights and sounds found in ports in the Far East, but in the town there was a bustle of colour and costume, a mixture of fine buildings and ramshackle huts, liquor stores and shops selling both quality goods and junk. There were sleazy streets with gambling dens and opium parlours, as well as secret areas forbidden to Henry by the captain. He had made the crew aware of his wishes in this respect, a request directed at one or two seamen who often returned to the ship looking dishevelled and obviously victims of a drunken brawl.

There had been a noticeable increase in American activity during September. The steam battleship *Powhaton* had arrived from the United States in August and, after leaving for a short time, it returned before going to Macao to await further instructions. Commodore Perry in the *Susquehanna* steamed in to Hong Kong harbour, followed at intervals by other ships from his mission to Japan. Apparently the *Powhaton* required an engine overhaul, possibly taking two months. This unwelcome news, plus the need of a general inspection for all his ships and the approaching typhoon season, all persuaded Perry to settle his headquarters at Macao. This decision also allowed him to grant some well-earned relaxation for the crews.

From now on, American activity increased. Storeships gradually built up supplies which were housed in new purpose-built warehouses. Hong Kong and other ports were alive with small groups of American seamen, many of whom had been to Japan with Perry. They were eager to brag about their success and were buoyant with confidence. Tales of strangely dressed men with peculiar hair styles and manners grew more fantastic with repetition. One thing was certain - they were going back to Japan.

Henry usually went ashore with crew members who were mostly American. This led to several noisy sessions in the popular bars. His companions proved their worth one evening when, trying to be part of the casual rivalry, Henry rather stupidly brought up the Shanghai incident where all four United States ships ran aground in the Yangtse. They stood between him and instant retaliation. Quite obviously something important was being prepared. The expectant atmosphere was exciting and recharged the interest and energy of Captain Cook's crew.

A short time later, probably resulting from shore leave in the port, intermittent fever hit some of the crew. Hong Kong and Canton were notoriously unhealthy during this season and resident families from the region used Macao as a summer resort, although even this area was not exempt from occasional epidemics. Some of the crew from the American fleet were also affected and several were taken to the overcrowded hospital in Hong Kong, where one of the older members of Captain Cook's crew had been transferred. The fever was of short duration for most of Henry's shipmates and their usual high spirits soon returned.

The repair routine and regular trips on shore reminded Henry of his days in Newport docks. It was the first time he had felt a genuine homesickness for his family. In the role of foster-father, the Captain persuaded him to write home and he promised to place the letter with a ship returning to England. It was a difficult letter to write and Henry was not sure who would reply. He remembered that Bridget had not learned to write, but his younger brothers and sisters should have received more schooling in Newport. The captain went ashore with Henry's letter, leaving the mate in charge as he intended being away for a few days. He was anxious to gain more official information about the American fleet's activities in Japan and the purpose of present preparations. He returned to his ship in thoughtful mood and stepped up the speed of maintenance work.

By early November the ship was ready. The fresh paint gleamed, seams were caulked, sails and rigging had been repaired, all at considerable cost. The captain had not been idle. He had been moving between Hong Kong and Macao gaining the confidence of some of the American officers, and had secured a contract for back-up assistance in delivering supplies. Except for one storm-ridden voyage to Formosa, the crew enjoyed the regular routine of calling at different ports along the mainland, returning to discharge the cargo at the storage depots in Hong Kong.

New Year's Day in 1854 was spent at anchor in Hong Kong harbour. Commodore Perry had now centred all preparations in Hong Kong and by the middle of January the American squadron, led by the flagship *Susquehanna*, set sail for Lew Chew on the first stage of the second mission to Japan. On 1st February the sail vessels were despatched for Yedo Bay in advance, to be followed by the steamships *Susquehanna, Powhaton* and *Mississippi* on the 7th, all calculated to arrive together. Storeship *Supply* would arrive later with extra supplies of coal and livestock. Coal was the life-blood of steamships and a search for future depots in the Pacific was one of Commodore Perry's priorities.

Gambling on the possibility of a coal shortage for Perry's battleships towards the end of their mission, Captain Cook had quietly decided to risk a private trading venture to Japan with a full cargo. He had secured a useful consignment for Shanghai, where he could also make contact with a reliable coal supplier. It was essential that coal be stored and shipped dry. Damp coal in the hold was highly dangerous. At best it would be a dirty cargo, but profitable. He estimated about fifteen days to reach the vicinity of Yedo Bay from Shanghai.

Commodore Perry arrived at Yedo Bay on 11th February to find the sloop *Macedonian*, one of the ships sent in advance, was aground. All attempts to free her had failed until this fortuitous arrival of the steamships. This incident confronted the Americans for the first time with a characteristic honesty in the Japanese which was difficult to equate with their traditional duplicity in negotiation. A container of bituminous coal, among other items which had been heaved overboard to lighten the *Macedonian* when aground, was washed up on the beach. The local Japanese took the trouble to return it to the squadron, by then some twenty miles away.

Sailing in line ahead, the three battleships with *Lexington*, *Vandalia* and *Macedonian* in tow, arrived off Uraga on 13th February. The storeship *Southampton* had already arrived in advance. The *Susquehanna* was to return to China after the conclusion of the mission, so the Commodore had his Cabin removed to the *Powhaton*. He continued with the same attitude of exclusiveness, never recognising the slightest personal superiority of any Japanese official however exalted his rank.

The Japanese were anxious to keep the Americans as far from Yedo as possible and had decided on Uraga as the place for negotiating a treaty. They completed a building for the purpose and Perry sent the captain of the fleet, Commander Adams, ashore to inspect it on 22nd February. Anticipating its unsuitability, Perry removed the squadron to a place within sight of Yedo while Adams was still ashore. Every devious argument to influence Perry to return to Uraga failed to move him. Finally it was mutually agreed that the small fishing village of Yokohama should be the venue.

The squadron could now expect to be at anchor for some days. Japanese officials were going aboard the *Powhaton* quite often but were always met by Commander Adams. The time seemed opportune to introduce to them the Japanese member of the *Susquehanna's* crew, known by the sailors as "Sam Patch". He was one of sixteen men swept away from the coast in a Japanese junk, rescued by an American merchant vessel and taken to San Francisco. All were given passage to China but only Sam remained with the squadron. The others stayed behind in China for fear of the death penalty required by Japanese law should they return.

As Sam was presented to the Japanese dignitaries, he prostrated himself at once, apparently completely awestricken. Sam had frequently been teased by his messmates about losing his head on arrival in his own country, and the poor fellow possibly thought his last hour had come. He was crouching in abject fear and trembling in every limb. Commander Adams ordered him to rise from his knees and reminded him that he was on board an American man-of-war, perfectly safe as one of her crew and had nothing to fear. Poor Sam was soon dismissed to his quarters as it was found impossible to reassure him. The Japanese tried every means to repatriate him but Sam could never be persuaded to leave his ship.

The Japanese aptitude for working collectively with speed and attention to detail was ably demonstrated as the building was constructed to accommodate all the officials negotiating the treaty. The "treaty house", as the Americans called it, was completed by 7th March. It was furnished in Japanese style with thick rice-straw mats, long and wide settees covered with red cloth and tables similarly draped. The windows were of oiled paper and hangings fell from the surrounding walls with paintings of trees and various animals. All was ready for the opening of the conference on the following day.

The Commodore planned every detail of this, his second landing on the soil of Japan. He knew the importance and moral influence of giving a display of great ceremony. All officers and sailors who could be spared were to accompany him, the officers in undress uniform of frock coat, cap and epaulettes and equipped with swords and pistols. There would be music from the bands of three vessels and all sailors would carry muskets, cutlasses and pistols. Five hundred officers and men in twenty-seven boats were rowed ashore in precise line abreast. The Commodore then left the *Powhaton* in his barge under a salute from the *Macedonian* of seventeen guns. It was indeed impressive.

The letter which Commodore Perry carried from President Fillmore was addressed, "To His Imperial Majesty, the Emperor of Japan". This was intended, not for the real sovereign in Kyoto, but for the *Shogun* at Yedo who ruled in his name. Throughout the weeks of negotiation involving endless discussions and hair-splitting arguments, it seems strange that Commodore Perry appears to have believed that he was dealing with emissaries from the Emperor. This error was caused by following the usage of the Jesuit Fathers and the Dutch writers on Japan, all of whom gave this title to the *Shogun*.

Finally, agreement was reached and on 31st March 1854 the Treaty of Kanagawa was signed. The port of Shimoda would be opened immediately, and that of Hakodate one year later, for supplies and American trade. Shipwrecked mariners were to be afforded help and protection, and American citizens allowed freedom of movement within defined limits. Perhaps even more important, it provided for the establishment of a United States consulate at Shimoda.

The metamorphosis had started. It had been agreed that gifts could be brought ashore from the American ships as from 13th March. There were thirty-four items of imaginative variety for the Emperor: a quarter-scale steam engine complete with track, tender and car; a set of electric telegraphic equipment; books, whisky, champagne, cloth, perfume, weapons, agricultural implements, down to two mail bags with padlocks! The Empress was to receive a flowered silk embroidered dress, perfume and a toilet dressing-box exquisitely designed and gilded. For other officials there was an assortment of clocks, wine and spirits, perfume, cloth and small arms. The Americans would never forget the circus-like antics of their hosts as they clung to the quarter-sized steam engine and carriage as it sped round its track. The Japanese could not disguise their amazed disbelief as they received messages by electric telegraph sent along a mile length of wire. They were unable to suppress their inordinate curiosity and followed the officers and men to examine every part of their uniforms. When admitted on board the ships, they peered in to every nook and corner accessible to them and made sketches, in their own peculiar style, of anything they could see.

On 24th March the Commodore had been invited ashore to receive the gifts ordered by the Emperor for President Fillmore, his government and, of course, for the Commodore and his squadron. The presents were arranged with the usual order and neatness which seemed almost instinctive to the Japanese. Three items which always form part of an Imperial present were rice, dried fish and dogs. Four small dogs of a rare breed of spaniel were set aside for the President and the fish was also there, but no rice. Another item regularly included was charcoal tied in bundles. Lacquer-ware with gold and silver decoration, fans, umbrellas, fabrics, collections of seashells were there and three hundred chickens for the squadron. The American party was led out from the treaty house towards the beach and taken to a pile of hundreds of immense bundles. Here was the rice! Each rice bale weighed not less than 125 lbs. There followed the awesome sight of twenty-five wrestlers, monstrous in height, bulk and strength, descending on the bales and removing them to a vantage point along the beach for transportation to the ships. Each wrestler lifted two bales at a time unaided, one even carried one in his teeth. It was a perfect marriage of utility and entertainment. The entertainment continued later with a demonstration of Sumo wrestling.

At last the mission had completed its main task and on 4th April the *Saratoga* left with Commander Adams who was to deliver the Treaty to President Fillmore in Washington. Commodore Perry, in a last flamboyant gesture, sailed the rest of the fleet further into Yedo Bay. After taking a look at the city, Perry gave orders for the squadron to proceed to the American anchorage off Uraga, and from there the ships were despatched at two-day intervals for Shimoda.

8

In The Wake Of Commodore Perry

Austen Cook was an anxious captain. He was running behind schedule and might have lost his gamble. The charts for the area were very sketchy but he chose to sail for Yedo Bay on a course between the island of Oshima and Shimoda on the mainland. It was almost three o'clock in the afternoon on 24th March 1854 when the look-out gave warning of an approaching steamship. It was one of the U.S. battleships. It passed no message and continued on its way at speed, leaving a bewildered Captain Cook to wonder if the whole squadron were leaving. This battleship was the *Susquehanna* actually returning to Macao on a new mission.

Again the look-out gave a shout. An American sloop was seen to be easing out from a starboard tack to take up a course parallel to their own. It was the *Vandalia* returning to Yokohama after patrolling the coast as far south as Shimoda. Information at last. Captain Cook was advised to make a safe anchorage before nightfall and to continue to Yokohama at first light next morning. He was to keep his American flag prominently displayed at all times. Confidence increased as tension was eased and the crew could view their situation with a more relaxed breadth of vision. There was a new curiosity among them in the steady flow of Japanese junks sailing and rowing, to both north and south, but always hugging the coast line. Even after dark their lamps could be seen like slow-moving glow-worms. Two boats, crowded with Japanese men, rowed out from the shore to view them with reciprocal curiosity, but made no attempt to climb on board. The crew was nervously alert and suddenly very aware that here was the notorious coast of Japan.

A useful southerly breeze influenced Captain Cook's decision to get under way a little before first light. The dawn revealed an interesting and varied coastline on the port side. Henry became completely captivated by a mountain that seemed to grow from its surrounding hills, snow-capped and majestic in its symmetry. It was Mount Fuji, sacred to the Japanese, and so often shrouded in mists. It was a scene to contemplate at leisure, but the mate was not inclined to tolerate his reverie for long.

Yedo Bay was undeniably a magnificent stretch of water and visibility was excellent. Yokohama could have been seen about noon but went unnoticed. All eyes were on the awesome, yet comforting sight of the American squadron. The individual ships had become familiar to Henry whilst at Hong Kong, but to see them here together on duty was different. The *Vandalia* was first in line and a pinnace moved away from her stern to guide Captain Cook to his appointed anchorage. This achieved, the pinnace came alongside and a lieutenant requested permission to come aboard. The captain took him to the privacy of his cabin. Henry found a vantage point in order to watch the door and it seemed a very long half-hour before they emerged. The crew were called to attention as a courtesy to the departing lieutenant. There followed a few seconds silence before all semblance of restraint vanished and, regardless of duties, the whole crew surged round their captain. For once he indulged their indiscipline, called for order and explained the sequence of events which had occurred so far in Yedo Bay and Yokohama. The men could not be allowed to go ashore, but they would be able to visit ships of the squadron from time to time. Permission was given for a relaxed evening with a minimum watch, but the ship had to be cleaned overall on the following day.

As a special privilege the captain invited Henry to his cabin for the evening, a concession rarely granted. For a few hours they were father and son, a relationship which now came easily each time without any initial embarrassment. Inevitably this intimacy would grow and Henry would gain many insights into the underlying experience required to finance and command a trading vessel. The next day would be an exciting example. The captain hoped to obtain permission to pay a business visit to the flagship *Powhaton* and Henry would accompany him with several other members of the crew.

Permission was granted and Henry enjoyed the exercise as he helped to row and weave the ship's boat through the vessels at anchor to the flagship at the centre of the squadron. It was a very happy occasion. A few seamen from each crew had already met each other in Hong Kong, so it was natural for a tour of the battleship to be arranged while Captain Cook went off to seek an outlet for his cargo.

The storeship *Supply* had arrived on 19th March, also from Shanghai, with coal and stores. The *Susquehanna* had refuelled from her before going to China, but there was still no immediate requirement of fresh supplies.

Fortunately, Captain Cook's quality of coal was equivalent and he secured a firm offer for his cargo if he undertook to remain with the squadron until it was ready to leave. A lieutenant was instructed to take the Captain to his waiting crew, where introductions took place. Henry would recall some fifty years later that it was Lieutenant Semmes, later to gain fame as Captain Semmes of the "Alabama".

To remain in the bay without shore leave for two or three weeks could engender problems, not only with a restless crew but also with stores and food. The Mate was instructed to draw up an inventory of essentials which revealed a looming problem regarding the quantity and variety of food. He was then sent across to the flagship with the details to seek assurance of help when needed. This was given with a further hint that it should be possible to pick up supplies at Shimoda before leaving Japan.

The following evening, there appeared to be a large-scale entertainment on board the *Powhaton*. Scores of Japanese boats were ferrying visitors from the shore through a sea of bobbing lights. A brass band was playing and, later, the sounds of a Yankee minstrel band echoed across the water, conveying odd snatches of Stephen Foster songs. Henry was bemused by the whole situation. His regular duties were largely supplanted by study of marine law and navigation with the captain, who insisted he also kept up to date with his independent practice Log, started as an exercise back in Hong Kong.

The crew had invitations to visit several ships in the squadron, all looking for relief from inactivity. On one of the ships, Henry met two seamen, Thomas Troy and Jonathan Goble, who claimed they were seeking permission to remain behind in Yokohama. For fourteen days life was infused with unreality.

Henry had become intrigued by the Japanese boats he saw always being rowed very purposefully. With a shipwright's eye he had noted a slender construction and sharp prow acutely angled. He amused himself by attempting to record the shape by simple sketches which he later tucked between the pages of his log. He often resorted to a sketch before embarking on any complicated carpentry job.

Captain Cook included Henry among the accompanying crew on two further occasions when he visited the *Powhaton*. Once, four days after the treaty had been completed, some welcome supplies of rice and other food items were given to them. The second time was on 13th April when they received orders to be prepared to sail on the 16th. *Southampton* and *Supply* were sailing for Shimoda on the 14th to survey a safe anchorage at this new treaty port. *Vandalia* and *Lexington* were to follow two days later, ahead of Captain Cook whose opportune cargo would be unshipped at Shimoda.

Henry was looking forward to reliving his first vision of Mount Fuji and kept a lookout on the starboard side whenever possible. This time a wall of mist, hovering on the tops of the hills, completely obscured even the slightest sign of the mountain. It was as though Fuji had never existed. Arrival at Shimoda was uneventful, although the scene was spectacular with the two harbours stretching inland to a series of sharply-peaked hills. Three ships of the squadron were in the inner harbour but Captain Cook was ordered to remain with *Vandalia* in the outer harbour. *Powhaton* and *Mississippi* would be arriving within two days requiring maximum space in which to manoeuvre, an operation finally completed in a manner which gained the nodding approval of the watching seamen.

It was arranged that the coal would be transferred to *Supply* as a reserve for the battleships. Captain Cook eased into the inner harbour and anchored alongside *Supply*. The coal had been shipped in containers, not only for clean handling but for securing in the hold to avoid the hazard of a shifting cargo in rough weather. The transfer was carried out with naval speed and efficiency, leaving Henry's ship noticeably higher in the water. Ballast, or preferably a good cargo, would have to be found but there were significantly few signs of commercial activity.

Captain Cook obtained permission to remain in the inner harbour. The crew spent some time in cleaning out the hold and scrubbing the decks to remove most of the coal dust which clung to the timbers. Uppermost in their minds was to spend some time ashore. An officer from the flagship came on board with a request that all hands be mustered on deck to be briefed on the rules of conduct to be observed at all times when on shore leave. They were to return all Japanese greetings with an equal politeness, avoid brawls whatever the provocation, and not to intrude on private or religious areas unless invited. Shops had been instructed by Japanese officials not to serve any Americans. This ban had been eased to a small extent through negotiation by Commodore Perry. A temporary currency value had been agreed that one American silver dollar should be equal to 1,600 Chinese copper coins - a currency understood by the Japanese.

This was such a different situation from any experienced before that Captain Cook made an exploratory visit with the Mate, leaving a few crew members in the ship's boat tied to a short wooden jetty. They found no active resentment. A few of the local men followed them everywhere, but most of the populace seemed to melt into their homes or peer from a distance. The strong naval presence in the harbour was reassuring. Shore leave would be granted.

For some reason, not entirely clear to himself, Henry wanted to explore Shimoda alone. Normally he would go ashore with some of the crew and invariably had a good time, but the pattern of pleasure was always the same, regardless of which port or country. Perhaps he was mesmerised by the continual boat building activity, so far only viewed from a distance. He was puzzled by the numerous labourers employed on building and repairing the boats and junks. He sensed something unusual in the whole atmosphere.

When Henry's turn came for leave, he scrambled ashore with the others and acknowledged a warning that the boat would return for them all in six hours time. After explaining that he intended to find his way alone, he strode off rapidly inland before objections could be effectively raised. Two Japanese immediately appeared, both wearing swords, and set off in pursuit but although they dogged his footsteps closely, they never interfered with his progress. They were undoubtedly local police acting on the instructions of an anxious administration.

Henry slackened his pace, having distanced himself from the rest of the crew, and could begin to satisfy his curiosity. The town was larger than he expected, compactly built with streets intersecting at right angles. The streets were about twenty feet wide and most were guarded with light wooden gates. He decided not to venture past them. There was a healthy look of cleanliness everywhere, when compared with his recollections of Ireland. Not only were there gutters but sewers channelled to drain the waste water and filth directly into the sea or into the small river which divided the town.

Very few houses were of stone; most were of dried mud and plaster over a bamboo or wooden frame. The roofs were wither-thatched or tiled, some with alternate black and white patterning. He wandered into an area where shops were open and seemed fairly busy. The people, perhaps feeling secure together, stopped as if commanded and turned to stare at him. Feeling embarrassed and not a little worried, Henry gave a nervous, rather hesitant smile and a very non-committal gesture of greeting. After a pause, one man made a small bow towards him and, as he straightened, he turned to those beside him with a broad grin. Others followed the example laughing and talking loudly to each other, the women with very high-pitched voices. The two policemen following Henry hurried across the street and shouted a torrent of sounds at the crowd, who were instantly silenced. Henry was not sure if he had been greeted or mocked, but he made one serious bow in return before continuing his walk. There was no more response.

As Henry progressed through the town, he recognised that the temples and shrines had the upwardly-curving roofs he had often seen in China. More strange was the footwear worn by most people, either straw sandals or wooden platforms supported by two wooden bars keeping the wearer about four inches above the ground and allowing only very short strides. His own progress had become less purposeful with legs unaccustomed to walking great distances and he began to regret the lack of a companion to share the burden of such condensed experience. Once again he sought relief in the familiar and made his way back to the harbour and the boat-yards. A low wall close to a stack of felled trees made an ideal resting place, from which Henry could survey the scene and absorb the aromatic smell of the cut timber. What he had seen from the ship was confirmed. There were hundreds of workmen, more or less busy, spaced round the different boats under construction or being repaired. Slowly a pattern of work emerged. Many of the men and boys were not craftsmen but were used collectively as machines to lift, to bend timbers and to hold for fixing. Men would never have worked like that in Newport. It looked so primitive yet obviously successful and, to a practised eye, showed a high standard of finish.

Tiredness and hesitancy slipped away as enthusiasm took over. He moved in closer to an area where men were shaping lengths of timber with tools obvious in their purpose but of a design unknown to him. Henry had forgotten about the police persistence and was startled when they leapt in front of him to bar the way. The carpenter looked up and stopped work. One of them moved closer and bowed to the policemen who returned the greeting briefly. There followed a flood of unintelligible conversation at high speed with much gesticulation. Henry began to panic and, perhaps prompted by having seen the temple roofs, he shouted out a few words in Chinese - boat! hammer! wood! - which he had learned in different ports. The effect was so remarkable it almost completely unnerved him. The shouting stopped and the men looked worried and uncertain how to act. Henry took advantage of their disquiet and began to demonstrate with gestures and repeated the same Chinese words. He seized a piece of wood and mimed cutting and hammering it, pointed to the

LITTLE FUJIYAMA, SHIMODA

Japanese Junk under repair at Shimoda

carpenter then back to himself, and finally across to the boat.

Obviously there had been some vague understanding of the Chinese terms which helped to convey the meaning of the mime. The carpenter's face relaxed a little but the eyes were still troubled. Henry was led to the work trestles and allowed to watch as the men resumed shaping the timber with double-handled blades which were beautifully made and very sharp. The workmen were skilful and Henry could see they knew how to avoid the vagaries of timber by constantly changing the direction of the cut. At ease in those surroundings and having a natural affinity with workmen, Henry instinctively picked up a piece of rough timber and moved to one of the trestles. He accepted a tool from the bemused carpenter working there and began to shave the surface of the wood. He knew that any tool produced the best result if used positively, so he proceeded to work quickly and confidently. The tool proved to be highly efficient. A group of workmen gathered round, talking very fast as usual, and making what appeared to be grunts of approval. Henry was enjoying the stir he had caused and played up to it by finishing his test piece with a quite unnecessary flourish.

Everyone was relaxed and laughing, even the two policemen. The carpenter, whom Henry took to be a foreman, gave two consecutive low bows without any hint of mockery. Henry gravely returned the politeness. With no common language to follow up the encounter they all stood rather awkwardly, smiling. The foreman then guided Henry to see one of the construction teams assembling the rib frame of a junk. The whole activity had a primitive appeal and yet was very sophisticated. He managed to memorise a few Japanese names for items in common use by carpenters, thereby evoking roars of laughter.

It was time to return to the jetty, but Henry could not leave before an exchange of bowing several times with the workmen. The foreman was inquisitive and followed Henry to the quayside, where the rest of the crew were waiting. Henry pointed to his ship, received a nod of understanding and left to join the crew after bowing farewell. They looked questioningly at him and he obliged with a few obvious remarks but felt too private to say any more. Suddenly he felt tired and very hungry, not having eaten since landing. Deep down, Henry knew that the day's events had changed him. He could act on his own ideas, he no longer felt tied to the crew for support; he wanted to be given more responsibility. Not everyone would like the change in him. Perhaps in time the manly aspirations would lose their urgency. After all, he was still only eighteen.

That evening, having mellowed a little after food and drink, Henry confided most of the day's events to the captain. He also ventured to suggest a possible cargo to take out of Shimoda. The sight of so much timber stacked in just one of the boatyards had reminded him of similar successful transactions in the past. The idea was good and the captain was quietly impressed, but there were difficulties. He was no longer in touch with the current demands for timber; also it might not be possible to persuade the Japanese to trade with him. He had discovered, during a visit to the *Powhaton* that day, the requirement that any major purchase must be made through the naval diplomatic chain. First, he must see the timber for himself and then decide.

Next morning the captain went ashore, taking Henry and the ship's carpenter with him. In the boatyard Henry was recognised and greeted in the usual manner. A deep bow was made to the captain after Henry pointed to the insignia of rank he wore. They were allowed to look around the yard but were closely followed. There was a fair mix of hard and soft timber, but the captain's attention was drawn to a pile of logs, not yet sectioned, outside the boundary of the yard. They were pine and other conifers, ideal for simple building purposes. There followed a useful exercise for Henry as he listened to the assessing of its probable value. The captain was satisfied, but its disposal would require another gamble. It was a challenge he was persuaded to accept.

The trio returned to the ship where a brief conference was held with the mate. It was decided that they should aim to leave Shimoda by 6th May if possible; that left only ten days for preparation. The captain wasted no time and enlisted the flagship's intervention to aid a fellow American. The purchase of the timber was made more possible by the presence of the chief interpreter from Yedo. He had already been called to the *Powhaton* on 25th April to deal with a strange incident. It had been about 2 a.m. when two well-educated Japanese men had rowed out to the *Mississippi* and, as they began to climb the ship's ladder, pushed their boat away to establish some permanence to their arrival. They were taken to the flagship where they confessed that their object was to be taken to the United States. Commodore Perry had no intention of offending the Emperor by being party to such a serious flouting of Japanese law. The men failed with their pleas to the Americans not to return them to certain execution. They were landed, still bemoaning their fate, at a place on the shore near the probable drift of their boat. In answer to his appeal for clemency, the Commodore was assured by the interpreter that the two men would not be put to death.

The task of buying in rations for the voyage was delegated to the mate. The crew had been living on the plentiful supply of fish and a good range of fresh vegetables bought via the navy in Shimoda. Poultry was rather scarce and fresh meat almost unobtainable due to the prevailing Buddhist influence. Cattle were also valued too highly as beasts of burden for them to be sold to carnivorous strangers. He was able to get an assurance from the storeship *Supply* for sufficient ships' biscuit and salt tack, with a good chance of a few hens or ducks and some vegetables. On 2nd May the sloop *Macedonian* returned from a survey on the Bonin Islands with a welcome supply of fine turtles which were distributed among the ships of the squadron. A generous supply of the meat was delivered to Captain Cook with compliments from *Vandalia* and the crew enjoyed a feast for kings.

The return of the *Macedonian* was providential in another way. Captain Cook learned from its captain that America was arranging to have storage bases on Peel Island (Chichi Jima), in the Bonin group, for coal and general supplies. It was seen as a useful stopping place for steamers travelling between California and China. Here was a typical outlet for a cargo of timber and a clear pointer to his next destination. The navy drove a hard bargain on his behalf and secured the timber for a surprisingly low price, including a commitment from the Japanese to ferry the logs out to the ship.

The crew were allowed one more trip ashore and this time Henry was pleased to stay with them. They were keen to buy some inexpensive souvenirs and, fortunately, the resistance of the shopkeepers had melted away and they were quite eager to collect American silver dollars. While strolling with a few friends into the suburbs of the town, Henry came upon the town prison. In one of the usual places of confinement, a kind of cage with bars in front and very restricted in area, were the two Japanese men who had been pursued and captured a few days after being returned to the shore from *Powhaton*. He later heard that these prisoners were taken to Yedo on the following day to a fate not recorded.

The hours of inactivity were over. Every man would be worked nearly to exhaustion for the next two or three days. The Japanese were ferrying the timber using several of their boats to ensure a continuous supply. No Japanese would venture on board, but all gave willing and energetic assistance with unloading. Stacking the timber into the hold at such speed was back-breaking work and proved the loyalty on which Captain Cook could depend. If a good profit were realised, the men could expect a sizeable bonus.

It was 6th May but loading was not quite finished. The *Macedonian*, *Vandalia* and *Southampton* sailed out of the harbour and set course for Hakodate to prepare for Commodore Perry's visit to the second treaty port. Captain Cook decided to abandon his schedule. His crew had earned a brief rest and he needed them to be fully alert for the first part of the voyage while skirting the coast of Japan. By delaying until the 18th, he would also be able to make a few farewell visits to the American officers who had been so helpful to him beyond the call of duty.

It was a more mature Henry who returned the gestures of farewell being signalled from *Powhaton* and *Mississippi* as his ship finally nosed out of the inner harbour.

9
Delights Before Disaster

From a seaman's point of view, the short voyage to the Bonin Islands was uneventful. Damp clothes which never quite dried out after torrential rain and strong winds which were rarely favourable were a nuisance but not unexpected. Captain Cook had been given good advice on the best approach to Peel Island and a safe anchorage. Some U.S. Navy personnel had been left to survey the island which seemed to have distinct possibilities for raising sheep and goats for fresh meat supplies in addition to the storage of fuel. Timber and water could be obtained in abundance but crews would always have to cut their own wood and take it on board green. Partly-seasoned timber for construction purposes was scarce so the cargo of building timber was welcome, although ferrying it to the beach without the advantage of a suitable jetty or Japanese help was laborious and time-consuming. The officer in charge agreed a Bill of Sale, drawn up by Captain Cook as a charge on the U.S. government and authorised in anticipation by the negotiating officer on *Powhaton*.

There followed a quite unexpected boost to the captain's plan to return to America after his long absence. A small quantity of coal had been accepted on Peel but was later found to be of a quality quite useless for refuelling steamships. It would not be a full cargo but was offered to Captain Cook as ballast with the possibility of its disposal for domestic use. There would be no better destination for such a transaction that San Francisco with its population explosion outstripping all local resources. It would be the longest single voyage he had ever undertaken, but he was certain of total support from an equally homesick crew. Henry had no such commitment and would be sorry to leave the Far Eastern influence which had helped to shape a highly impressionable stage of his life.

Ample stores were made available by the survey team but water supplies would need strict supervision for a period exceeding two months. To insure against such a shortage, the captain planned a southerly deviation from the direct route to replenish supplies on one of the Sandwich (Hawaiian) Islands.

Henry was given the task, as an exercise under very close scrutiny, of plotting a route due west from Peel Island. He would have to log every change of course required to compensate for unfavourable winds and drift. After twenty eight days a small island was sighted but it was surrounded by treacherous reefs which were such a common hazard in that part of the Pacific. A second island marked on the chart was reached on the following day. The chart gave no name to it but did indicate a deep water approach. The captain directed the crew with seamanship of a very high order and successfully anchored within sight of a group of palm-thatched huts.

A boat put out from the shore to greet them but when a loud voice hailed them in English it produced something of an anticlimax. Many American and European travellers had settled in the islands and married the well-endowed island women. Sailors generally referred to the Sandwich islanders as *Kanakas* perhaps through the larger population on Kanai Island. Water could be supplied from several running streams without depriving the small settlement, so the crew were able to combine some inland excursions with ferrying casks of water back to the ship. The sudden freedom among such idyllic scenery made the idea of jumping ship a topic for amusement during the evenings. The men were relaxed and risked having fun at the captain's expense by suggesting he must be related to Captain James Cook who named the group of islands and, on his return two years later, was murdered there in 1779. He let the story grow for a while before confessing that he was not remotely connected with that great explorer.

Realism returned after a few days. The captain took a north-easterly route for the second part of the voyage, hoping to hit the advantageous westerlies which could drive him north of San Francisco without too many deviations from the course. The south-moving Californian current would then play its part in bringing the ship to its final destination.

Thirty-seven salt-weary days after leaving paradise, the crew were rewarded by their first sight of San Francisco. As they sailed through the entrance to the harbour a wide stretch of calm water opened up before them, secure from the vast Pacific Ocean.

After completing such a long voyage, which followed an already extended period away from families, many crew members were frustrated in their eagerness to begin overland journeys to their homes. The crew had to remain with the ship until Captain Cook could make arrangements with the banks to allow credit on the various Bills of Sale which had accumulated. He was able to pay off the crew to everyone's satisfaction and Henry was rather awed at possessing such a sum of money which had accrued over many months.

A few of Henry's shipmates had no special roots and declared they would remain in the area and be willing to sign on again when required. Most left the ship never to return, including the chief carpenter whose supportive opinions Henry would miss. There had been a very competitive market for the coal in response to a notice that the captain had displayed on the quay. He could have shifted a cargo several times larger.

The captain helped Henry to find a clean-looking lodging ashore but seemed unwilling to reveal his own intentions. He had never confided to Henry any details of family background, whether or not he was married, nor from which part of America he had come. His religion was Christian but his short services on board were confined to simple bible readings without comment and basic Christian prayers. He promised to be in touch again after one or two weeks.

The routine renewal through Catholic worship and example had not been available to nourish the sincerely practised origins of Henry's faith. Several of his shipmates had been Catholic but more from unquestioning acceptance than through devotion. Quite naturally he had drifted into a similar attitude but something of the devout Catholic atmosphere at home had stuck to him and made him avoid, if sometimes reluctantly, the excesses indulged in by many seamen.

One evening he was seeking entertainment in a seaman's hostel which was visited by all sorts of travelling missionaries and Christian evangelists seeking souls. On this occasion Henry found himself talking with a Catholic priest for the first time since leaving home. It was a disturbing encounter which inspired improbable resolutions and a promise to find the address given to him where the priest would be saying Mass and hearing confessions.

Henry felt insecure during his leave in San Francisco. He was not at ease in company with the hard-drinking, rough-talking groups of men who frequented the bars. They displayed a callous indifference to everything around them. He was used to high spirits and enjoyed those times with the crew in Hong Kong and other Far Eastern ports, but the veneer of oriental politeness invariably leavened hot tempers. In lonely nostalgia Henry, relieved by an occasional meeting with old friends from the crew, waited for the return of the Captain and the therapy of work.

His lodgings were comfortable. The terms included a good breakfast and one other meal, usually served early in the evening. Hot water was brought to the room every morning and, if he was too lazy to get up in time for breakfast, a tray of food would be dumped on the table in his room without comment, for him to eat or leave as he pleased. One morning there was a startling change to the routine. The tray was not brought in by the usual maid but by the landlady herself. Instead of leaving, she picked up an extra mug of coffee that was on the tray and sat on the edge of his bed to drink it. While she was drinking she talked to Henry, asking him about his home and plans for the future. Henry could not make up his mind whether he should get up and eat breakfast while she was chatting or to wait for her to go. He decided to wait, remembering he was only wearing drawers, and had no wish to embarrass his landlady, who was a very pleasant, mild-mannered woman in her early forties.

She finished her coffee and returned her empty mug to the tray. Henry was about to make some suitably trite remark as she left when he noticed a distinct hesitation followed by a questioning uncertain glance back in his direction. She seemed to make up her mind about something and without a word, as though frightened of breaking her resolve, she slipped off a type of housecoat and plunged into the bed beside Henry, pulling the covers up to her neck. Each was wide-eyed with surprise at the sudden move until mutual laughter eased the nervous tension.

She was the first to speak and guessing from Henry's reaction a worried innocence, she confessed to her own confusion in indulging a sudden desire so out of character. Henry was not so naive as to be unaware of what was expected of him but was uncertain how to set about it. He need not have worried. This pleasant, rather motherly, woman took the initiative with a sensitive understanding and seemed able to satisfy her own desires and yet allow him to respond without feeling inadequate. After a while she left him, pulled on her housecoat and giving him a smile of thanks she left the room. It was the one and only occasion.

After a few days the whole affair was reduced to a dream sequence. His landlady never changed her previous attitude to him. There was not even a hint of a knowing smile or any extra attention. Henry found it difficult to meet the landlord's eye with his usual frankness. Did he suspect anything? Was she like that with other lodgers? Henry was full of unanswered questions. He would come to realise how fortunate he was to have had such a considerate and skilful tutor compared with many sordid opportunities he had resisted in the past.

The captain returned as promised, having been away for little more than a fortnight. Henry was feeling rather self-conscious and watchful to see if there was any reaction from someone who knew him so well. There was none. Captain Cook seemed preoccupied with his own plans although he greeted Henry warmly enough. The captain had been master of his schooner for several years and owned a two-third share in her. He had been responsible for her trading, maintenance and profitability, and had secured a good reputation in the process. His return to America had given him the opportunity to meet his partner and persuade him to agree a change of policy. He wished to use his reputation as sufficient guarantee to become assigned to a large trading company, thus avoiding some of the risks and uncertainties. A suitable arrangement had been made with an American company of international repute who wished to use his experience for the benefit of their branches in the Far East. His first voyage would be in part ballast with small crates of goods consigned to their branch in Shanghai, which was to be his centre of operations.

It took several weeks to prepare the ship and to sign on a crew of the calibre expected by the captain. An important change came for Henry. He was promoted to chief carpenter and allowed to assist in interviewing applicants for his previous job. The captain also recorded the completion of Henry's apprenticeship as shipwright. He had been groomed for early promotion but the captain allowed it only because of his proven aptitude, tested by the ship itself. Rising to his new position of responsibility, Henry decided to make a further change to his image. He began to let his beard grow during the weeks of preparation, hoping it would show its potential before they set sail. In contrast to the captain's beard, it was light in colour and rather thin in density but satisfied Henry's vanity when it was close-trimmed.

They set sail in the final week of October 1854, knowing that the seasonal wrath of the Pacific lay between them and Shanghai. Life on board soon drifted into traditional patterns, oscillating between calm and emergency. Responsibility broadened Henry's view of the ship. He began to see the unity of it, the vessel and the crew as one organism using the forces of nature to achieve its own will.

For the next two years Henry followed many familiar routes throughout the Far East with an ever-increasing sense of command encouraged by the amount of trust placed in him by the captain and the mate. Fortunately, the mate had rejoined the ship at San Francisco and knew he had nothing to fear or resent from this quiet challenge to his own authority. The relationship between the captain and his adopted son was friendly, familiar and rewarding for both of them in mutual affection. Henry was finding it difficult to recall details about his family back in Newport and his mental pictures of them had dimmed. One voyage took him back to Hong Kong where the captain was able to trace a reply to the letter sent home the previous year. It contained news of each member of the family, even John who was only a baby when he had escaped from Newport, but there was no warmth in the letter. It was as though someone else had written it for them. Perhaps someone had, the writing was very legible. It left him feeling rather sad and quite lonely, in spite of so many companions.

Trading for a major company had brought new status to the ship and an easy confidence to the outlook of the crew. Towards the end of September 1856, the ship was returning to Shanghai with a light cargo from Formosa and the crew were looking forward to satiating their various appetites. The captain was more concerned with the heavy swell coming at the ship from the east. He could feel that it was different from the usual run of the sea. It had a power and weight as though summoned from the depths. The crew was called to action stations and the ship prepared for rough weather in the normal routine.

It was only mid-afternoon but the light was fading at an alarming rate as dense black, turbulent clouds were swept across the sky by a rapidly increasing wind. On a clear day, the entrance to the Yangtse would be visible from about eleven miles, and Captain Cook was tempted to race for shelter but his ship could not respond against the dictates of the wind and waves. The regularity of the swell had been broken, giving freedom to individual waves, each gathering power to itself. About a mile distant on the port side, Henry spotted a tiny cone-shaped island, momentarily revealed as the ship was thrust into the air. It was the island of Gutzlaff (Dajishan), a landmark familiar to him which had a series of rocks extending from it for some four hundred yards to the east, terminating in a prominent nine foot high black rock. Knowing it was there made little difference. A huge wave, out of sequence, caught the stern of the ship full broadside, smashed the rudder and removed all pretence of control. Before the ship could get back on an even keel, a second wave lifted it like a petulant child with a toy and smashed it hard on the Gutzlaff rocks.

Typhoon - Taifū (great wind)

The mind can conjure strange thoughts in times of crisis. Henry was struck by the flimsy weakness of wood as he heard the hefty bottom timbers split open like a cigar box. The sea rushed in, but as a third wave pulled the ship free the sea spewed out again, sucking cargo from the hold. The Captain ordered the ship to be abandoned, but the wind drowned his commands making them a waste of effort . A few sailors had already leaped into the sea, taking their chance with the floating debris within reach. Both the ship's boats had been torn away by the second wave. Henry wondered what could be gained by leaving a ship he had learned to trust. It was safer on board and still the largest piece of debris. He made his way to the man he had come to know as father who immediately became the Captain, not the father. Worried about the closing darkness, he ordered Henry to leap to the first possible makeshift raft. The sea suddenly gathered the ship closer within itself and a large packing-case, securely lashed with ropes, surged to the surface. Angry at Henry's hesitation, he pushed his son over the side. Henry missed the case as he landed in the sea but managed to seize a rope from it as it bore down on him.

Although severely bruised, Henry was able to heave himself up and straddle his body across the top of the box about a foot above the surface of the sea. The waves were mountainous and for a while at each summit he looked frantically in all directions but could see nothing. Panic gave way to a determination to survive.

71

It was dark. He remained spreadeagled across the surface, aware of intense cold. He felt numb with exposure. His hands were locked round the ropes with the rigidity of cramp. If he let go with one hand to relieve the pain he knew he would never be able to close it round the rope again. He had hoped to be thrown onto Gutzlaff Island but obviously by now the sea had carried him too far. The next possibility was the Shanghai landfall forming the south shore of the mouth of the Yangtse.

There was darkness, never-ending darkness. All strength had gone, he was mechanically fixed to the ropes by sinew and bone. He could no longer use prayer to keep hope alive, but something guided his surging progress to land. The packing-case was smashed against a low-lying rock and Henry was flung into the sea in a horizontal cartwheel. His mind was dead to any thought of swimming; his body had no survival instinct left.

He had no way of knowing how long waves had been sweeping over his feet. A faint glimmer of light in the sky lit up a smooth stretch of sand ahead of him. Straining his head round he could see that the waves were as gentle as in Ireland. Where was reality? He was almost too cold to feel cold. He began to make little painful movements, rubbing fist against fist, not yet aware of fingers. Drawing upon his youth and fitness, Henry began to crawl up the beach and out of the water. He staggered to his feet but collapsed, unable to balance on legs he could not feel. He rested content to practise small movements. The light improved. The second attempt to stand was successful and he managed to reach a patch of coarse grass before falling once again. Sucking the juicy ends of the blades of grass did little to ease a raging thirst.

Rays from the early sun had some warmth in them and Henry lay still as if in a warm bath as his clothes began to steam and dry. He had noticed a few rough dwellings in the distance but he had no hope of reaching them. Occasional sounds of voices came from that direction. He saw the grass moving to his right and two hens wandered close to him, intent on their search for insects. As one of them came sufficiently close, Henry gathered all his strength and caught it in both hands. The other bird rushed away flapping ineffectual wings and squawking loudly. Henry was about to dispatch his catch, a skill he had learned as a boy in Ireland, but stayed his hand. The close contact with something living and warm was sensuously pleasant after the night of pain. His mind raced over his loss - everything he owned, probably many of his friends, perhaps even the Captain. Exhaustion took over and he wept.

The hen was food and without thinking ahead how to use it, he killed it. At that time Henry was kneeling over the bird revealing his presence to three men from the village who had been alerted by the squawking hen. With loud shouts the men rushed at him and, in vain, he got to his feet and tried to run. He was pulled down and the men stood over him, anger evident in every movement, one holding the dead bird. Henry had mastered a simple working vocabulary in Chinese which he tried to put to good use. At first the men were too hostile to listen and kicked him several times. Slowly they pieced together snatches of his story, confirmed by his weakness and dishevelled appearance, but still shook the hen at him in a threatening manner.

The men carried Henry back to the village quite carefully; he was taken into one of the huts and given some food and drink while seated on the floor by a charcoal fire. His body responded with a drowsy feeling of well-being. Henry was puzzled why a group of men and women outside the hut were directing so much fiery language over the dead hen rather that at him. Perhaps the villagers were strictly Buddhist. He vaguely remembered this might forbid the eating or killing of animals; he thought it wise to remain ignorant.

His clothes soon dried and he rummaged through his pockets to see what was left. His pay-book and ship's papers were there, though blotted with ink stains, and four silver Mexican dollars had remained in the tangle of a pocket lining. He had no shoes.

The three men came back into the hut with a more friendly manner and explained that they had searched along the shore for other survivors. They had found only broken crates and small pieces of wreckage. Henry gathered from their description that he was at a point south-east from Shanghai. He begged for some simple straw shoes and for help in getting him to Shanghai. He offered them the four dollars in payment. The men conferred, then nodded agreement. The straw sandals were much too small but they had none larger. It was also decided to give Henry passage on one of their small open boats that would be skirting the coast to Shanghai on the following day.

After a small meal of rice with chopped vegetables, and plenty to drink, Henry slept on the floor with a hard pillow for his head and covered with a single old blanket. He slept as though in comfort.

10
To Full Maturity

True to their word, the villagers gave Henry passage to Shanghai in their small boat. He shared it with crates of the seaweed which had been swept in by the storm and gathered by the enterprising boat owners for a quick profit. Some types of seaweed were valued for medicinal purposes and others were used extensively in cooking. Shanghai was within easy reach up the Wusung River (Hwang-Pu), about twelve miles from the mouth of the Yangtse. The boat was sailed into the harbour and moored to a small quay convenient to the centre of the town where scores of other small boats jostled for favoured berths. There were no formal farewells, which seemed appropriate after such anger and hostility had been directed at him.

As Henry approached the head office of his employers, his heart was thumping with anxiety. Did they know about the wreck? Would there be news of his captain and the rest of the crew? The company had heard nothing; the ship was a little overdue but that was not unusual. Henry gave an account of what had happened in the storm and of his own rescue and return to Shanghai. It was explained to him that news of other survivors might take many days to arrive, depending on where or how they were rescued. The company manager was very sympathetic to his state of mind and unkempt appearance. They kitted him out with some fresh clothes, arranged for him to be fed, and given somewhere to sleep undisturbed.

Three days later, four crew mates were brought to the hospital suffering from exposure and severe damage to the legs. They had been clinging to debris with legs trailing in the sea and, although they had been flung to safety on Gutzlaff Island, their legs had been smashed on the rocks in the process. Henry went to see them and came away feeling ashamed of his own understandable self-pity .

A further week passed without any news to lighten his sorrow. Some wreckage had been found at several points south of Shanghai but no more survivors. The company wisely brought the days of idle waiting to an end and instructed Henry to sign with one of their vessels which was due to sail for Hong Kong. Henry might have resented the decision but he liked Hong Kong with its happy memories. His papers were renewed and brought up to date and all money due to him was paid in full. A semblance of dignity had been restored but his deep sorrow was pushed only fractionally below the surface. All his roots had been severed, even his sea chest had gone with all those oddments he used to rummage through when feeling homesick or lonely-letters, souvenirs, precious tools, special clothes, even the bible brought with him from Newport which was often held and sometimes read.

The voyage to Hong Kong was not a happy one. He had been given responsibility at various times for almost every aspect of running his old ship. As chief carpenter he had almost reached officer status and the captain had been his foster-father. What other ship could possibly have offered such a situation? Henry's position was reduced to that of a semi-skilled carpenter and his offers to help in other ways were firmly rejected. He felt under-used and frustrated and found himself giving vent to a latent temper that had rarely surfaced before.

While on shore leave in Hong Kong, Henry picked up news that a British barque, the *Henry Ellis*, was signing on some fresh crew. He found his way to it and managed to get taken aboard where he was interviewed by Captain W.A. Baillie and the chief officer. They asked him some very searching questions about his experience but, although convinced of his competence as a shipwright and carpenter, they exchanged glances of scepticism at some of his replies. They had not heard about his shipwreck, only that several vessels had reported damage after being ravaged by the storm. The position of chief carpenter had to be filled and it was offered to Henry on condition that he obtained full legal discharge from his present ship.

It took several days, but his discharge was granted; the captain was quite pleased to let him go. Captain Baillie heard from a chance meeting in Hong Kong with this captain that Henry was surly and had too high an opinion of himself. The shadow caused by this biased view would be dispelled within a few weeks. Henry was signed on and soon became totally absorbed in getting to know his new ship. The *Henry Ellis* was a barque of 412 tons, some 80 tons larger than his first ill-fated ship. He was pleased with the equipment on board and liked the general construction and clever design of fittings to allow for easy maintenance. He set about making a list of work priorities, in some order of urgency, giving simple drawings where it was helpful by way of explanation. He submitted the schedule to Captain Baillie for approval and was given permission to purchase the timber he would need to have on board for the next few months at sea.

There were times when he felt guilty in his newly-found happiness but he had always gained therapeutic renewal from hard work. All his efforts in seeking news of Captain Cook failed to provide any crumb of comfort. Of course news travelled slowly, but deep in his heart Henry knew that he would never see his second father again. He had decided not to worry his family in Newport with any details of the shipwreck and he became reconciled to his loss through a sincere belief in the Christian view of death. He confided much of his personal history to Captain Baillie, including his relationship with Captain Cook. The captain needed very little persuasion before agreeing to conduct a full burial service at sea for Captain Cook. The ship's crew were assembled on deck for the service and sang the hymns with gusto when asked. Henry had made a crude but effective wreath using rope and vegetable leaves scrounged from the galley. This he cast into the sea at the appropriate moment as a sacramental sign of his acceptance of the Will of God.

The crew found it easy to sympathise with Henry. Through their experience of him as a hard worker, fair in his dealings with them and conscientious with his training of the junior carpenters, he found himself accepted into a new family of shipmates. This was important to Henry as he had become so used to the influence of an American crew and their allegiance to the American view. His observations about American supremacy when dealing with the Japanese were sharply countered by details of British naval prowess in India and in the war with China then in progress.

The fact that Great Britain was by then the dominant power in Eastern waters was a situation used to good effect by the Americans for their own benefit in Japan. In August 1856 Townsend Harris had arrived in Shimoda to take up his duties as Consul-General of the United States. His attempts to arrange a full commercial treaty with Japan, with rights of residence and American legal jurisdiction over its citizens, were met with all the usual procrastination. Harris was a stubborn and very shrewd man. Early in 1858 he sowed seeds of anxiety for Japan by emphasising that the British were at war with China because of Chinese attempts to evade treaty obligations. By the end of July he was able to apply more pressure with the information that Britain had made a peace settlement with China and was planning to send an expedition to Japan. His treaty was signed on 29th July!

Japan's virtual isolation from the world was about to end. On August 18th and 19th, similar treaties were concluded with Holland and Russia just as the British squadron arrived at Shimoda, bearing Lord Elgin as plenipotentiary. The mission included a steam yacht, the *Emperor*, sent as a present for the emperor of Japan by Queen Victoria. Lord Elgin resisted all efforts to keep him at Shimoda. The British squadron set sail and with a show of independence it swept past Kanagawa to an anchorage off Yedo, where it took a mere two days of negotiation before a treaty with the British was signed, based on the formula used by Townsend Harris. Baron Gros concluded a similar treaty for France two months later.

During the British conflict with China, Captain Baillie had kept away from the Chinese mainland even though some parts were relatively safe. A new confidence that reception in the designated ports in Japan would be less hostile had opened up the possibility of fresh trade routes. It was while negotiating stores at Hakodate, on Japan's northern island of Hokkaido, that Henry first had close contact with fur hunters returning from an expedition to the Kuril Islands. He was attracted by the strong lines of their ships, built to withstand extreme conditions of weather. It was after being invited as a guest on board two of the ships that his enthusiasm for their sturdy perfection evoked a resolution that at some time in the future he would design and build ships. It was probably just a dream, but one that concentrated his observation and sketching at every opportunity for the next three years.

Captain Baillie was more interested in the collection of fur pelts, which were of sea otter, fur seal and sea lion. Normally these would fetch their highest price in Europe, preferably London, but he was sure that the trading company to which has ship was assigned, Sassoon & Co., would welcome such a valuable cargo. After long discussion over the proposed deviation from their usual practice, the captains of the hunter ships agreed to sell their cargoes at a fair price charged to Sassoon & Co. The quick sale would provide time for a second hunt in the Kurils before returning to their home port. While the furs were being transhipped, Henry indulged his delight in these small vessels and learned about the hunting methods used, the curing of the skins and how to price them. It was a tough life but lucrative.

During 1858, the *Henry Ellis* sailed along routes then so familiar to Henry that his knowledge of navigation and expert general seamanship no longer remained hidden. Captain Baillie knew for certain that his scepticism at the first interview regarding Henry's wide experience was quite unfounded. He was going to need a new Second Mate and had come to the conclusion that Henry was an ideal candidate. Henry's abilities were rigorously tested for several weeks under the critical supervision of the First Officer. This was just the situation in which Henry could give rein to his instinctive and well-trained handling of a ship under sail or in port. Still only twenty-two years of age, he was officially promoted to officer rank and could now take command of his ship should the need arise. With this new status came extra privileges when ashore. The need to use the Japanese harbours of Shimoda and Nagasaki had become more frequent and, in spite of the very restricted zone of access, Henry was able to add an increasing number of phrases in Japanese to his early limited vocabulary.

News was beginning to filter through to the major trading companies early in 1859 that Japan was going to allow a foreign trading settlement to be developed at Kanagawa and that Nagasaki and Hakodate would be opened to foreign commercial activity. There was intense rivalry between the Far East offices of companies such as Jardine Matheson, Walsh Hall, Dent and Oliphant. Henry's present employers, Sassoon & Co., were determined to establish an agent in the new settlement at the first opportunity. The date set for the official opening was to be 1st July. Captain Baillie and his officers were instructed to be there with a company agent as passenger, whose task would be to establish early roots along with their illustrious rivals.

For Henry to return to the scene of his first meeting with Commodore Perry's squadron in 1854 was an unbelievable stroke of good fortune. He expressed his doubts about finding suitable deep water at Kanagawa, remembering the American ships' preference for the deep water off Yokohama. That problem could be dealt with on arrival.

11
Kanagawa Versus Yokohama

Mr Rutherford Alcock arrived at Yedo in June 1859 as British Consul-General and secured the temple of Tozenji as his residence and Legation. He then proceeded to Kanagawa to prepare for the opening of the port on the appointed day. Here he met Mr Townsend Harris who had also arrived from Shimoda for the same purpose. Kanagawa was so situated that the foreign settlement could steadily expand inland from the coast without restriction. Both consuls were determined not to be subject to Japanese control like the Dutch at Deshima. Unfortunately, Kanagawa also gave access to the Tokaido which was the traditional main highway for noble families and clans to travel and process between Yedo and their domains. The Japanese were equally determined to prevent foreign use of this route, even to consuls and ministers, and proceeded to implement an alternative plan.

Henry Cook's memory of shallow water on the Kanagawa side of the bay proved correct. Although adequate for the shallow-draught Japanese junks, the allocated site had insufficient depth of water for even the smaller classes of foreign ships. Naturally the British and American officials had to dispute such an impossible location, thus giving the Japanese an excuse for delay while a new site was negotiated. Meanwhile the Japanese expertise in mass organisation was put into action. They selected a site at Yokohama which, although hardly meriting its enhanced description as a fishing village, had already been noted by Commodore Perry as having adequate deep water.

Yokohama was nothing but a collection of huts on a small strip of hard ground bounded on the north by the sea, on the south by an extensive swamp, and on the west by a creek which was tidal for about a mile and then separated from a freshwater stream by sluice gates. To the east was an estuary into which a river flowed from the hills. Not satisfied with these natural barriers, the Japanese cut a canal through the saltwater swamp, joining the creek and the estuary. Yokohama was now an island from which there were only two exits, one via three bridges leading into a single street across the creek into the village of Homura. The other exit was by a bridge across the eastern estuary leading to a long viaduct specially built across salt marshes to Kanagawa, a distance of about three miles. Each exit had its own guardhouse in which *yakunin* or Japanese police would always be on duty - for foreigners' protection of course - to search all who entered or left the proposed settlement.

Both consuls opposed the offer of Yokohama as the new site, recognising an attempt virtually to imprison the entire foreign settlement and prevent any free movement inland. It reproduced the very situation that they were in agreement not to accept, that of the Dutch at Deshima. Even so, they underestimated the enterprise of the Japanese who still went ahead with their plan. At vast expense, they constructed an *hatoba*, or landing place, of two granite-faced jetties jutting out into the sea. The harbour was undeniably good with excellent deep water. A few houses and godowns (storage huts) were thrown up but were adequate for merchants to move into at once. Immediately in front of the *hatoba* was a large official-looking Custom House.

The *Henry Ellis* arrived from Shanghai, via Nagasaki, and anchored in deep water away from Kanagawa towards Yokohama. The British warship HMS.*Sampson* was also anchored in the same deep water. It had remained after bringing Rutherford Alcock from Yedo. Captain Baillie obtained permission to visit the warship and took Henry with him in case his previous knowledge of the area was of use. They learned that Yokohama was to be the centre for the foreign settlement, but negotiations were still under way for a Kanagawa option to remain open. The consuls had not relinquished the belief that the shallow water problem could be overcome. Indeed, the Japanese, after a long delay and apparently against official policy, granted a site where foreigners might purchase as much land or property from the Japanese owners as they liked and consuls would be provided with residences. The Japanese had intelligently anticipated an ally not suspected by Harris or Alcock, namely the greed of merchants.

Captain Baillie and Henry returned to their ship and, acting on the advance information, weighed anchor and sailed to a more advantageous position closer to Yokohama. Here they remained for the next three days, rather tense with anticipation. From this vantage point they had a clear view of the preparations ashore. Hundreds of workmen were swarming from one area to another moving huge quantities of material. Simple structures of buildings grew at an incredible speed. This hive of activity took Henry right back to his experiences in Shimoda. What motivated this collective energy? Could a foreigner like himself harness it?

Waiting in the bay for three days gave Henry plenty of time to reflect on past experiences and to consider what could lie in the future. He had many long discussions with Sassoon's agent who was ready to be put ashore at the first possible moment. These talks gave Henry some insight into the cut and thrust of shore-based trade and nourished an ever-growing desire to be his own master. Yokohama was going to be a frontier-town in the Far East. Worldwide commercial interests would be able to gain a foothold in Japan with endless future opportunities for every type of profession. In a country where most construction was designed to be built in wood, surely his own particular expertise would be in demand for many years?

The *Henry Ellis* was no longer the sole merchant vessel in the harbour. Several other ships had arrived and were anchored in different parts of the bay. At last, on the 1st July 1859, boats were seen leaving HMS. *Sampson* and heading for the shore ready for the official opening of the settlement. A signal was sent to Captain Baillie giving clearance for him to proceed to the *hatoba*. The *Henry Ellis* became the first foreign merchant ship allowed to enter Yokohama, open at last for trade and residence. To be an officer on board this ship filled Henry with the heady sense of making history and it drove home the final nail into a resolution to play a full working role in that history.

The First Officer was left in charge of the ship. Henry was to lead a small party on a preliminary exploration of the situation ashore while Captain Baillie escorted the Sassoon agent. They reported at the Custom House where an efficient interpreter had been employed for the occasion. A number of offices were attached to the building, many still in the hands of the carpenters. On leaving the Custom House, Henry led his companions into a wide street where they had a close view of the reason for all the bustle witnessed at a distance from the *Henry Ellis*. Both sides of the street were bordered with well-built houses of timber, the walls infilled with mud. Some of them were occupied by Japanese merchants who appeared to have arrived only that morning. Their goods were still being unpacked as servants and porters made frantic efforts to display them for sale. It was as though a conjuror had waved his magic wand over the marshy deserted bay and produced an instant settlement of Japanese merchants. In general, the articles for sale were very attractive; cloth, fans, pottery and beautifully lacquered wooden boxes. Some stalls carried a few items of food. The men with Henry were anxious to buy some souvenirs eventually to take back to England. Many of the goods were priced in the Japanese currency of *ichibus*, very quickly shortened to "bu's". Henry remembered using coins valued at one and half *ichibus* when in Shimoda. He had kept some of them but remembered, saddened for a moment, that they were lost in the wreck. He agreed with the men that some of the items were fair bargains.

They returned to the Custom House to exchange their dollars, a currency acceptable throughout the Far East. According to the treaty it had been agreed that one dollar was to be matched weight for weight with two Japanese coins, each valued at one and a half *ichibus*. Two officials were on duty with scales and a pile of glittering new coins. The men watched the exchange in weight with close attention and were agreeably surprised with the accuracy. They hurried back to the stalls to join an ever increasing number of foreigners disembarked from the ships in the bay. Henry no longer had that sense of urgency; he knew he would be returning to stay.

As they approached the stalls, Henry was aware of angry shouting, particularly from some of the newly-arrived trading agents who were conspicuous among the seamen. The Japanese merchants were demanding three times the number of *ichibus* marked on the prices displayed. Further inspection of the coins in his hand to refresh his memory of them, revealed a difference that he was not proficient to translate. In fact, the currency value stamped on these specially minted coins was only half an *ichibu* instead of the usual one and half *ichibus*! Once again the Japanese government had tried to gain advantage over the foreign visitors. The bright new coins were indeed the correct weight, as decreed by treaty, but their face value had been changed! This ingenious attempt to devalue the dollar by two-thirds was to be subsequently nullified by the enterprising foreign merchants in a manner not pleasing to the Japanese.

Henry returned his crew to the ship where, aggrieved but still pleased with their purchases, they schemed with the next group going ashore how to beat the system. They failed.

The *Henry Ellis* remained at Yokohama until the Sassoon agent had completed his report and made the few trade arrangements possible within the Japanese tight control of foreign enterprise. His task would not be an easy one.

So here was a small, undeveloped piece of Japan ready to be organised into a flourishing centre for trade. It was a situation analogous to the 'wild west' of the United States, exciting, risky and probably dangerous. At twenty-three years of age, Henry Cook, a highly-skilled shipwright, experienced in shipping and foreign trade and sensing a fertile situation for his own future, could not resist the challenge. He resolved to devise some means of starting a business based in Yokohama. First, he had to return to Shanghai on the *Henry Ellis*.

12
Birth Of A Partnership

The *Henry Ellis* returned to Yokohama at the end of November, but this time there was little excitement on board. It was cold with flurries of snow sweeping across the harbour. Captain Baillie anchored away from the *hatobas,* allowing Henry to go ashore in one of the ship's boats with a Captain Elmstone, who was to be the new chief agent for Sassoon in the settlement. As he approached the jetty, the scene was a picture of desolation, so unlike the frantic bustle of the July opening. The harbour was full of kelp swept in from the outer bay by the storms. A few empty sampans were moored at the landing-place but no living being was in sight.

After passing the guardhouse at the end of the *hatoba*, Henry intended to seek directions to the Sassoon office on Lot 75 from the Custom House, but it was closed. By chance, two Americans were walking past and offered to escort Captain Elmstone to the Lot, allowing Henry to return to his ship. He was at a loss to understand so radical a change in the atmosphere of the settlement - perhaps it was the cold weather.

Henry felt obliged to declare his intention to seek an opening for business in Yokohama and so give Captain Baillie ample time to find a replacement for him. The news was not entirely unexpected and Henry was given considerable extra leave ashore for the next few days to test the feasibility of his plan. The weather had improved for the second day in harbour, which encouraged Henry to go ashore to explore changes made since July and to talk to some of the residents. As the day progressed he was able to piece together the pattern of response made by the pioneer settlers to their very restricted circumstances.

There were now two main streets, cross-linked with small access roads. The land was divided into lots and numbered haphazardly as new arrivals with sufficient money bought the lot of their choice. A few bungalows had been built and occupied whilst several others were in course of construction. Men who had arrived early enough to purchase the bungalows often shared their dwellings with the less fortunate until a hotel could be built. One or two even rented Japanese houses in the straggling native village. With such a limited area of land suitable for development, it was obvious that the unscrupulous among the early settlers would reap fat profits from later arrivals eager to purchase whole or part lots.

Seven or eight trading companies now had registered branches but Henry could detect no signs of urgent business. Most visible activity was centred on the sites where houses, offices and godowns were being constructed. He called into the Sassoon office to renew acquaintance with Captain Elmstone where he learned that trade in exports was very limited. The Japanese refused to allow them to export silk, a trade jealously guarded by their own merchants. So far, the principal items for export had been copper wire for China, palm fibre, dried fish, seaweed and even Japanese swords. As the community grew there would naturally be great opportunities for imports from Europe and America to sustain the style of life to which most settlers were accustomed. The news, like the weather, was disappointing.

Two days later Henry was able to go ashore once again. Some of the crew, intent only on having a good time, had found a couple of makeshift bars where food could also be purchased. Henry followed their directions and to his delight spirits were raised in two senses of the word. A good number of young settlers gradually gathered there, apparently for the sole purpose of killing time. Few ships were arriving at Yokohama and trade was very slow. There was insufficient work to keep the young merchant community fully occupied. During fine weather, they organised themselves into all manner of sports activities, walking and sometimes shooting on the marshes. This shared endeavour to remain buoyant during a time of frustration had fostered a strong sense of camaraderie. How were they able to afford such a non-productive way of life? Some had a basic retaining fee from their parent companies. Others had found an ingenious way of misusing a Japanese discrepancy in the international values of silver and gold. Although by changing the face value of the *ichibu* the Japanese had succeeded in restricting trade and profits to the foreigners, they still had an 'Achilles heel' in their relative values of gold and silver. For centuries they had adopted their own standards of value without any regard to those recognised in the rest of the world. Consequently, whilst the world relative value of gold to silver was about 1 to 15, the Japanese value was only about 1 to 6.

This discrepancy, combined with a successful insistence by the foreign ministers that the false half *ichibu* be abandoned and the correct weight for weight treaty regulation be observed for the first year, gave the young settlers an opportunity to make profits that they could never have thought possible. After exchanging their dollars for "bu's", then using them to buy the undervalued gold *kobangs*, they were shipping the gold to China where it was sold for its true bullion value. In this way the traders were making upwards of 150 per cent profit within a month or six weeks through simple cash transactions with no other trading involved. The Japanese government complained bitterly about this rapid flow of gold from their country and even the foreign ministers condemned this unseemly scramble for quick profits. Nevertheless the tables had been well and truly turned and the Japanese had none but themselves to blame.

Tough commercial competition in Shanghai and Hong Kong had schooled Henry to recognise survival tactics in trade. Back at the ship he mustered every dollar he could legitimately claim ready for the first stage of his own currency switch. It was prudent not to broadcast his intention as the quantity of gold he would be carrying back to Shanghai could foster avarice in the best disciplined crew. He thought it wise to delay the purchase of *kobangs* until the final day before sailing.

Perhaps the most important undertaking since he ran away to sea was about to confront him. Time had been passing without any light shining at the end of his tunnel of ambition. The *Henry Ellis* was due to set sail on 12th December for Shanghai and already it was the 8th. The bar he had been frequenting was empty except for a few men, not of the usual crowd. He was swapping yarns over a drink with a man, slightly older than himself, who confessed to being a Dutch ex-seaman, a ship's carpenter by trade. The man's name was Henry Frey. He had been impressed by the rush to build housing and business premises in Yokohama, all constructed in timber, and he had judged that the situation offered the ideal time to leave the sea and ply his trade where it seemed more profitable. He had been working with Japanese labourers under several different contractors, two of whom had been European. Through them he had gleaned a little understanding of how to price jobs which had led to an urge to set up his own business. Unfortunately he still needed financial backing for the initial expense of buying in supplies, hiring premises and labour.

Henry Cook and Henry Frey had the same Christian name, a similar ambition and a common language in timber, although each had different experience in its use. Henry was an experienced shipwright and as an officer was used to giving orders and able to instruct men in whatever tasks needed to be done. Frey, on the other hand, was basically a competent ship's carpenter who had gained some knowledge of local business practice and problems of supply. As they talked with ever-increasing enthusiasm, it was inevitable that they would see the advantage of coming together in partnership, each hoping to find support from the other when launching into the uncertainties of such a venture.

Frey was annoyed that Henry would not consider leaving his ship before it sailed, a suggestion that offended Henry's sense of duty and integrity. The aspect which worried Henry was that he had too little time in which to make a wise and balanced decision. Both men agreed to spend the following day separately considering their position and how best any partnership should operate.

Deep within himself, Henry knew that this was the chance he had longed for and one in which he was prepared to take the risk; nevertheless he sought an element of safety by taking the initiative. Acting on impulse, he went to Sassoon's office to consult Captain Elmstone who would have some understanding of company documents. Together they planned what seemed a fair and practical basis for a partnership where neither partner knew anything of the character of the other. To Captain Elmstone it was foolhardy, but he was sympathetic to Henry's wishes. It was arranged that Henry and Frey should agree the details at Sassoon's office.

Captain Baillie was not surprised when Henry confided in him the sequence of events. He promised to arrange for Henry's discharge after the next return voyage from Shanghai, towards the end of February or early in March. With that certainty to offer Frey, Henry met him as arranged and persuaded him to conduct their business st Sassoon's. Frey's command of the English language was adequate for general use but any Agreement needed to be in simple unambiguous terms. The final document was very much as prepared by Henry and Captain Elmstone:

Each was to contribute $100 as first capital for the business.

Henry would look after all shipbuilding and repairs.

Frey would manage all other building contracts and general carpentry.

The business was to be conducted for mutual benefit with equal interests and profit. Neither man was highly educated but, as Frey had gained some recent local experience, it was agreed that he should keep the accounts and books for the joint venture on condition that Henry would have access to inspect them. Any dispute arising would be settled in a British Court of Justice.

A paper headed "The Articles of Partnership" listing all these details was drawn up and signed by each man on 10th December 1859. Captain Elmstone was to hold the Agreement until Henry's return.

Henry left Yokohama on the *Henry Ellis* for his last trip as an employee His elation was tinged with that strange excitement which feeds on apprehension, but his hidden store of golden *kobangs* was a security he found easy to understand!

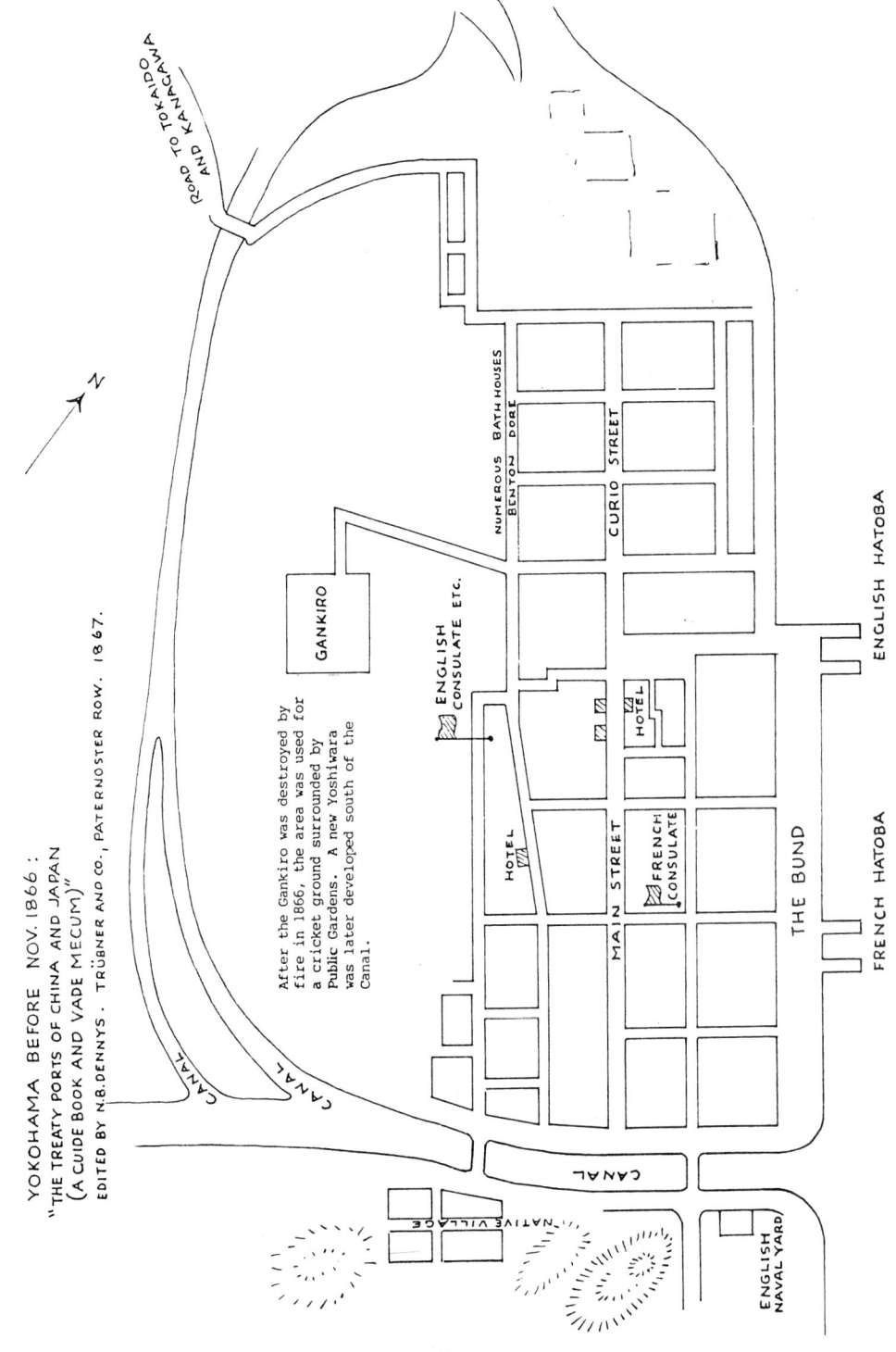

YOKOHAMA BEFORE NOV. 1866:
"THE TREATY PORTS OF CHINA AND JAPAN
(A GUIDE BOOK AND VADE MECUM)"
EDITED BY N.B.DENNYS. TRÜBNER AND CO., PATERNOSTER ROW. 1867.

ROAD TO TOKAIDO AND KANAGAWA

N

CANAL

CANAL

CANAL

CANAL

NUMEROUS BATH HOUSES

BENTON DORI

CURIO STREET

GANKIRO

ENGLISH CONSULATE ETC.

After the Gankiro was destroyed by
fire in 1866, the area was used for
a cricket ground surrounded by
Public Gardens. A new Yoshiwara
was later developed south of the
Canal.

HOTEL

HOTEL

MAIN STREET

FRENCH CONSULATE

THE BUND

ENGLISH HATOBA

FRENCH HATOBA

NATIVE VILLAGE

ENGLISH NAVAL YARD

13

Yokohama's First Shipwright

The *Henry Ellis* returned to Yokohama from Shanghai in February 1860. Henry's discharge was to take effect from the 26th, which gave him about ten days in which to clear all his obligations on board and to reassure himself that Frey was still firmly committed to their partnership. It was during this time that Henry first met George Rogers, shipping clerk to Oliphant and Company, who came on board to discuss business with Captain Baillie. A friendship grew between them during the next few months, occurring naturally from the shared experience of shipwreck. Rogers had been shipwrecked whilst travelling from Shanghai to take up his post and, with others who were rescued, was finally escorted to Yokohama by a detachment of *samurai* shortly after Henry had left in December.

Henry had mixed emotions when leaving his ship for the last time. She was a fine seaworthy vessel with a happy crew and a likeable captain. For the past eight years he had lived and worked in the well-ordered security of shipboard life. Now he was to turn his back on an established pattern of life and, instead of being absorbed into a disciplined community, he would be one man in a settlement of unpredictable complexity, matching his wits against hundreds of equally determined people. February 26th was to open his eyes to the new reality in quite a violent manner.

He had arranged to meet Frey that evening after leaving the ship. They were going to plan future strategy over a few drinks at the Yokohama Hotel on Main Street. This bungalow hotel, the first in the settlement, had been completed only recently at high speed to fill an urgent need. Accommodation was at the rear but a billiard room took pride of place in the front. It was almost dark, just after six o'clock, when George Rogers rushed in looking very white and highly agitated. He had left his house on Kitanaka Dori, to the west of the settlement, with the intention of visiting a friend in the next street. Two or three *samurai*, recognised by the two swords each carried, hurried across the road ahead of him and into a side turning. He thought little of the incident until he almost tripped over what he at first took to be a drunken sailor lying on the ground.

Stooping down and turning the body over, he discovered that the man was dead and minus one hand. He had a deep cut through the shoulder and another cut down his face severing the nose. Not a soul was in sight but looking round for help he saw a second body further away on the opposite side of the road. A Japanese came by with a lantern and by its aid Rogers found the hand and a tall silk hat. He put the hand inside the hat, left them by the first body and rushed off to give the alarm first to the *yakunin*, then to Thomas Troy, the U.S. constable who had been a sailor with Commodore Perry's fleet. No wonder the poor man looked agitated!

Frey had agreed to allow Henry to share his accommodation until separate lodgings could be found. Instead of leaving the hotel for home they remained behind to attend an emergency meeting of residents called to discuss the murders. It was resolved to divide volunteers into several watches to patrol the streets at night armed with revolvers, rifles and shotguns. An atmosphere of excitement prevailed rather than one of fear, now that collective action was to be taken. Henry and Frey declined to take part; neither had personal weapons to offer and they had too many private problems to occupy them.

Returning to Frey's bungalow on the east side of the settlement added more confusion to Henry's first day. He was used to the inky blackness of night at sea but navigating in similar conditions on land was far more daunting, especially when coupled with an uneasy watchfulness for a murderous attack. Frey found his way with little difficulty and seemed able to distinguish streets from field though both were ankle-deep in sticky mud. The life Henry had left behind only that morning was already beckoning to him with its ordered cleanliness and would continue to lure him for the rest of his life.

Both men were eager to begin work as soon as possible. Large companies could withstand idle months in anticipation of future profits but Henry's savings were very limited. Not without some misgivings, Henry handed over his $100 share of the partnership's capital to Frey who was to keep accounts of all income and expenditure. Henry required premises with easy access to water for building and repairing seagoing craft. The same access would enable Frey to receive a continual supply of timber for his construction work. They succeeded in renting a site, lot No.69, right on the edge of the Creek which isolated the settlement on the south-east boundary. Frey knew where he could call on a pool of Japanese workmen, including skilled labour and coolies. In a very short time they had an adequate office and several work and storage sheds erected. Henry was amazed how quickly he was able to converse with the Japanese with so little knowledge of the language. Using phonetic equivalent sounds together with some Chinese to support his practical demonstrations, quite complicated instructions were followed expertly. He could appreciate the skills of the carpenters even though they used their tools backwards! When cutting or planing wood, they pulled the tools towards them instead of pushing the cutting edge away as in western practice. The result was equally good.

It was time to publicise the services they now had to offer. All the men in their social group knew about the partnership. Even secrets were hard to keep in the Yokohama of 1860. Henry and Frey thought it wise to make their entry into business more official and produced a number of hand-written notices for the larger trading companies and several for the regular meeting places where visitors congregated. Fortunately no more murders had been committed and residents had eased their nightly vigilance in spite of rumours which filtered through concerning the growth of *samurai* unrest. The murder victims had been reported to be two Dutch captains, Dekker and De Vos.

Business began to flourish quite quickly. Henry had been worried about the financial state of the partnership as initial outlay on materials had amounted to more than anticipated, but Frey assured him they would soon be out of debt. They continued to inform each other of orders that came in, however small, so that Frey could keep the books up to date. The number of vessels coming to Yokohama was steadily increasing, often with storm-ravaged superstructure needing repair. The fashioning of new masts was becoming one of Henry's specialities. Much of his work was carried out on the ships still anchored in the harbour. Several companies had ordered small cargo-carrying boats for use between their ships and the *hatoba*.

Prosperity had allowed the partnership to employ up to thirty-five Japanese workmen on a permanent basis paying them wages of eight *tempos* per day, roughly equivalent to sixteen cents. With business progressing well, more time could be spared to take part in the social life of the settlement which fostered a sense of security in a foreign land. The great centre for meeting and hearing the latest news was the Yokohama Hotel. It was here that Henry soon became a welcome companion and confidant to other residents. He was at ease in their company, enjoyed a drink and had a fund of yarns to keep them amused.

THE FOREIGN SETTLEMENT, SOUTH-WEST OF THE CREEK, YOKOHAMA. 1889.

A regular topic of conversation was the poor supply of nourishing western food. Some poultry was available but the men longed to sink their teeth into some real butcher's meat, a food the Japanese never touched. They had failed to persuade the Japanese to kill any cattle, not realising that, historically, anyone who earned a living by killing animals, even to profit from the cured hides, was loathed and outcast. Henry made a proposal which endeared him to his friends for a long time. He offered to slaughter a beast for them. Cattle were cheap and a decent animal could be bought for five *kobangs,* about seven dollars. Some of the residents clubbed together and bought one. It was taken to one of the stables belonging to the hotel where Henry demonstrated another of his skills as he prepared and sectioned the carcass. His old ship the *Henry Ellis* often shipped live animals to be slaughtered for fresh meat at sea and Captain Baillie had given him expert tuition with pigs and cattle. Being the first butcher in Yokohama was a record in history he had never anticipated!

Henry's growing popularity in the community was beginning to sour his relationship with Henry Frey. Advice from friends had secured a better lodging for Henry where a young Japanese woman cooked and kept house for three of them. Some of the men had hired native women on permanent contract as housekeepers and female companions.

After Henry moved away, his contact with Frey was usually confined to business and they still kept meeting regularly every Friday to exchange details of work in hand. On several occasions at these meetings Henry had asked to see the accounts but Frey always found some excuse, generally that the books were not quite up to date. It was not satisfactory but he had to admit that the partnership was successful and money was flowing comfortingly. Profits were estimated as averaging two hundred per cent over outlay.

Whenever the *Henry Ellis* sailed into Yokohama, Henry made time to go on board to meet the crew and Captain Baillie. The captain congratulated Henry on his growing success but when he heard about the shortage of meat in the settlement and Henry's entry into the slaughter trade, his interest quickened noticeably. Would there be enough trade to support a resident butcher? Would the Japanese object? Henry was not slow to realise that his old captain was succumbing to the lure of quick profits ashore.

Christmas seemed to arrive long before it was due, but Henry managed to attend a special Mass in the French quarter of the settlement where a visiting priest was staying. It was useful having Latin as the common language in the Catholic Church. The Japanese were happy to find any excuse for a festival and added their own excitement to the celebrations. The rather forced enjoyment of men away from their families was relieved by some genuine solid entertainment. A group of sailors from a visiting British warship gave an excellent impromptu show in one of the empty godowns where an array of lanterns and plenty of bunting produced a creditable atmosphere of theatre. Some of the sailors were most convincing as women and aroused the traditional bawdiness of such a concert.

The memorable year of 1860 came to a close but the events live on in history. The Japanese archives faithfully record Henry's three "firsts" as a modest beginning to his improbable future in Yokohama.

It was time for Henry to write home to Newport.

14
Prosperity And Pleasure

Writing letters was not one of Henry's best accomplishments nor indeed was any form of writing. It had been so long since he had written to Newport that it would seem mean to send just one page to declare he was fit and happy. To give the full story would take a book. As a compromise he gave an account of the more recent events, that he was now in business and could receive letters within a few months of their being sent. He had become aware of an increasing demand for skilled metal workers in his own shipyard, as well as among other workshops, so he had been seriously considering the idea of inviting his younger brother Anthony to join him. Anthony was apprenticed to a blacksmith in Commercial Road when Henry ran away to sea and would be at least twenty years of age. A firm proposal to Anthony was included in the letter with a promise to reimburse him or his parents with the whole cost of the voyage should it be accepted.

The number of ships in the harbour at any one time was increasing. Since the 'weight for weight' treaty for the first year of currency-exhange had ended, the Japanese had no option but to align their relative values of precious metals with those of the outside world. Although this had stopped the easy profits enjoyed by the merchants, it made legitimate trade more possible. The influx of shipping kept Henry busy and he began to feel the confidence that money brings in a commercial world.

Captain Baillie made a firm decision to quit the sea and set up a butcher's shop. Henry promised to prepare the way for him and managed to secure rented premises just behind, but attached to, a general store owned by Messrs. Baker & Co. On October 14th Captain Baillie brought the *Henry Ellis* from Shanghai to safe anchorage at Yokohama for the last time. It was a sad wrench but he knew it was time to retire, taking with him a reputation for dependability.

The "Nagasaki Shipping List and Advertiser" of brief duration in 1861 was the first English newspaper in Japan. This was followed by the "Japan Herald", a weekly published every Saturday evening and launched in

Yokohama on 23rd November 1861. Henry and Frey agreed to take immediate advantage of it and composed a suitable insertion for the second issue.

FREY & COOK,
Shipwrights,
Boat-builders and Mast makers,
also
House Builders and General Carpenters and Blacksmiths,
On the Creek near the Residences of H. B. M's Minister and Consul.
All work in connexion with the above trades executed in the best manner with despatch, and on reasonable terms.

The famous firm of Lea & Perrins also seized the opportunity to warn an unsuspecting public to beware of foreign spurious imitations of their well-known sauce. Purchasers should check that the company name appeared on the wrapper, label, bottle and stopper! Also, empty bottles should be broken to prevent fraudulent refilling.

Captain Baillie had quickly installed himself in his new shop and announced his presence in Yokohama with a very personal notice in the fifth edition of the paper.

```
        W. A.   B A I L L I E

late Master of ship "Henry Ellis"
    BUTCHER AND PROVISIONER
(In the premises at the rear of
 Messrs. Baker & Co.'s Store)

     YOKOHAMA  JAPAN.

N.B.   W.A.B. trusts that by strict
attention to business he will merit
a share of the Public patronage.

   YOKOHAMA, 14th DEC. 1861.
```

The "Japan Herald" owed its existence to Albert W. Hansard, the head of an auction and commission business and the pioneer English journalist in Japan. He aimed to bring to its readers news from Japan and abroad in a fair and temperate manner with space for open discussion. At once it became the official organ for the notices and publications of the treaty powers in Japan. Of primary interest to Henry were the details of shipping movements and trade statistics. He could never have envisaged the extent to which his own activities would be reported in subsequent newspapers right up to the time of his death, thus confirming the recollections of his descendants.

The closely-knit social life of the young merchants continued and extended Henry's education for living at every meeting. A favourite outdoor recreation was pony riding, a sport quite new to Henry. Sometimes parties of ten or more would make excursions to Kanasawa and Kamakura to visit the great bronze idol of Buddha, knows as "Daibutsu". As all riders were accompanied by their *bettoes* (grooms), it made quite an impressionable cavalcade. Although up to that time no rider had been attacked on such journeys, all carried revolvers for protection. Henry found travelling by pony to be quite luxurious once he had mastered the rhythm of motion, certainly when compared with the agony of even a short journey in a *kago*. This was the most uncomfortable means of transport to all but the Japanese; it was a simple bamboo structure with matting in the base, carried on the shoulders of two runners. The men made light of their journey and the load, but the occupant was shaken unmercifully. The agony experienced during the forced conveyance of captured seamen before Commodore Perry's intervention was hurtfully demonstrated. One benefit was the cost. It was possible to travel some twenty miles for as little as two dollars compared with fourteen to eighteen dollars for the hire of a pony.

The limits for foreigners to travel from Yokohama were set at ten *ri*, about twenty-five miles, but the adventurous nature of many of these early settlers led them to nudge these arbitrary boundaries and stay overnight instead of returning to the settlement before dark. Part of the challenge was to find lodgings in one of the small villages with the possible chance of sampling the charms of Japanese women. Henry had made excuses for declining to go on these trips. In fact many of his companions were well-cushioned financially and he was beginning to realise he was not in that league. For other reasons his decision was wise. The Japanese governor of Kanagawa complained to the British Consul that he could not sustain any security for foreigners in those

DAIBUTSU or Great Buddha, Kamakura

TEMPLE, Kamakura

A KAGO - the most uncomfortable method of travel in Japan

Pounding Rice in a Rice-Mortar

circumstances unless he were given previous notice. It was not safe or expedient for foreigners to pass the night away from the settlement in the current restless state of the country, particularly without competent knowledge of the language or means of communicating with local people. The Consul let it be known that such behaviour would be made a penal offence in future.

Glowing accounts from some of his friends sparked off a curiosity about the Yokohama *Yoshiwara* quarter, known as the *Gankiro*. This was situated on the far side of the swamp area and was reached only by the Yoshiwara-machi, a filled-in strip of land guarded at the far end by *yakunin*. Turning away from the native area of the settlement, recently devastated by a tragic fire, Henry walked along the 'machi' one Saturday afternoon with a few companions, feeling rather guilty about the reason he had given Frey for his absence from the yard. They idly looked at the small shops and stalls that lined the route until they came to the only entrance and exit available. Privately owned, the *Gankiro* was run more or less on similar lines to the traditional Japanese houses of prostitution. There were facilities for eating and bathing, together with a comfortable bar and an area for large-scale entertainment.

Henry's group enjoyed a steaming hot bath together, which caused a great deal of laughter between them as they became almost parboiled in the intense heat preferred by the Japanese. Several of them were becoming used to the custom of washing thoroughly before entering the communal bath and to using the cotton bags filled with rice bran, the Japanese equivalent of soap. These gave a softening effect, similar to oatmeal, without the obvious lather of soap. Even whilst luxuriating in the sensuous warmth, Henry's professional eye marvelled at the efficient workmanship and strength of such a huge wooden tub needed to contain that volume of hot water. Having dried themselves and dressed casually in the robes provided, each went his own way to satisfy the anticipation in his loins. This routine was quite acceptable for the men in Japanese society. The girls on offer were mostly under a term of contract for which their parents had been paid. They were trained, educated and cared for by the owner *mama-san*.

The casual bragging comments made by men over drinks often bear little relation to the truth, so Henry was agreeably surprised when he first saw the girls. They were in a long narrow room partially screened by slats, but he could see them quite clearly and was soon smitten by the dilemma of choice. They were typically short in stature but were well-groomed and wearing colourful kimono. He was relieved to see that the heavy Japanese make-up was restrained and there was no evidence of the unsightly blackened teeth affected by women of married status, a custom to which he was never reconciled. The tallest one was the only criterion of choice he felt able to use and the overseer *mama-san* beckoned to her. From that point he was absorbed into the practised routine.

He was led in silence along a short corridor to a small room where several *futons* were arranged on the floor, which was covered with a thick layer of the usual *tatami* matting. To break the silence he asked the girl, in Japanese, for her name. She smiled and replied,"Rumika". Did he require tea or *saké*? No. Another smile. So far Henry had not fathomed the meaning behind a Japanese smile. They smiled whether in agreement or disagreement, whether understanding or not. It was confusing, deceptive and disarming, but socially very acceptable.

Feeling conspicuously tall in the small room, Henry squatted on one of the *futons*. Rumika came over to him and began to massage his shoulders, a manoeuvre she expertly carried out while removing his loosely-buttoned shirt. It was all so unhurried. He tried to read the thoughts behind her eyes but the gentle smile was an effective barrier. Had he wished he could have relaxed into total passivity confident that Rumika's skill could achieve its ends, but she had aroused a desire in him to be an active participant. She quickly sensed his change of mood and proved herself to be equally efficient in her receptive role.

She left him alone for a while, giving Henry time to reflect on his afternoon in the *Gankiro* . How different it was from his initiation in San Francisco. There was no sense of shame or embarrassment. Perhaps it was the civilised detachment of the girls which made such behaviour acceptable in Japan. He felt vaguely angry that some of the rough brutish men he had met might ravage the tranquillity of the place and bring it into disrepute. In some measure he was prophetic. Rumika returned with a hot towel and some tea, then left him to dress himself and depart. She had come in silently with a smile and departed still silent, still smiling. Henry was puzzled why, in some strange way, he felt privileged.

After dressing, Henry made his way to the waiting area where his companions had agreed to meet and leave together. Conversation had dried up, each preoccupied with his own thoughts. They made their way back along the Yoshiwara-machi where their minds were jolted back to the precarious realism of life in Yokohama as once again they were confronted with the blackened remains of homes in the native quarter. A damp acrid smell still drifted on the breeze. Such extensive fires were endemic to Japan, caused by primitive lighting and heating and the close proximity of buildings constructed in timber. The foreign quarter had suffered a similar fire on 5th January, just before Henry became a resident. The Japanese make little fuss when it happens and soon begin to help each other to build anew, as indeed they were busily engaged as Henry walked through. A sense of awe was very evident in the crowds who came to watch such events. It was a common belief that fire was a god who honoured their dwellings by his visitation. Perhaps this was the reason for their resigned acceptance of the situation and spirit of collective cooperation.

As he reached the corner of Ota-machi, he burst out laughing. A short Japanese man was standing in a small brook which ran in front of his house, beating clothes on a round stone in the deeper part of the water. He had been the first Japanese laundry man to set up in the business of washing foreigners' clothes. The brook looked far from clean, particularly since the fire, but still he persisted to give a service. The incident cleared Henry's introspection and he walked home briskly, though still musing that the Japanese certainly were different!

15
A Hard Lesson

Damage caused by the fire in the native quarter amounted to the destruction of six hundred and eighty houses at an estimated loss of *ichibus* 435,000 or £40,000 sterling. Although modest by Japanese standards, it would have been much worse but for the removal of some of the intermediate buildings ordered by the British Consul - a task carried out by men from the various men-of-war anchored in the harbour. George Alcock, later a close friend of Henry, likened it to an echo of the Great Fire of London. Enterprising advertisements soon appeared offering space to rent in so-called "Fire Proof Godowns".

During the summer of 1861, Henry became more closely acquainted with the French priest, Abbé Girard, through his still infrequent attendance at Mass. He was a genial and good man who was not only a fierce protector of his own flock but also very active in the welfare of the other Christian communities. His plans were well ahead for the building of a permanent Roman Catholic church which would be the first place of Christian public worship to be opened in Japan. A measure of the Abbé's popularity were the donations for this purpose sent in from all sects and denominations. Henry was unsuccessful in his efforts to obtain part of the building contract for Frey and was oddly relieved that he had failed.

For over a year, Frey had not produced the partnership accounts for Henry's inspection in spite of continued requests. That in itself was highly suspicious and, when coupled with a slowing down of essential supplies needed to complete orders on time in the shipyard, Henry had good cause for concern. Although he had no proof, he was fairly sure that Frey was accepting building contracts without informing him, thus steering profits away from the partnership accounts. Henry felt a little more secure after gaining possession of their Deed of Partnership, a fact he was careful to keep to himself. Captain Elmstore had continued to hold the Agreement since it was first signed, but he had decided to take over the captaincy and part-ownership of the *Henry Ellis* after Captain Baillie had resigned. He left for the Cape of Good Hope on 11th January 1862, sailing via Hong Kong. Before leaving he had returned the Agreement to Henry, advising him not to release it to Frey. The legal profession was not adequately represented in Yokohama at that time and Frey had become rather too friendly with a man who had gathered sufficient knowledge of conveyancing to make himself useful in some of the building projects. The man was Frederick Crutchley and Henry distrusted his pompous pretence to knowledge of legal matters which had coloured most of their conversations. He felt justified in not disclosing his retention of the document.

The letter from Newport, which came in reply to his own, revived feelings that years of absence had dimmed. As he read the little items of news about each member of the family he was happy to allow sentimental emotions and memories to engulf him. Only the news that his brother John was then nine years old had no meaning for him. Henry never knew him or ever thought about him. John was only a few weeks old when Henry left Newport. Like the last letter received from home, this one was written in an educated hand, as though someone had written a story for him.

Anthony had agreed to come to Japan to join Henry's business but unfortunately had been unable to raise sufficient money for the journey and suitable clothes. Henry scolded himself for not having foreseen that probability and immediately set about making amends. By leaving a deposit with a trading company that had a branch in Bristol, he was able to send a covering note from them to Anthony who would then only have to make his way to Bristol to receive the help he needed. In this way Henry could expect his brother to arrive by May or June that year.

During the latter half of 1861, the swamp area to the south and west of the foreign settlement was being filled in by the Japanese. Hundreds of workmen were transporting soil dug from the hills on the edge of the Kanagawa side of the Creek. Narrow canals had been made into the swamp to allow small boats to deposit their loads of earth right into the centre of the area. The work along the Creek was distracting the workers in Henry's shipyard but he was more annoyed when hundreds of tons of hillside collapsed into the Creek as a result of indiscriminate tunnelling for the earth.

Although the Japanese Governor of Kanagawa was allowing this work to take place and he was treating the safety of foreigners quite seriously, there were many problems he was failing to deal with. Street lighting, drainage of surface water and sewage, and a sufficient water supply for fighting fires were all causes for concern. Residents were beginning to look for some form of municipal council to deal with these essentials. Petty interference with trade still persisted, typically illustrated by a story passed to Henry by Frey, who gleaned it from his own Dutch Consul:

> One of his fellow countrymen had imported a tiger from Singapore to sell for an agreed price to a Japanese entrepreneur, giving the merchant a huge profit. Unfortunately the Customs officials would not allow the tiger to enter Yokohama and could not be persuaded to change their decision after days of argument. Finally the Consul resorted to a deviousness refined by experience and declared that, as Customs would not allow entry for the tiger and the ship could not possibly take it back, the Dutch merchant would have to lose his money and release the animal. Horrified at the certain consequences of their action, the Japanese reversed their decision and the tiger was bought for public exhibition.

Henry was never wholly convinced by the story but agreed that it illustrated the intransigence of some Japanese officials.

During the year, Henry made two more visits to the *Gankiro* to see Rumika. She had become rather special to him and when, on the second occasion, she was not available he left at once preferring not to ask or speculate on the reason. Perhaps she was ill. This attachment to Rumika had achieved a hint of blind innocence in Henry's mind and did nothing to inhibit his occasional attendance at Mass. One service he was determined not to miss was the Dedication of the newly-built church. At 11 a.m. on Sunday, 12th January 1862, the Pro-Vicar Apostolic and Superior of the Mission of Japan and Lew Chew presided over its dedication to "The Sacred Heart of Jesus". Henry was not surprised at the number of non-Catholic residents who attended out of respect for the well-loved priest, the Abbé Girard. On the 16th a Mass was celebrated for the repose of the soul of Henry Heuksen, the Dutch interpreter and friend of the U.S. Minister Townsend Harris. One year earlier almost to the day, Mr Heusken was returning home on horseback from his official duties as interpreter when he was attacked by six Japanese with drawn swords. His *yakunin* escort fled leaving him with a horse whip as his only weapon for defence. His callous murder shocked the whole settlement.

The Japanese became so curious about this Christian Church that several groups of twenty to thirty "pilgrims" defied the law forbidding visits to foreign places of worship. Each group was quickly arrested by *yakunin* and taken to Tobé prison. The *Shogun* eventually ordered their release after strong protests from the French Minister, but gave a warning that future cases would be treated with the utmost rigour.

By February, Henry had come to a firm decision to have his partnership with Frey dissolved. He was convinced that no proper accounts had been kept and all efforts to see any books had failed. He was incurring time penalties for delays in completing some orders in the shipyard caused by late delivery of materials. There was no doubt now that Frey was accepting contracts privately and leaving work unfinished. Henry's pride and integrity were being sorely tried and the partnership was beginning to damage his reputation for competence and reliability. He decided to invoke the clause in their agreement regarding disputes and applied to the British Consulate for a court hearing of his case.

Public notice was given that the case would be heard on 12th May 1862 before H.B.M.'s Consul F. Howard Vyse with Henry Cook of Yokohama, shipwright, as plaintiff and Henry Frey, of the same place, as defendant. Two assessors were appointed.

Henry managed to obtain the services of Mr Hoey, a newly arrived solicitor, who claimed in court that Mr Cook's sole object was a dissolution of the partnership. He asked the court to get possession of the accounts of work done and money received. The Deed of Partnership was handed to the court. Captain Baillie was called to give testament on Henry's behalf and another friend, Allan Cameron, who had known both partners ever since Henry arrived in February 1860, gave a fair account of his knowledge of Henry's difficulties with Frey.

Under cross examination Frey declared he never understood what he was signing and had no intention at the time of agreeing to disputes being settled in a British court. When asked, he replied that he was willing for the partnership to be dissolved. One witness claimed he had been employed by Frey for a little more than a month to act as book-keeper. The books had been taken from him a week before the court hearing and returned with a 'money paid entry' crossed out.

When the case resumed on the following day, Frey requested that he be allowed to re-open his case with Mr Crutchley appearing on his behalf. The court decided against the application stating that Mr Crutchley had presented no credentials to practise as a solicitor and had no right to appear in court in that capacity. Henry was relieved that he had followed Captain Elmstone's advice!

The Court appointed Mr Bruyn and Captain Macdonald to inspect the books, prepare a balance sheet and report back to the Court on 13th June. They reported that no books had been kept and business had been conducted in a very loose manner indeed. The balance sheet presented was a result of information from documents and assorted papers and from parties who had advanced or paid money due. In the statement of wages paid to Japanese and foreigners the amounts were left blank, but both partners agreed it should be about $3,000 at least. The report noted that work on a schooner and a new godown was unfinished and severe cost penalties were accruing.

It was at this point in their report that Bruyn and Macdonald seemed to exceed their brief and appropriated the duties of the court by making judgements and apportioning blame. They claimed that at a conference they had advised both Frey and Cook to seek further cash advances and extra time for completion of work outstanding on contract. Frey was willing to follow that course but Cook refused to consider such action until he had a settlement. In the opinion of these gentlemen, "the conduct of Mr Cook is highly reprehensible".

Henry had in mind that both he and Frey had asked for dissolution of their partnership so how could they expect further loans of cash? He also objected to the manner in which the conference had been conducted. The "Japan Herald" was critical of several aspects of the court hearing which it reported at length, including Henry's comments:

Here is the statement of one of the parties whose books the Accountant and his assistant were appointed to inspect.

June 20th, 1862.

"I was called into Mr. Bruyn's office—he told me that Capt. Macdonald and he had agreed that it would be better for me to get further advances on our contracts"—I said "as for settling any of my affairs in your office I shall not." He said "it's no use your acting ugly or *I will make it worse for you.*" I said "I should be sorry to come into his office to insult him but I declined to settle my affairs in his office."

(Signed) HENRY COOK.

Perhaps we shall learn that Accountants appointed to inspect Books and draw Balance-sheets can—in a proper performance of their duty—make it better for a man who toadies to their officialdom—or worse for one who ventures to ask them to embrace in their inspection something he produces We feel assured that we shall not be told that this meets the approval of the Court.

On 13th June the Consul issued public notification of the final dissolution of the partnership. In fairness to Bruyn and Macdonald, they closed their statement to the Court by acknowledging that Mr Cook had given them all assistance in his power by handing in an account from memory of work done for shipping and of monies he has personally drawn from the Firm, whereas Mr Frey pertinaciously refused to assist them with his memory. They left it all with the Court to endeavour to extract such information from him. This bad publicity prompted Frey to insert an advertisement in the "Herald" of 21st June in an attempt to claw back some creditability:

NOTIFICATION.

BRITISH CONSULATE, YOKOHAMA
13th June, 1862.

The Undersigned, H.B.M.'s Consul, publicly notifies that a dissolution of the Partnership of Messrs. Frey and Cook at Yokohama has this day been decreed by the Undersigned, and that the whole of the property of the Firm will be disposed of for the benefit of those concerned.

All parties having claims against the Firm are requested to send in the same to Her Britannic Majesty's Consulate before the 15th of July proximo.

F. HOWARD VYSE,
H. B. M.'s Consul.

ADVERTISEMENT.

The Proprietors of the *Japan Herald*. Please insert this as an advertisement in the *Japan Herald* until further notice.

H. J. FREY.
YOKOHAMA, 14th June, 1862.

To the Editors of the
"THE JAPAN HERALD."

SIRS,—I have been informed that a judgment was delivered yesterday, the 13th inst., in H. B. M.'s Consular Court, decreeing a dissolution of Partnership between Mr. Henry Cook and myself; I beg to state that I am not cognisant of the same, nor do I acknowledge either the justice or legality of an "exparte" trial imposing upon me an obligation after having been denied similar advantages granted to my partner an Englishman.

I am, Sirs,
Your obedient servant,
H. J. FREY.

The "Japan Herald" summed up the popular verdict in Yokohama with its own observation:

> "We believe Mr Cook can afford to put up with the gratuitous 'reprehension' of his conduct, supported as he will be by the approval of all those whom he has wisely declined to draw further into complications of the quondam partnership matters."

Henry's first entry into private business had many successes, including a reputation for top quality work, but it ended with a bitter warning that in future he would need to keep personal control of his affairs.

16
Mounting Tension

Although relieved that he had successfully severed his partnership with Frey, Henry still had to face his debts and fulfil an outstanding contract. The work on Mr Eisler's schooner should have been finished on 2nd May and a penalty of $15 per day had been accumulating. Most of Henry's friends had supported his action and were quick to offer temporary financial help, a solution he firmly rejected. His stubborn independence was appreciated by Mr Eisler who volunteered an advance on the final payment to secure a speedy completion of his refitment programme.

Henry's debts had been cleared by July and his Japanese workers paid off, yet still leaving him in credit with a little money and a few pieces of useful equipment. The pressures of the previous months had occupied his mind totally and the arrival of his brother Anthony surprised him as though it had never been planned. Both men had changed almost beyond recognition and Henry's beard was a disguise Anthony found difficult to penetrate.

Anthony was not worldly-wise, having lived the simple life of a black-smith in the Newport area for the past thirteen years. He had found the courage to leave England secure in the knowledge that his brother was successful and could guarantee employment for him. The news of Henry's split with Frey left him feeling vulnerable and bewildered. Henry found suitable lodgings for him, unfortunately not very close to his own. That evening they went to one of Henry's regular haunts so that Anthony could meet some of his friends and feel more at home in the community. It was a sad mistake, leaving Anthony feeling more isolated than before. He had nothing in common with their extrovert brashness. His efforts at joining in the conversation were brushed aside, albeit without malice, leaving him silent with his beer. Even his name was wrong. They had become so used to Henry that any brother of his must surely be 'Cook' - why had he changed his name to 'Carrol'?

There was an awkward silence between the brothers as they walked to Anthony's lodgings. Both men realised it was impossible to recapture boyhood feelings and that a gulf of experience now separated them, one not easily bridged. Well into the night they exchanged memories of the family in Newport with Henry greedy for news of Bridget and his mother and father. At a distance he could still cherish that love he had for them, but would the reality of it be sustained if they ever met face to face? He began to doubt it and felt more lonely, as though they had suddenly died.

Henry's spirits were quickly restored as he pursued the rebuilding of his business. He had been particularly friendly with Allan Cameron ever since settling in Yokohama and was very grateful for his support during the court case. Their experiences were complementary to each other and Henry had secretly wished that his partnership had been with Cameron instead of Frey. When approached, Cameron was not slow to see the logic of joining forces with Henry, knowing him to be the most competent shipwright in the settlement. The idea was even more attractive when he learned that Henry planned to offer a full shipbuilding service to plans of his own design. It was an enterprise close to his heart. Partnership agreement was reached within two weeks.

Cameron had premises on the coast with a convenient jetty running eastwards into the bay. It was easily reached by crossing the Creek at the first bridge, the Yaytobashi, and had plenty of space for development. The firm of "Cameron and Cook" soon earned itself a solid reputation. Their first order came from Jardine, Matheson & Co., the great international trading company, who required a new schooner for the China run. At its launching it was named "The Pearl" and was reported by the "Japan Gazette" to be the first ship built by foreigners in Japan, certainly since 1859.

The firm was able to employ Anthony Carrol in their workshops and so give him a useful introduction to the problems and pleasures of working with the Japanese. Unfortunately, he and Henry failed to rekindle the brotherly closeness of their boyhood.

There was a growing superstition among the foreign community, based on a considerable amount of fact, that the major tragedies affecting them always happened on Sundays. Sunday, 14th September 1862, certainly added to that conviction. Henry had been standing on the jetty attached to his shipyard gazing out into the bay as several vessels of the British fleet sailed in, commanded by Admiral Kuper. Nostalgia satisfied, he was returning to the settlement across the Yaytobashi and stopped to yarn with his old friend George Rogers who had been watching the fleet from the bridge. An employee of Rogers ran across to them in a highly agitated state with some very garbled news that a woman had just arrived back in great distress claiming that her three male companions had been murdered but she had managed to escape. Henry and Rogers hurried to the house where she had taken refuge to find that a crowd of anxious residents had also gathered there, hoping to learn that the rumour was false. There were too many rumours, but it could not be ignored that attacks and murders were on the increase - a trend fuelled by civil unrest within Japan over the foothold that foreigners now had in their country.

Advisers to the Emperor, whose Court was centred in Kyoto, were all in favour of driving the foreigners out of Japan and closing the treaty ports to them. This course of action appealed to many of the *samurai* class who were losing status and traditional security of livelihood as the despised merchant class gained importance. On the other hand, the *Shogun* who was the political ruler of Japan was beginning to realise the inevitability of world influence in his country's future. His advisers, the *Bakufu*, were cautiously and reluctantly conceding the value of foreign infiltration. Disgruntled *samurai* decided to take matters into their own hands and remove the foreigners in their own skilled two-sworded manner. They became *ronin*.

A *ronin* was literally an outcast. Every person in Japan was supposed to belong to one of the country's *daimyo* or lords, who was in turn accountable for the actions of his clansmen and responsible for their protection. However, it was possible for men, particularly those of the *samurai* class, to resign their allegiance but in so doing would forfeit all rights of protection. The *daimyo* would no longer be responsible for any action of the outcast.

These *ronin* had organised many murderous attacks on foreigners and seemed able to move about the country quite freely. They had attacked the British Legation in Yedo in July of the previous year, 1861. Lawrence Oliphant, the new Secretary to the Legation, was badly wounded but fortunately recovered. In June 1862, a second attack was easily contained although two marines lost their lives. It was the first incident to confront the new Chargé d'Affaires, Lieutenant Colonel Neale, who had arrived earlier in the month.

Henry and his companions were aware of these assaults on the Legation, the "Herald" covered the news efficiently, but Yedo was not Yokohama and the danger appeared more remote. The outrage that this woman described struck at the heart of their fears and it was much closer to home. Her name was

Mrs Borrodaile. She was the wife of a merchant in Hong Kong and was visiting her brother-in-law, Mr Marshall, a Yokohama merchant. Making up a party of four were Mr Clarke from Yokohama and a Mr Richardson who had just retired from business in Shanghai and was visiting Japan before returning to England. The party left Yokohama about two o'clock for a country ride on horseback. They intended to cross to Kanagawa by boat and then continue on horseback to Kawasaki where there was a fine temple.

This journey took them along the notorious Tokaido and when nearly halfway to Kawasaki at the village of Namamugi they had ridden into the middle of a *daimyo's* entourage coming from Yedo, consisting of a large body of *samurai*, some of whom signalled for them to move aside. Mrs Borrodaile claimed they had complied with the request and, in consequence of repeated signs to go back, they turned their horses to return to Kanagawa. Quite suddenly and without further warning some of the retainers drew their swords and fiercely attacked them. A cut from a two-handed sword was aimed at Mrs Borrodaile's head. Instinctively she ducked and the blow swept the hat from her head. The three men, entirely unarmed, were badly wounded and could do nothing but try to dash through their assailants. She saw Mr Richardson fall from his horse, apparently dead. Her brother-in-law shouted to her to ride for her life as he and Mr Clarke were too badly hurt to keep up.

From that moment she scarcely remembered anything. She recalled riding into the sea, ignoring the risk of drowning, and then along the shingle. Her horse regained the road and continued its headlong gallop towards Yokohama, twice falling under her. She had arrived about half-past three, smeared with blood and in a fainting condition. News came that Marshall and Clarke had managed to reach the American Consulate.

Some of Henry's friends who owned their own ponies joined the British Consul, Captain Vyse, and his escort in a search for Mr Richardson at Namamugi. They found him just off the roadside, dreadfully mangled with ten fatal wounds from sword cuts. Two old mats had been thrown over him. A litter was constructed and the body taken to Kanagawa.

The murder was the subject of speculation and interpretation. Certainly it was not committed by *ronin*. The *daimyo* in procession was the Prince of Satsuma, Shimazu Saburo, a powerful lord said to be in favour of expelling foreigners. It also came to light that Richardson and Mrs Borrodaile were leading their party and were not familiar with the strict rules governing the conduct of people in the vicinity of such processions. At the very least, they should have dismounted from their horses until the long cortège had passed. The *samurai* had possibly been carrying out their professional duties with ruthless efficiency.

The foreign community wanted immediate action. Henry found Anthony and made him attend a meeting that evening at which nearly all residents were present. Captain Vyse chaired the meeting which requested that ample reparation be demanded of the Japanese government and that the person of the *daimyo* be secured to guarantee speedy compliance.

Colonel Neale of the Legation could see cause for serious repercussions and wisely waited for positive instructions from England. Meanwhile he persisted with efforts to gain reparation but the Yedo government confessed their inability to deal with Shimazu Saburo in the off-hand way demanded of them. He was far too powerful.

The waiting game of diplomats was hard to bear. Another public meeting was held, this time at the house of Mr Clarke, who was wounded at Namamugi, for the purpose of forming a Volunteer Force. The object was to invite any willing men to join and form themselves into a Rifle Corps for the defence of their lives and property. Henry had committed himself so completely to Yokohama that he felt he had no option but to join the Corps, as did many of his friends. His brother declined, pleading no experience with fire-arms.

The Race Course on reclaimed swamp land

Momentous though these happenings were, they could not be allowed to interfere with business or pleasure. As soon as the work of filling in the swamp area was completed, a start was made on dividing it into new lots although no building could be allowed for some time. This did not prevent devotees organising a very presentable racecourse on the reclaimed land, complete with grandstand. The opening meeting was a welcome festive occasion attended by officials from the Legation and Consulate.

Even Anthony revived his latent Irish love of horses by entering into the spirit of the event. A badly bruised cheek dampened his enthusiasm only for a short time. He was hit by a bottle thrown from a refreshment booth where a dozen or so people were hotly engaged in a brawl. Captain Vyse and some of his men were called to break up a potentially serious and destructive incident.

The fear of being murdered was only one of many anxieties faced by settlers in this frontier town but it remained the general topic of conversation for several years.

17
When Diplomacy Failed

The Cameron and Cook partnership was fast becoming a victim of its own success. The demand for small working boats was increasing and orders for two more schooners finally stretched their resources of space and equipment to the limit. Realising that Henry was still a key figure in a growing industry, though others would arrive before long, several enterprising people had approached him with offers of partnerships and other inducements. He was always willing to discuss any such ideas but secretly knew he was ready to strike out alone. He respected Allan Cameron too much ever to take him to court and vowed to himself that any dissolution of their partnership must be arranged with mutual consent.

Looking to the future, Henry began to search for a vacant site suitable for a large shipbuilding complex with workshops capable of producing the metal fittings and constructions in current use. He found an ideal location on the recently filled-in swamp area. Lot 115 stretched right down to the side of the Creek, giving good access for ships and shelter from the fierce gales to which Cameron's beach was exposed. Adjacent to the rear was Lot 120, ideal for the workshops. Allocations of land were made by the Japanese government, free of charge to early settlers. The only stipulations to the grants were that a fence be erected round the plot immediately and that a yearly ground rent be paid according to the number of *tsubo*, about four square yards. Henry sent his application through the Consulate, having in mind that the site could be used for any overflow of work before launching his solo enterprise.

Early in July 1863, sailors coming into Yokohama were complaining that the Japanese had closed the entrance to the Inland Sea, a long stretch of water bounded by Honshu and Shikoku Island, which forced them to make a long detour round the island of Kyushu when sailing from Korea and North China. They were not aware that influential advisers to the Emperor had forced the rival *Bakufu* to agree that moves to expel the foreigners from Japan should begin on 25th June 1863. The *Bakufu* had no wish to provoke hostilities and were torn between wishing to obey the Emperor and maintaining good relations with foreign representatives. Not so the governing body of the Choshu domain who were fanatical in their desire to be rid of foreigners. On the appointed day, Choshu steamers attacked an American vessel in the Shimonoseki Straits, the entrance to the Inland Sea, which their territory controlled from the north side. Then, in early July, ships and shore batteries fired on Dutch and French vessels inflicting damage and casualties. Short punitive raids by American and French naval ships had been ineffective, so the Straits had been considered closed to foreign shipping.

Rumours that *ronin* were gathering for a mass attack on the settlement at Yokohama caused some panic, not entirely eased when the rumour was declared false. Henry found some comfort and security by wearing a revolver strapped round his waist when moving about at night, as did most of the residents. They could still laugh in pantomime fashion at the sight of themselves playing billiards, or sitting at card tables, armed with guns as though in a Californian mining town!

It often happened in those early years that news of some major event caught the interest of residents and details leading up to it would filter through a day or two later. Some of the usual crowd at the Hotel were stunned by news that the British had declared war on Japan and that the navy was already bombarding the coast. Reception of the news was mixed; some gave ill-considered cheers, others were silent with disbelief. A group hurried to the Consulate, too anxious to wait for the next copy of the "Herald", where they were relieved to hear it was an action to force Satsuma to accept their responsibility in the Richardson affair, not calculated to lead to war.

Colonel Neale had received his official instructions and authority to use force if necessary. He was to demand from the Japanese government a full apology and an indemnity of £100,000 and from Satsuma an indemnity of £25,000 and execution of the murderers. The *Shogun* had no wish to provoke war and agreed to pay the indemnity; Satsuma would give no such undertaking so Neale resorted to force. He ordered a British squadron to enter Kagoshima Bay, the heart of the Satsuma domain, and seize three Satsuma steamers to be held until compliance. This action led to an exchange of gunfire with the shore batteries which resulted in the destruction of most of Kagoshima, fortunately with little loss of life, and the sinking of the steamers. The British squadron suffered heavy damage and withdrew. When negotiations were subsequently resumed, Satsuma at last agreed to the terms. Strangely, this action led to a mutual respect between the British and Satsuma navies which continued for many years.

Once again it had happened on a Sunday, 15th August 1863! Sailors were relieved when the entrance to the Inland Sea was declared open and safe to use. The destruction of Kagoshima failed to act as a warning to Choshu, who continually refused to negotiate a settlement. A combined force of British, Dutch, French and American ships carried out a heavy bombardment of the Shimonoseki shore batteries on September 5th and during the next two days men were landed to destroy guns and emplacements. By September 14th conditions for a truce were settled and once again the *Bakufu* accepted responsibility for the cost of the action, agreeing an indemnity of three million dollars.

The continuing intrigues between Kyoto and Yedo were not a lasting concern for Henry. Incidents peaked and captured interest but day-to-day pressures for economic survival posed problems of greater importance to most of the merchant community. Diplomatic and administrative officials quite properly monitored every twist and turn of the Japanese political struggle and were comfortably cushioned against the need for commercial struggle. The tolerance gap between them widened with the merchants accused of being interested only in making money, an activity easily disdained by their accusers. Fortunately for Henry, he had been able to bridge that gap and was gaining respect from all sections of the community, including the Japanese.

His application for land was approved and, on receipt of the title deeds from the Consul, he diverted some of his carpenters to the task of fencing. Henry was the second person to build on the reclaimed land, the first being an American firm of naval stores contractors on Lot 117. Captain Baillie quickly laid claim to Lot 116. There had been public complaints about the slaughtering of cattle and pigs near Main Street and the accumulation of stinking offal left to rot in the gutters or on the beach in front of the offices. A deserted beach area at Homoco, about a mile from the foreign settlement, was allocated for this work and had become known as the 'Butcheries'. Baillie found the journey tedious and inconvenient and was eager to save time by ferrying his meat round the coast and along the Creek to his new premises.

Frey moved his business to 114, next to Henry but just across a narrow street. He was hoping to obtain contracts for new buildings by moving into the reclaimed area. Since the court action brought by Henry, possible clients had used other contractors and the distrust still continued on the new site. He shortly moved to 113 and finally closed his business in 1865.

NISHINOBASHI - Bridge spanning the Creek.

The nearest bridge for crossing the Creek from 115 was the Nishinobashi. When viewing various sites in September 1863, Henry came across a notice in Japanese posted up at the entrance to the bridge. It appeared to be official. His recognition of Japanese characters had improved sufficiently for very rough translation, given the time, although he was still completely incapable of writing the characters on paper in spite of his ability as a draughtsman. The notice referred to the *Gankiro* and stated that if the *Gankiro* at Yokohama was not removed, the house called "Iwatsukiya" (owned by the same person) at Shinagawa would be burned. He was bemused by such a strange form of public notice and not convinced until his translation was confirmed, in essence, by a compradore that Cameron often employed. He had not been to the *Gankiro* for a while in spite of his infatuation with Rumika, or perhaps because of it and the hurt occasioned when facing the truth of her work. Perhaps the subtle influence of Abbé Girard had something to do with it? Not a subject yet to be thought about too deeply.

18
Dark Clouds And Silver Linings.

It was difficult for Henry to resist spending too much time and money on the new site to the detriment of his work for the partnership. He made up his mind to be quite open with Allan Cameron about his plans for the future. Cameron was not surprised. He had recognised the signs and guessed correctly at the dual purpose behind the project at 115. However, he made it quite clear to Henry that he had no intention to disband such a successful partnership until he could devise his own means of ensuring a sound continuity of business. Henry offered the possibility of working together where practicable after eventual independence.

Several strongly-built schooners had been ordered by companies interested in the lucrative trade of seal and sea-otter hunting. While working on these designs, Henry had formulated in his mind certain ideal innovations of a highly practical nature that had fostered in him an ambition to build such a vessel for himself and commission it for hunting otter. He could still recall the thrill of his first contact with the hunting schooners at Hakodate whilst serving on the *Henry Ellis.*

There was in November 1864 a day when work almost ceased throughout Yokohama. On 21st November two English officers, Major Baldwin and Lieutenant Bird, were brutally murdered at Kamakura by two fanatical assassins. Sorrow and outrage were so intense that every resident felt the need to attend the funeral of the victims to give expression to his feelings. Henry and Cameron had dismissed their workers for the day in order to leave themselves free to become part of this unprecedented demonstration. The Japanese acknowledged the demand for justice to be done by sending many of their high officials to the funeral.

The first assassin was caught, interrogated and sentenced to be decapitated on 30th December. First, he was paraded round the streets of Yokohama preceded by a board proclaiming his sentence. Throughout the route he shouted and sang his hatred of foreigners and called upon all Japanese to follow his example. The majority of residents made their way to the ground inside the execution enclosure. Henry felt he could not face such a gruesome spectacle, a decision he never regretted when later he was told that the executioner had had to wield his sword three times before the head was finally severed from the body.

In the afternoon, Henry made his way to the Yoshida-bashi, the main bridge across the canal boundary, to deliver a complaint to the *yakunin* stationed there about one of his workers who had been arrested for stealing. A crowd had gathered round one corner of the bridge and he moved across, curious to know the cause. That was a mistake. The third part of the assassin's sentence was being carried out. His ghastly head was impaled on a spike mounted on a stand. It was still wet and bloody with the remains of the neck buried in a block of clay. How could the guards remain there on duty beside it! Henry was instantly sick as never before at sea, and for a few moments became the new centre for the mild-eyed curiosity of the Japanese viewers. When the second assassin was captured about three months later and the whole sequence was repeated, he remained resolutely in the shipyard.

Following this display of Japanese justice, similar cowardly attacks ceased for a considerable time, to the relief of all foreign and native residents. Henry liked the ordinary Japanese people and often made excursions through the native quarter to enjoy being among them. They worked hard and seemed to play even harder at appropriate times. He was often invited into a home as he passed and offered a little rice cake and perhaps a drink. He liked the bare simplicity of their rooms, owing more to tradition than to poverty. Each house had its own shrine in the main room and was accorded a touching devotion beyond any given to a Christian crucifix. Sometimes whole families enjoyed games in the street with a boisterous energy and the effervescent high-pitched laughter he first heard in Shimoda. It was all so different from the aggressive posturing of their leaders.

Experiencing the basic friendliness of the Japanese changed the critical attitude he had shown when some of his friends began to arrange for wives, families and girl friends to join them from home countries. Conditions were still far from ideal but the political unrest had to end soon, surely? He had to admit it was very pleasant to see the ladies bringing charm and western elegance to the all-masculine monotony and yet he felt ill at ease in their company. He could not match the effortless flow of trite conversation indulged in by his strangely sober companions. It was a sophistication that

Henry had never been in a position to experience before and it exposed to himself a class difference which had not surfaced when dealing with men from many walks of life.

Since moving into his new premises on the Creek, Henry had been approached regularly by an acquaintance, Samuel Rowell, with a view to establishing a new partnership. Henry got the impression that Rowell was particularly interested in the light craft he was building at 115, mainly yachts and racing boats. Money was more plentiful and pleasure craft were much in demand. Henry had discussed the proposition in some detail but his heart was not in it and in any case he was still tied to Allan Cameron. Rowell began to increase pressure to extract at least a verbal agreement from Henry who disliked this new attitude. Not wishing to offend a possible business ally, he hedged, using the need for Cameron's agreement which he was sure would not be given.

Rowell was furious and took the matter to the Consular Court, asserting that Henry had given firm verbal assent to a contract and claimed $500 in compensation. He won his case.

Henry was sure that he had successfully avoided ever giving a positive verbal commitment which would have been binding in law. He lodged an appeal which was heard on 2nd May 1865 by Charles Winchester, H.B.M.'s Chargé d'Affaires and Acting Consul General in Japan, who examined the pleadings and evidence with great care. He commented:

"It is evident from the nature of things that antecedent to the formation of a partnership there must be a time when the interests, wishes and intentions of the parties must be the subject of negotiation and discussion without being legally bound to each other to carry these intentions and desires into effect. Otherwise no two individuals wishing to join in business would be safe in opening their mouths to one another on the subject .... To create a foundation for such a claim for damages the terms of a verbal agreement must be absolute and not conditional, and they must be clearly proved."

The court found in favour of Henry; Rowell had to pay all costs of his original lawsuit and of the appeal. It was the first case of its kind in Yokohama and the "Japan Herald" considered that the points at issue warranted a special verbatim report.

Just over a month later, His Excellency Sir Harry Parkes landed in Yokohama on 18th July, replacing Sir Rutherford Alcock as British Minister. Affairs linked to Sir Harry were to enter the lives of Henry's family for the next hundred years.

It was inevitable that in the merchant community, faced with so many uncertainties and disasters, some would seek the mutual support and influence of Freemasonry. Several friends of Henry had been suggesting that he would be considered acceptable should he contemplate the serious step of becoming a Mason. As a Catholic, nurtured in prayer by his parents rather than in doctrine, he had but a very hazy and inconsequential knowledge of its condemnation by the Catholic Church. Any attempt to foster social contacts would be welcome. At a preliminary meeting, Brother John Black, editor of the "Japan Herald", had proposed that a Masonic Lodge, working under the Constitution of the Grand Lodge of England, should be inaugurated. It was carried unanimously and on 26th June 1866, Yokohama Lodge No. 1092 was consecrated. Henry was Initiated on 15th August 1866 and Passed on 21st November. Finally he was Raised on 24th January 1867. The Lodge first met at 72 Main Street but was soon forced to move after one of Yokohama's greatest fires.

Henry had moved into a very simple but adequate house of a temporary nature erected on the site at 115 Creek Road, as it was then called, and was looked after by a Japanese housekeeper. He had been working in his room since early morning checking some drawings he had prepared the previous day, 25th November 1866. His housekeeper had rushed in about 10 a.m. and pulled him to the door without her usual polite ceremony. Across the far side of Yokohama, in the native quarter, he could see sharply-angled palls of black smoke being driven by a fierce wind. Flames seemed to be leaping from dozens of different locations not closely connected, but it was difficult to see clearly from that distance. Henry issued safety instructions to his foremen and gave them permission to release some of the men whose homes were in that area.

He made his way towards the centre but could make little headway against the panic measures being taken by frightened families. The Japanese servants were frantically pulling furniture out of the houses, blocking access along the streets. Measures being taken were crazy even hazardous to his practical mind. Destruction was total and a changing wind blew lighted embers along Main Street starting fires as far as No. 72.

There was nothing Henry could do in such a conflagration. Fearing for his own property and the ships in his care, he turned his back on the desperate scene and returned to the shipyards to prepare for the worst. The wind was kind to him and by seven o'clock in the evening it had veered to seaward and the fires burned quietly without further menace.

The next morning Henry saw the full extent of the destruction. Yokohama would have to be rebuilt, even redesigned. The fire had obeyed the notice on the Nihonbashi. It had totally destroyed the *Gankiro* and thirty-five people there had died. He could trace no list of names but was sure that Rumika, gentle Rumika, would be one of them - - - all because some grease had dropped on to the fire in a small cookshop and started an inferno.

Already some of the Japanese were beginning to set up shanties among the still smouldering ruins of their former homes. Don't they ever despair?

There was an infectious air of renewal all over the settlement. Great changes were being planned. The fire was being praised for its timely demolition of piecemeal development.

A Fire Watch-Tower

The New Masonic Hall, Yokohama, built after the fire.

Henry and Cameron were caught up in the same fever and agreed to dissolve their partnership and go their separate ways. On 16th January 1867 Henry gave the news to Yokohama via the "Japan Herald":

H. COOK,

THE OLDEST ESTABLISHED Naval Architect, Ship and Boat Builder in Japan, begs to inform his numerous patrons that he still continues to contract for building every description of vessel adapted to sea or river navigation, Yachts, Gigs, and Racing Boats.

He has on hand large quantities of the best wood to be procured in the country, Oregon Pine spars to suit vessels of any size; he has also engaged the services of a first class Mechanical Engineer, who will supply Iron and Brass castings, either for ships or other purposes, with the utmost despatch. His workshops posesses every appliance necessary for the repairs of ships or steam machinery; the shipwright's and blacksmith's shops are equally well supplied with plant and the work is entirely carried on under the supervision of experienced Europeans.

Estimates and particulars forwarded to his patrons with quick despatch on application to the undermentioned address.

H. COOK,
115 Creek Road.
Yokohama, Sept. 13th, 1866.   s12ptf.

19
Another Partnership

The weather had been unsettled for some days with gales blowing from the south-east. Henry had abandoned his plans to refloat a small schooner, which had come in for repair a month previously, and closed the yard early. It was too soon to expect his evening meal to be ready, so he made his way to the Grand Hotel for a drink with his friends. They were sitting in the lounge when they noticed a bedraggled-looking group of westerners being escorted to the desk by a naval officer. All attention was focused on the new arrivals, a rare enough occurrence in this community. Their obvious state of distress caused further speculation, especially as a lady and two children were in the group and there was no luggage to be seen.

Henry and his friends did not like to intrude, but on making subsequent enquiries they learned that a ship had gone aground in the storm near Shimoda. The passengers had been taken aboard a naval vessel and landed in Yokohama. By chance, Henry overheard that the lady was Irish and he resolved to return the next day to satisfy his curiosity.

Any news soon spread among the English-speaking community; there were so few resident in the port in 1867, although each year brought many newcomers. The Irish family had been on a world cruise and the father, recently widowed, had brought his cousin to act as governess to his children during the long absence from school. She was from a well-known talented Catholic family of priests and doctors and had returned home after keeping house for her brother while he was studying medicine in London. Soon after he had established his own practice, Mary Julia Butler was offered the opportunity of a world cruise. Rather restless at home without any meaningful work, she had been delighted to accept and they had set sail some six months earlier.

There were few passengers on board the vessel and no lives had been endangered. The crew had managed to refloat her at high tide and the ship was now laid up at Shimoda awaiting minor repairs to the hull. Henry thought it likely that the passengers would be able to continue their cruise in a few weeks, so he hoped to devise a means of introduction as soon as possible.

The next day was Saturday, so he went to the hotel in the evening but only met up with his usual colleagues. Perhaps they were still recovering from their ordeal - Henry did not feel he could question the staff on this matter. Then he remembered - Mass was at 10 a.m. on Sundays at the Sacred Heart Catholic Chapel in Yokohama - she might be there. He had not attended very regularly of late, but the priest knew him well and would be eager to introduce any newcomer to his flock.

Henry rose early and put on his Sunday-best suit. He was a personable young man, still only thirty-one years old, but with a maturity beyond his years. He arrived early and chose a seat near the back so that he could see who came in. It was not long before he was rewarded. With a rustle of silk and light footsteps, a very smart young lady shepherded two children into a pew and whispered something to them. They bent their heads, ostensibly intent in prayer.

Henry's heart missed a beat. How ridiculous he thought to himself. She's probably much too superior to want to talk to me. But in spite of himself he determined to meet her after the service. Henry's prayers during Mass were confused. He had always turned to God for guidance, so now he prayed only that he would acquit himself well and not reveal his underlying apprehension.

Abbé Girard greeted Henry warmly outside the church and asked after his business. Henry felt obliged to make excuses for his occasional absence and blamed pressure of work, saying urgent repairs could not wait, even on Sundays. The Abbé smiled in agreement. Then, incredibly, he said he wanted Henry to meet some visitors who had arrived unexpectedly in Yokohama. He took him over to the small group waiting by the door and introduced Henry Cook to Mary Julia Butler and the children. A fellow countryman he explained to them, born in Kilkenny, but a much travelled gentleman. Mary Julia smiled knowingly and said she would like to hear about some of his adventures, adding that she was sure the children would be enthralled.

Henry had always acted positively and promptly invited them all to his home for Sunday tea. He immediately regretted it, picturing her in his plain and humble parlour and with a solitary Japanese maidservant. However, it was only momentarily, for Mary Julia explained that her cousin, Francis, was somewhat indisposed and she did not feel she could leave him for too long. But if Mr Cook would honour them with his presence at the hotel, she was sure

Francis would be delighted to make his acquaintance. Henry could not have wished a happier outcome to this introduction and a time of 3.30 p.m. was agreed.

Other meetings inevitably followed as a result and Henry realised how homesick he had been for female companionship from his own background. In spite of the difference in birth and upbringing, there was a natural affinity between the two, both had a spirit of adventure, and the variation of experience seemed to complement the relationship. The children were always eager to watch the activity at the boatyard and sometimes Henry took them for short trips in the bay. Their father was anxious to return home; he felt that Henry was becoming too fond of his cousin. He regarded him as an ordinary working man despite his acknowledged skills and reputation as a shipwright with his own business.

After a month had elapsed without the anticipated return of the ship from Shimoda, he decided to book a passage with the next P. & O. vessel going to London. Francis discussed this intention with his cousin and was somewhat surprised at her reaction. She was unhappy about leaving so soon; the children were enjoying the experience and she was keeping up with their lessons. Japan was so beautiful in the spring - could they not wait for another month or two when the weather would become hot and humid? Francis was adamant. He was concerned about his estate in Ireland and felt that his bereavement had caused him to neglect his affairs for long enough.

That evening, Mary Julia told Henry of the decision and could not conceal her emotion. Their friendship had ripened into love and Henry gathered the desolate girl into his arms and comforted her. His thoughts were in turmoil; he had not faced the reality of a parting during the happy weeks spent in her company. Now the prospect appalled him. Never to see her again! Japan was the other end of the world from Ireland - again he made a positive decision and asked her to marry him and stay in Yokohama. Mary Julia looked up at him and suddenly she, too, knew that this was the only solution.

Henry escorted her back to the hotel to confront her cousin. He was shocked at the idea and pointed out to Mary Julia that her family would never agree to such a liaison. She replied that she was nearly twenty-eight years of age and did not need her parents' consent to marry. Henry was able to support her and would be a kind and considerate husband and a good Catholic father if they were fortunate enough to have a family. Henry glowed inwardly with pride at her words. She had spirit; he admired her and loved her with every fibre of his being.   He had never been in love before - it was a new and wonderful experience.

20
Married Bliss - A Shadow Falls

Several weeks passed before Mary Julia's cousin, Francis, could secure a passage home. He persistently voiced his objections to her liaison with Henry and it was only her love for the children which prevented her from abandoning her responsibilities. It was obvious that he intended to convey his anger and disapproval to her parents when he returned to Ireland but Mary Julia was not easily swayed from her own judgment, a characteristic she was to pass on to future generations.

Much of Yokohama was still scarred from the great fire and presented a depressing background to Mary Julia's first impressions. Spared from damage in that catastrophe, Henry's shipyard was full of bright prospects and she quickly perceived a role for herself in reorganising the management of his office as well as bringing love into his home. Obviously a busy life lay ahead but she had no second thoughts and relished the challenge with a confidence inbred from birth. So, yet another family thread was being drawn into the tapestry of Japanese history at a time when events were moving rapidly.

In late August 1866, the young Shogun Iemochi had died and had been succeeded most reluctantly by his guardian, Tokugawa Keiki. A few months later on 3rd February 1867, Emperor Komei died and he was succeeded by his fifteen year old son who was to reign for the next forty-five years and became known as the famous Emperor Meiji. From the beginning of his accession he gave proof of his good intentions towards foreigners by inviting the Ministers of the Treaty Powers to visit him at Kyoto. It had been arranged for Sir Harry Parkes, the British Minister, to be received at Court on 23rd March.

The procession escorting Sir Harry was led by the Mounted Police Escort with Inspector Peter Peacock at the head. The procession was quietly wending its way through the streets when suddenly, as it rounded an awkward bend, armed Japanese sprang out of the houses and began slashing indiscriminately with their swords at horses and men. The Escort was taken by surprise and given no time to use their lances. Before anything could be done to meet the attack, nine out of the eleven policemen were wounded, some severely, and four horses. The Emperor was outraged and quickly issued a proclamation that he regarded such attacks as infamous and detestable. Any guilty *samurai* would have their swords removed and be beheaded as common criminals. It proved effective and attacks were few from then on. Inspector Peacock, who was wounded in his defence of Sir Harry, became a close friend of Henry and his family. He married a Japanese lady, Sato, who bore him a son, Charles and a daughter. The friendship fostered intriguing consequences some hundred years later.

BUNKICHI (with the stick) the Japanese tailor used by Mary Julia

Henry could not fail to be aware of these great events which provided such colourful news for the Yokohama journalists but, with a business to run and deeply in love, he naturally had a different notion of priorities from the journalist and diplomat. He and Mary Julia were married on 5th July 1867, first at the Legation for British registration, and then at the Catholic Church of the Sacred Heart. A few close friends gave their support at both venues, anxious to maximise happy occasions in the community. They marvelled at Mary Julia's wedding dress which displayed a sense of fashion rarely seen in

Yokohama. She was generous by nature and gladly shared the secret. There was a Japanese tailor (or *shitateya*) called Bunkichi who had a small shop on the other side of the Creek, almost opposite Henry's shipyard. She found him quite able to translate her sketches into reality in spite of the complications of western fashion. He had even arranged for assistants to attend the hotel where she was staying.

The sheer wonder of his marriage overwhelmed Henry. He was living in a fairyland where the impossible happened and it took time before he could regain that clear perspective essential to his shipbuilding enterprise. Mary Julia's education and upbringing brought a refinement to his life that he had never before experienced. His house was made a home with fresh decoration and furniture. Extra Japanese servants were hired and carefully instructed. She seemed to absorb the Japanese language so naturally in contrast to his own years of laborious endeavour. The office was buzzing and workmen appeared to be moving more purposefully. Friends he used to meet in the town came to visit him at home and were charmed by their hostess. Gradually Henry realised that his wife relied absolutely on his own particular strengths and experience in a restless foreign country. Each was contributing to the other's needs; in no way had she diminished his own prestige but only added where he had lacked, and he loved her for it.

Henry began to move in business circles where previously he had felt ill at ease and trade increased in the shipyard. When appropriate he was invited to municipal meetings for consultation, reflecting the improved status of his already solid reputation. The young, self-made Irishman could be forgiven the trace of pride which crept into his very practical nature. Something in that pride prompted an urge to write to his family in Newport to give them news of his marriage and other successes. A letter from England arrived to spoil the spontaneity of his intention. It came from his sister Bridget.

She had married a Bluenose, the common term for a native of Nova Scotia; he was a seacaptain and a widower, Lynam Durkee, who preferred to use her second name, Sarah. The marriage had taken place at St. Bride's Church, Liverpool, in August 1858, and she had acknowledged this name on the marriage certificate with her cross, not being able to write. Her letters were always written for her by friends. On this occasion she was reminding Henry that their parents were nearly seventy years of age and were anxious to have his young brother, John, settled in a steady job. Would Henry be willing to employ him in Yokohama? Her husband was offering to pay his passage to

Japan. This possibility had never occurred to Henry. John was a baby when Henry ran away to sea and was still only fifteen. He would be a stranger, an unknown quantity as a brother and as a person.

Mary Julia pointed out that bringing Anthony to Japan had not been a great success. He resented his workman status, not realising how unsuited he was to enter any partnership with his brother. Jealousy had even kept him away from Henry's wedding. Mary Julia had tried to befriend him but her overtures had been rejected rather boorishly. After lengthy discussion it was agreed that at least John would never be short of work in Yokohama and might be better disposed towards Henry, having no early relationship to overcome. So it was decided to suggest that John should complete his apprenticeship with the blacksmith before coming to Japan. By then he would be seventeen and qualified in a skill that Anthony had found much in demand in the area.

After this lengthy exchange of ideas Mary Julia was strangely quiet for a few minutes, her eyes betraying indecision. Henry was quick to notice the change and coaxed the reason from her. She was almost certain she was carrying their first child. His excitement and pleasure came easily and honestly, but she realised, perhaps for the first time, just how far away she was from Ireland and her family. Mothers-to-be in Yokohama needed to find great reserves of courage.

In November 1867, the reluctant Shogun Keiki voluntarily surrendered his administrative powers to the young Emperor. Unfortunately his supporters were not satisfied and an army of the ex-shogun advanced on Kyoto. After three days of civil war, Keiki's forces were defeated. The unrest continued at intervals and during March 1868 the residents of Yokohama had genuine cause for concern. A considerable number of Japanese, wearing two swords and claiming the rank of *samurai*, were visiting the settlement. Japanese officials gave warnings of suspicious bands of *ronin* in the area and requested that any foreign nationals who could muster armed men should place guards at all entrances to Yokohama.

Henry tried to keep the anxiety from his wife, who had only eight weeks before the baby was due, but the Emperor himself could not have suppressed that sort of news. The American marines gathered at the U.S. Naval yard at 112 Creekside, just two plots away from their house. Gradually every two-sworded man was driven out of the settlement unless he had an official pass from the Governor of Kanagawa.

The danger passed, but Henry in his desperation and despair could only blame the unrest for the death of his first born. Poor Mary Julia! Her baby son was born prematurely and, in spite of attendance by the doctor and careful nursing by the Japanese servant, the little chap died after a few hours' struggle to live. They buried him in the foreign cemetery, an area set aside on the high ground on the other side of the Creek called The Bluff, which was being developed for foreign residents. They marked the grave with a tiny headstone:

"Sacred to the Memory of the Infant Son of H.COOK.
Died on 25 March 1868."

Mary Julia, young and strong, recovered quickly and the tragedy reinforced their love for each other. Conscientious practice of her Catholic faith had rekindled the simple devotion of Henry's youth and together they received much consolation and help through Abbé Girard.

The rapid changes in Japanese politics overshadowed such personal tragedies. The Emperor was poised ready to move his Court to Yedo and resume the historical and Holy Office which was his right. In October 1868 the name of the capital was changed from Yedo to Tokyo (the Eastern capital). The Japanese authorities wished foreigners to have the opportunity of seeing the royal procession as it approached Kanagawa, along the Tokaido, on its way to Tokyo. A favourable spot was selected for them but they were particularly requested not to cheer, to avoid spoiling the 'charm'. Henry decided this was an opportunity to bring some excitement and social contact back into the life of his hard-working wife.

The Emperor left Kyoto on 29th October but would not arrive in Tokyo until 26th November. When the procession neared Kanagawa, special Japanese officers directed them to the vantage point. By Japanese standards the procession was notable for its simplicity, in spite of a thousand soldiers and eight drum-and-fife bands quietly playing a single theme over and over again. Mary Julia had a good ear for music but even she found it impossible to catch the theme precisely. The silence among the watching crowd was most impressive and all bowed low as the Emperor approached in his plain whitewood *norimon* carried by numerous bearers.

Henry and Mary Julia each sensed a new beginning for Japan and hoped it also heralded a new life for them. Mrs Cook was pregnant again!

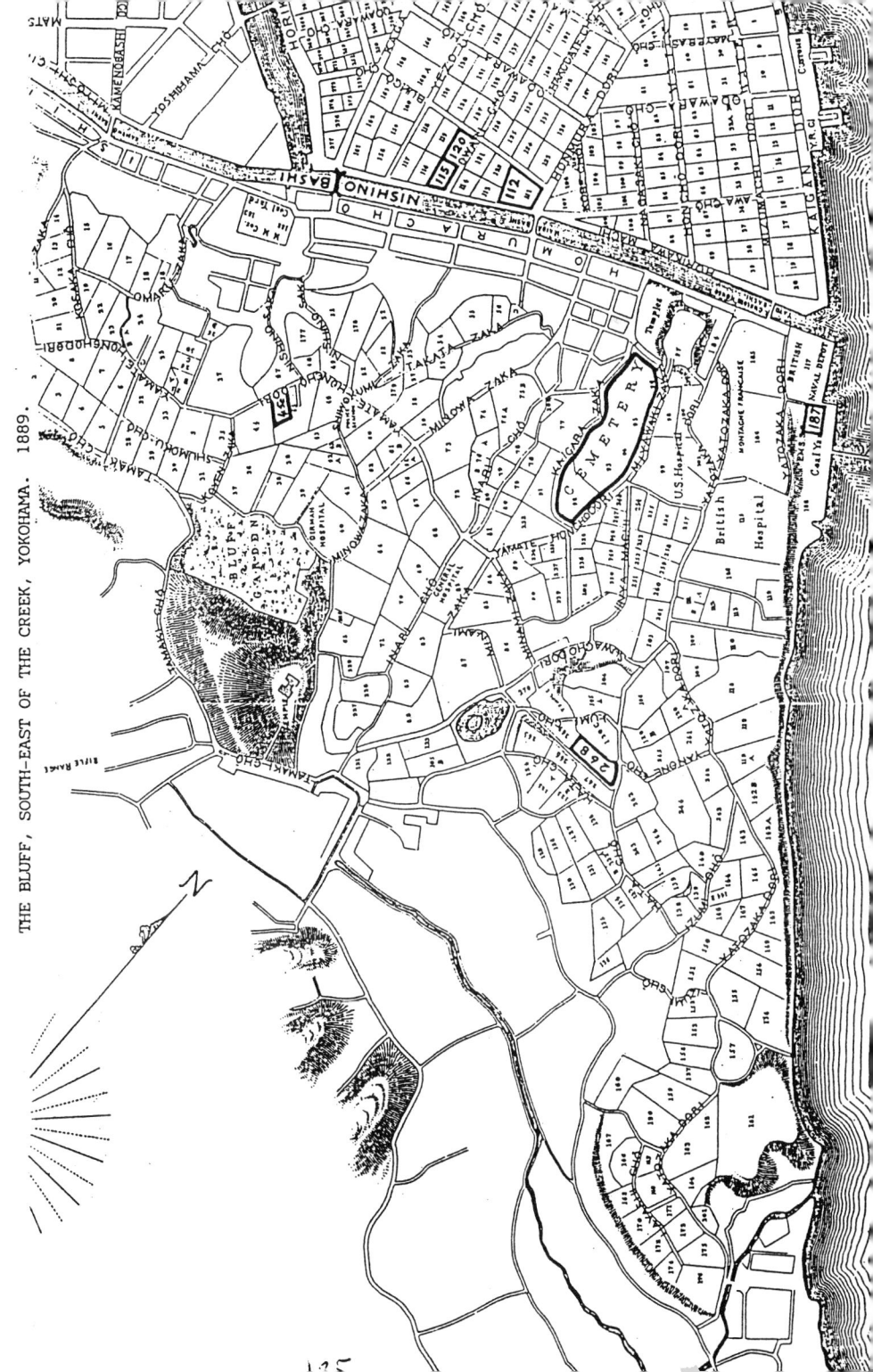

THE BLUFF, SOUTH-EAST OF THE CREEK, YOKOHAMA. 1889.

135

21
Disinherited

A messenger from the Grand Hotel brought a letter to the house, addressed to Miss M.J. Butler. It was a much-delayed letter from Mary Julia's parents. As expected, Francis broke the news of her intentions with a bias which shocked them into outrage. They wrote immediately condemning her action, forbade the marriage and threatened to disinherit her if she ignored their wishes. Even without the delay en route, the letter would have arrived too late. It would have been equally ineffective had it been received before her marriage. Mary Julia had no regrets. The Ireland of her childhood was so far away and she had already dismissed any idea of returning. A little choke of sadness was quickly put aside and she was able to show the letter to Henry and set his mind at rest in all honesty. Any loss of family fortune was amply compensated by her present happiness and their income was more than adequate.

The young seventeen-year-old Emperor was known to be in favour of reducing much of the ceremony traditionally surrounding his movements. He seemed to be giving emphasis to his role as Sovereign and playing down the sacredness of his office. News travelled fast in seaports and, towards the end of January 1869, a strong rumour was spreading that the Emperor had broken all convention and had been seen on board a small steam yacht out in Tokyo Bay. He appeared to be looking at the Japanese vessels anchored there. It was the first time an emperor had been afloat! Henry also learned from a friend at the Legation that there were some indications that the Emperor was having a yacht specially prepared for his own use. The seafaring fraternity began to see him in a new light.

Mary Julia's pregnancy was giving no cause for concern. The pace of events had eased and began to flow more smoothly, giving her a welcome peace of mind. Yokohama was at last losing some of its frontier appearance as solid, respectable-looking buildings rapidly covered old fire-ravaged areas. The town's early reputation as a wild, irresponsible town of free-living merchants surrounded by houses of ill-repute had somewhat modified, but was still relevant as in any international port. Although Henry was careful to socialise with most of his old friends and he still enjoyed a drink with them, a happy home life had steered him away from any excess.

Happiness at home reached a new height when, on 2nd July 1869, Emily Julia Cook was born easily and safely. Feeling a little guilty in his joy, Henry stopped for a few moments to think of the little boy who had died; he offered a heartfelt prayer of thanksgiving for this new blessing. He insisted that Emily should have the same second name as his wife, hoping she would develop the same qualities - it was a prophetic wish. Henry began to celebrate in the way he knew best. His mind toyed with the idea of designing a racing yacht, something special to be called the "Emily". It was not long before the design was committed to paper. The Japanese servants were as delighted and excited as Emily's parents and were all set to spoil the baby. By the sounds emanating from around the cot, Mary Julia guessed that her daughter would be speaking Japanese almost as soon as English.

Although more acutely aware than Henry of the Church's attitude to Freemasonry, Mary Julia had come to accept the practical and social aspect of his membership. Nevertheless she was surprised when later that month, on 29th July, her husband was one of the ten members of the Yokohama Lodge who increased Masonic potential in the settlement by founding the O'Tentosama Lodge, No. 1263, which could be freely translated at 'The Lodge of Light'. With the help of Sir Harry Parkes and other foreign Ministers, the Japanese government had granted in 1868 the provision of Lot 70 for the erection of a truly monumental stone building for Masonic activities. Public comment was made that "Freemasonry flourishes all through the East, but in no place more than in Yokohama, considering its size."

The Japanese were always ready to utilise western technology to their own advantage. An expert from England had already successfully installed a telegraph system between Tokyo and Yokohama. With foreign financial help plans were made for the construction of a railway between Tokyo and Osaka with a branch line to Yokohama. Mr. Morel, a man of great experience, was engaged as Engineer-in-Chief, and he began to advertise for suitably skilled workmen to accept a long term of employment in the project. When Henry heard about the offer, he immediately thought of Anthony who was ideally qualified. He lost no time in putting the idea to his brother who, true to character, wrongly accused Henry of trying to be rid of him. When his temper cooled, Anthony recognised the sense in Henry's suggestion. He began to see advantages in being independent for a few years, particularly now that he could understand the Japanese language adequately. In October 1869 Anthony vacated his lodging in Yokohama and joined Mr Morel's team. He was sent to the Tokyo end of operations and found a suitable lodging in Shimbashi on the outskirts of Tokyo.

Although Henry disliked Anthony's general attitude, he acknowledged the competence of his work and found it difficult to replace him in the shipyard. He had been working on the conversion of a schooner to steam-assisted power involving extensive work in metal. Fortunately it was almost completed. As this type of conversion was new to the yard, Henry had promised the owners to give it a thorough test at sea and personally to supervise its delivery to an anchorage at Nigata. The ever-present thrill of putting to sea took the edge off his sorrow at being parted from Mary Julia and the baby for several weeks. It was November when she watched him steam along the Creek towards open sea and she returned to the office determined not to show her emotion.

Henry was still away at sea and his wife had settled to a routine of managing the home and business when, on 9th December, a *jinrikisha* (a small two-wheeled cart drawn by a man) stopped outside the guarded entrance to the shipyard. Henry had found it necessary to employ a guard to prevent increasing theft of valuable materials. The passenger alighted and several boxes and a large canvas bag were deposited at the gate. The westerner could not make himself understood so he was taken to Mary Julia in the house. He then explained that he was Mr Cook's brother from England. She regarded him with a high degree of scepticism and suspicion - John was not expected until some time in the following year and Henry was not there to identify him. Then she remembered that her husband would have the same problem, having seen his brother only as a baby.

John was invited into the house where he was able to give a proper account of himself. He had impetuously abandoned his apprenticeship and hoped to try his luck in Henry's business. That explained his untimely early arrival. Hard-pressed with responsibilities during Henry's absence, Mary Julia let her Irish temper surface to complain about his thoughtless behaviour but as quickly regretted it. She agreed to let him stay until Henry's return. She was sorely tempted to open the presents from England but resisted, knowing that they had really been gifts for Henry.

Two weeks passed and still her husband had not returned. John had been protesting daily that he was supposed to be given a job in the shipyard. Mary Julia had no intention of allowing that to happen knowing how particular Henry was about the skills of his workers, most of whom were Japanese. Although he employed European foremen, he still reserved to himself the task of hiring labour. With the intention of forcing the issue, John made the mistake of airily declaring that he would find employment elsewhere in Yokohama. Mary Julia seized the initiative and praised his intention, thus making it difficult for him to back down. She even provided an interpreter guide to help him search the town.

John had enjoyed his voyage from England and rather fancied himself as a sailor. The vision persisted while searching the notices along the dockside until realism forced a regretful admission that he was unqualified and had no valid certificate. The best offer was for him to be employed as an unskilled water tender on the Pacific mail steamers. An enterprising Japanese millionaire, Iwasaki Yataró, had seen a great future for these foreign-built steamships. He had accumulated a fleet of such vessels and formed the Mitsubishi Mail Steamship Company. By judiciously selecting European directors, captains and engineers, it became the most important commercial undertaking in the Japanese empire.

John signed on to begin work on 29th December; this meant spending an uneasy Christmas under Henry's roof. Mary Julia tried to hide her feelings for the few days left before his departure, but she had too many worries to be sincere. Her spirits were certainly not raised by the discovery of a dead man floating in the Creek on the day following Christmas. He was a seaman from H.M.S. *Ocean* and it was presumed he had been drunk and incapable. There was no fencing along the edge of Creekside and two similar drownings had occurred earlier in the month. The relief of tension after John's departure left her feeling lonely and listless.

Mary Julia had felt imprisoned as her duties kept her close to the works and, of course, to her baby daughter whom the servants tended to monopolise. It was not safe for her to go out alone at night, even when accompanied by one of the servants. Yokohama was still without street lighting. The total darkness, as experienced by Henry when he first arrived, continued to encourage murder and housebreaking by Japanese criminals without fear of interruption. Henry had been in the forefront of residents demanding gas lighting and an efficient police force of both Japanese and European officers and men.

Midway into January of the new year, 1870, Mary Julia had a surprise visit from two great friends who had known Henry since the break-up of his partnership with Frey. They were George Alcock and his wife Mary. Mary Julia, not knowing they had gone to Kobe for a holiday, was disappointed not to have seen them at Christmas. George was full of apologies about not renewing contact sooner, but they had no idea Henry would be away for such a long time. Emily was the centre of attraction and at six months the firm chin, characteristic of her mother, was already evident. Sharing her love for Emily with friends intensified her own feelings, and a few tears welled silently in place of words.

They were distracted by voices and heavy footsteps on the gravel outside. The door was pushed open by a fit-looking Henry, just saying goodbye to the engineer and fitters who had sailed with him to Nigata. The weeks at sea had given him an alert, eager appearance that his wife had never seen before - it was love at first sight all over again. As they hugged each other she knew that 1870 was going to be a good year. George and Mary shared their joy for a few minutes. Henry remarked that she looked well and he was pleased to see she had company, which prompted Mary to rejoin that men always see the bright, easy side of running a home!

22
An Imperial Commission

The joy of being reunited was all that mattered until Mary Julia brought them back to earth with the news about John. Frustration at not seeing this unknown brother for himself, forced a sharp rebuke to his wife for not keeping John until his return. A wave of anger was directed at his brother for the arrogance of his actions and breach of trust in breaking his apprenticeship. The anger passed and together they shared the fun of opening the presents from England. Both parcels were quite heavy. The first one contained a huge family bible weighing every bit of eleven pounds. It was profusely illustrated with engravings and he could already picture Emily being fascinated by this huge book when she was older. What moved him most was that his sister, Bridget, had planned the gift over a year previously. On the flyleaf, in copperplate script, was written:

> Cardiff. 11th December 1868
> Presented to our Beloved Brother
> Henry Cook by Mr. & Mrs. Durkee
> as a token of their love & esteem.

His hand moved across the words as though to touch his sister and he felt chided for his hasty judgment of John. The second present brought delighted comments from Mary Julia. It was a true Welsh tea-set with pictures showing the national costume round the cups. The note inside was brief, written by his father, and brought a touch of sadness:

> "To Jeremiah, with love from Mother and Dad."

They remembered him just as he was all those years ago.

Unfortunately two of the cups were damaged a few months later, but not beyond repair. Mary Julia had become used to the small, fairly regular earth tremors, so common in Japan, and had learned to ignore the signs of a restless subterranean force. The one she experienced in May 1870 was far more severe and frightening. The servants grabbed Emily unceremoniously and rushed out of the house. The packs of uncontrolled dogs roaming the area howled in unison, adding to the sense of unreality. The rooms inside the house were covered with dust but there was very little structural damage. Some areas of plaster had fallen away from the timber framework leaving holes in the walls. Much of the crockery was broken, including the two Welsh cups. Torrential rain followed, adding to the confusion.

Japan was well supplied with water and, in all the towns and villages, large public wells were available from which anyone could draw water on payment of a very trifling sum. Yokohama had an ample supply of good, spring water found a few feet below the surface. Unfortunately the larger part of the Settlement, including Henry's house and works, was on ground reclaimed from a salt-water swamp, and nothing but salt water could be obtained by digging. Henry had organised a team from among his coolies to keep a reasonable supply for the house and works carted from the older part of the town. He was glad to be relieved of that responsibility when, in August, an enterprising Frenchman, M. Gérard, completed laying down pipes to supply excellent water from the gullies about a mile from the Settlement.

Another good sign of civilised progress came with the news, that as a result of protests about the lack of street lighting, the Japanese authorities had ordered lamp-posts from Shanghai. They had arrived and were being put into their places but, although intended for gas, they were to be illuminated by kerosene until gas became available.

Henry had spent so many hours at sea, reacting to every shift of wind, that even the comforts of home and a land-based business could not dull his sharp awareness of changes in the weather. Perhaps it was the deep grey in the sky overlaying an unnatural stillness that persuaded him to call his foremen together and instruct them to make fast any loose materials on unfinished structures. They looked at each other but made no comment; they were used to carrying out his orders with a fair degree of confidence. He was to become a legend to them later in the day, the 2nd October, when the sky blackened like night and Yokohama was hit by a typhoon of a ferocity rarely encountered there before. He had urged his men to seek the stoutest cover they could find, and crammed many of them into his own house where they helped to cover windows and bar doors.

The angry power of the wind and the wall of water it flung across the town dwarfed all human concepts and reduced man to insignificance. As the danger passed and men began to leave their shelter, Mary Julia was nonplussed by the apparent indifference displayed on the faces of the Japanese workmen as they set about restoring order. Henry told her how he had noticed that same look in response to the great fire which had destroyed most of the native quarter before she arrived. There was an acceptance that tragedies will occur.

Mary Julia had work to do. The boatyard had suffered some minor damage and several of the men had received small injuries from flying debris. She bound their wounds, continuing a responsibility she had accepted for this hundred-strong workforce. The premises on the next plot, No.114, were severely damaged. Messrs. Wilkie and Laufenburg lacked the benefit of intuition and their newly-erected sheds were flattened and some of the vessels and small boats under construction were smashed to pieces.

After any major storm at sea, ships put into port for emergency and sometimes extensive repairs. Henry's ingenuity and well-equipped yard had restored many a damaged vessel and he had the deserved reputation of being a specialist in the field. His stock of timber was low, just at a time when he could anticipate extra demand. He was expecting a consignment from Hakodate which might have been hit by the typhoon had it been arriving on schedule. He decided to make his way to the Custom House, by the English *hatoba*, to seek news. He was surprised that so many buildings had survived with only trivial damage considering the amount of rubble and debris lying in the streets. Many of the ornamental trees of which residents were so proud were lying at unnatural angles.

There was good news at the Custom House. The vessel carrying his timber had sheltered successfully at the French *hatoba* before the storm broke. Some of the smaller boats in and around the English *hatoba* had not been so fortunate. Broken masts, split timbers and tangled strips of canvas were being smashed by a still-restless sea against the foot of the Bund, which acted as the sea wall for Yokohama. A ship's dinghy had been thrown onto the Bund and one glance showed it to be beyond repair. The bleak, unfriendly-looking sea stirred painful memories before Henry turned for home.

The following afternoon the timber consignment was being unloaded at Creekside. Henry still found simple pleasure in wandering among a fresh batch of timber, approving its colour and quality, but this time his musings were interrupted. One of his coolies came rushing to him, wide-eyed, with a message that two officials wished to speak with him and were waiting in the office. They must have looked highly important to produce such an agitated response in one so humble and, indeed, they did. They were two Japanese government officials, one of whom spoke good English and requested to speak to Henry in private, looking pointedly at Mary Julia. She took the hint and Henry locked the door against further intrusion.

He was told that the pride and joy of the new young Emperor, the recently-commissioned steam-assisted yacht, fitted out for his personal use, had been blown ashore during the typhoon. It was already a highly sensitive issue that he intended to break with tradition and be the first emperor to use this mode of transport instead of being restricted to processing by road. An excess of publicity could bring popular protest, with fears for his safety used as an argument by those in government who disapproved. Henry had been recommended as the man most likely to be able to refloat the yacht without calling on outside help. He accepted the awesome task and, after much deep bowing and smiles of assent, he was given all the information to hand, which contained none of the essential technical details.

The officials left and Henry went across to the house to confer with his wife. They agreed on certain measures to avoid undue publicity although, of course, the incident would eventually become common knowledge. Perhaps the Emperor hoped to rely on a courtesy restraint by the Press. Henry left for the scene in his small launch which he used when visiting ships in need of repair at anchorages along the coast. It had a reliable turn of speed even without the use of its sails. He took his chief foreman and several trusted craftsmen to help him survey the situation. They would not be returning that night; the survey would need to be thorough and the beach was some twenty-five miles distant.

The captain of the stranded yacht was Dutch and part of his duties was to instruct Japanese crew members in the management of the new technology, a fact which may have brought the rather embarrassed expression into his eyes. Henry was fair in considering there was little else he could have done in the circumstances. Apparently the yacht had rounded Shimoda, on its way to Tokyo, when the captain became aware of the storm gathering to the east of them. He had calculated they would reach the comparative shelter of Tokyo Bay ahead of the storm and increased his engine speed to compensate for the precaution of lowering sails. Henry was surprised that the captain had failed to interpret the warnings that nature had given, but he was not there to investigate the captain's actions. As the power of the typhoon began to nullify the power at his command, the captain had seen his vessel relentlessly being pushed towards rocks at the southern point of the Yokosuka peninsula. He was familiar with a small stretch of sand east of the rocks and knew it to have a fair width before reaching high ground. What he did not know was the depth of sand - were more rocks concealed just below the surface? Henry had to admire the captain's decision to go for the sand. Using full power on one paddle to turn and direct the bow towards the beach, he had avoided the certain disaster of being driven broadside onto it. All power had been shut off as the gigantic sea lifted the vessel, almost on an even keel, and thrust it well up the beach.

Henry could see that the yacht had slewed slightly broadside which would add to his problems. Successive waves had pushed it more deeply into the sand as the ferocity of the storm increased, but had at the same time given it extra protection. The captain had saved his crew and probably his ship. Interior damage was considerable because of the refinement of furnishings, but that did not bear heavily on his shoulders.

The survey revealed no major damage to the upper hull which remained above the sand. The yacht must have had a surprisingly soft landing. Most of Henry's previous salvage operations had been for vessels aground on hard rock, but Henry remembered a cargo ship which had become fast in mud in the estuary at Newport. As a boy he had watched fascinated as a cradle was built round it and used to lift and drag the vessel from the suction of the mud. Inspired, he checked the depth of sand at intervals to the sea and, when satisfied, his mind was made up. A sceptical foreman was grudgingly convinced that a cradle could be built without experienced labour. Henry had learned to have confidence in the Japanese gift for absorbing new ideas and techniques.

It took two days to assemble all the ropes, timber and tackle he was likely to need on the beach. Half of his labour force was transported in junks, followed by three of his 'workhorse' launches. The captain and crew of the yacht stood back and watched as a co-ordinated pattern of work was started and continued at a speed only possible by a team used to working together. The main structure of the cradle was placed to support the hull as sand was rapidly excavated. Careful inspection of the emerging hull was reassuring and Henry called the captain over to confirm his opinion. As the captain viewed the minimal damage, which was undoubtedly the result of good luck, a revived confidence in his manner showed that in his own mind he had tipped the balance towards seamanship and skill. It was a pity that the paddle housings were so badly buckled!

Four Japanese officials had been despatched overland to monitor the operation. They had remained on the higher ground noting every move and probably making sketches, as was their practice. They approached Henry for the first time, as soon as the captain had finished his inspection, to inform him of the Emperor's wishes. Henry gained the impression that those wishes could be changed by his officials according to the condition of the yacht. However, Henry was not to be given the contract for repair as the Emperor was anxious to view progress at his personal anchorage near Tokyo. It was an obvious solution to a delicate problem. A steam-assisted vessel was on its way to give the yacht an unobtrusive tow direct to Tokyo. Henry was glad to be relieved of that final responsibility.

All preparations were completed ready for high water. The yacht was secure in a structure almost as complicated as its own and was poised as though for its first launching. Henry favoured a swift tow into deep water and had laid timber-ways to the sea, slightly angled to realign the yacht for an even-keeled stern entry. The sea was only twenty feet away and would just touch the stern at high water.

The scene was common in Japan where human power was more readily available than machines. Henry's men were divided equally on each side of the yacht grasping the cradle lashings. Out at sea the three 'workhorses' had lines secured to the cradle and the captain and crew were aboard once again. At a given signal, men and machines pulled together producing not an inch of movement. The men shouted encouragement to each other. Their energy was instant but the machines at sea had to build power slowly. It was all over so quickly once inertia lost its hold. The cradled yacht slid down the ramp and was dragged out into deep water with bows scraping the sand under water before reaching flotation depth. The cheers were of relief and approval. The Japanese had tumbled over each other at the water's edge as the speed of entry took them off balance and they were too slow in releasing their hold. As the yacht floated, its crew released the securing beams of the cradle which fell away into the sea, restoring some dignity to the ship which seemed so much smaller and far less daunting in her proper environment. The launches cast off their lines and one of them towed the cradle towards the shore for dismantling.

The yacht had an easy tow into Tokyo Bay, leaving Henry to salvage his equipment, clear the beach and ferry men and materials back to the shipyard.

23
Unexpected Rewards

Reunions after Henry's quite frequent absences were still something special for Mary Julia. She was to reflect, in a couple of months, that her new pregnancy had a great deal to do with his homecoming from salvaging the imperial yacht. Back in the office, Henry gave an account of events to her, as he would to any business partner, and she helped him to cost the whole operation. It had been an unusual commission and not clear to whom the account should be sent. There was no obvious name or department to contact, and so avoid any accidental breach of confidence. Henry had no intention of sending the bill to His Highness and was in favour of standing the cost himself as a goodwill gesture to the Sovereign ruler of a people that he was beginning to value very highly. He doubted whether a European workforce could have risen to the team work required on the beach at Yokosuka, in spite of superior experience; but he had to admit that his own European foremen were also essential. Mary Julia agreed the Books could stand the loss and entered the details to account for this amount.

The two Japanese government officials who had given Henry his first instructions returned a few days later again wishing to speak with him. On learning that they had come to settle the account, Henry explained that he had made no charge. His comment was ignored as though never spoken and a paper was handed to him for agreement. Together with his wife he scanned a costing of the salvage operation in disbelief. The observers on the beach had listed every item of timber, labour, etc. and had it valued. Even the wages he paid his workmen were there, with the omission of the extra earned by his foremen. It was an insight into Japanese efficiency never before experienced by Mary Julia, although Henry had come to respect it long ago. Henry signed for the cash, which was handed to him in a canvas bag, and after a few brief bows the officials left.

Henry and his wife had a meeting with all the shipyard foremen where it was decided that minimum jealousy and maximum goodwill would be fostered by calling the entire workforce together when work ceased at the end of the day to explain what had happened. Each man would receive an equal share of the money in addition to his normal wage, whether or not he had worked on the salvage. Judging by the wide smiles and back-slapping among the coolies and craftsmen, Henry felt he had made a wise investment.

It was almost noon the next day when Henry was called to the house by a message from his wife. At the entrance were two Japanese soldiers, armed with swords in the usual manner, who bowed to him as he went inside. Mary Julia greeted him with the news that two officials from the Court had come to see him on behalf of the Emperor. This also explained why the servants were so ill at ease, caught between the instinct to kneel in obeisance and continuing their duties for Mary Julia. They were told to leave.

The Court officials were richly dressed and the exchange of greetings with Henry was solemn, the bows lower than he would have expected. They bore personal gifts from the Emperor in recognition and gratitude for his expertise in salvaging the yacht. The Emperor had been given a detailed report of the whole operation. They placed in front of him a beautifully lacquered casket and a number of tapestries, secured in a roll by ribbons at each end. The officials stepped back to await his inspection of the gifts. Mary Julia came to Henry's rescue with her natural confident bearing and broke the tension with excited comments as she joined him. Both were awestruck when the opened casket revealed a considerable sum in gold coins. Together, they unrolled the tapestries which were of traditional Japanese design, some bordered with gold thread. Their very obvious pleasure and amazement pleased the officials who, in turn, relaxed and smiled relief to each other. No wonder they had arrived with an armed escort!

Henry and his wife expressed their appreciation with the inadequacy imposed by mere words. Suddenly, remembering the youth responsible for such lavish gifts, Henry strode across the room and took from the shelf a small model schooner he had carved whilst serving on the *Henry Ellis*, and asked the officials to present it to the Emperor as a modest token of his thanks. They were delighted with the gesture, realising it would add prestige to themselves when reporting back to the Emperor.

The servants were called in to show their respect during the formal farewell and remained with heads bowed as the Emperor's envoys left the house to be escorted back to Tokyo. Before leaving the room the servants were allowed to see the gifts, although the casket was not opened for them.

Alone at last, Henry and his wife could savour the honour and inspect the presents more closely. Henry removed the gold and placed it in the heavy safe kept in one corner of the room. Banks were beginning to establish themselves in Yokohama but habits die slowly and Henry rarely used them. The casket was put on display in the centre of the table. Mary Julia saw the tapestries as ideal wall coverings to give the main room a richly furnished appearance. Strangely, these first spontaneous decisions introduced a practical utility which slowly replaced the historic honour they at first represented.

Only special things were kept in the casket at first. Years later it housed the sewing and mending requirements for the family and found its way into the workroom. By the 1920's it was used as a door-stop by Henry's younger daughter, Beatrice, who came to Britain in 1900 and eventually settled for many years at Ilford in Essex. The tapestries continued as wall hangings and, in England, as door coverings to exclude the draught. Their final indignity came several years later; hearing that the drama group, attached to the Catholic Church of SS. Peter & Paul, were rehearsing Gilbert and Sullivan's "Mikado", she donated the tapestries for authentic stage furnishings. The drama group never knew how truly authentic they were!

Familiarity and time can dull the magic of first acquaintance but not of the Emperor's message symbolised by those gifts. It was a very worthy trait in Japanese families, whether noble or peasant, that a truly-felt obligation was not finally repaid by presenting a gift. The honour of obligation continued, sometimes with succeeding generations, as Henry's family were to experience. The Emperor, too, was not found wanting some fifteen years later when Henry's family were in great trouble.

24
Creekside Health Fears

By January 1871 Emily was six months old, healthy, and to Henry, even more beautiful than her mother. The health of his family was to be of great concern for the next two years. A violent epidemic of small-pox had been raging through Yokohama throughout the winter. The residents were alarmed at the apathy shown by the local government which had failed to take any steps to define or limit the disease with vaccination or improved sanitation. Parts of the swamp area were still being filled from excavations on the far side of the Creek, but it was the condition of the Creek itself that alarmed Henry and his neighbours. They were convinced it was becoming a source of disease and were dreading the onset of a hot summer.

The Creek was in the process of being cleaned. It was to be dredged for a greater depth of water and confined by a sea wall on each side. Instead of hiring a mechanical dredger, the work was being done by manpower only. This involved draining the Creek for long periods and interrupting all normal trade. Not only was the foul condition of the bottom of the Creek laid bare but heaps of black ooze were piled up on the banks just a few feet from the houses. The smell was atrocious and a cause of discontent among Henry's workers. Lack of access meant that more work was carried out in the harbour and kept Henry away from home for longer periods. He was desperately concerned for Mary Julia, who was carrying their third child, especially during the months of hot weather, noted for an increase in epidemics of dysentery and cholera. He began to use one of his larger vessels when working in the harbour or at sea so that she could be with him and away from Creekside as often as possible. Emily and her Japanese nurse always accompanied then. These short trips became quite frequent as he even encouraged them to go without him, in the charge of a trusted foreman.

Life expectancy in Yokohama was not very high, particularly among European women. A list of 114 persons buried in the General Cemetery between 11th July 1870 and 25th February 1871 showed an average age of only twenty-eight and half years. Increased public fear of catastrophe had been given ample justification where fire, shipwreck, water damage and theft were concerned. This had led to a proliferation of insurance company advertising in the press. In just one edition of "The Japan Weekly Mail", twenty large advertisements were inserted by such companies, all offering the solace of reparation.

Mary Julia's peace of mind was not improved by two further earthquake shocks of major severity during the month of June, which caused some damage in the town. Habitually now she measured each shock against that first bad experience and guessed they were less severe. These occurred while Henry was away at sea once again. His reputation, as an expert in the salvaging and refloating of vessels which had grounded on rocks or shore, had increased still further as news of his success on Yokosuka beach had filtered through. Insurance companies were seeking his advice and sometimes requested his personal supervision. He tried to satisfy these fresh demands but regretted the time spent away from building ships.

It was to fulfil one of these contracts that Henry had to leave his wife barely six weeks before the baby was due. A large steamer, *Ocean Queen*, had been driven hard on shore and required specialist assistance. He tried to get messages back to Mary Julia as often as possible via passing vessels. Confirmation of his homecoming seemed more certain when she read an official report of his progress in a June copy of "The Far East":

> We hear that the party who left with Mr. Cook for the West Coast, to get off the stranded steamer "Ocean Queen", have been very successful. On the 9th instant she was within four times her length from the shore so, if all goes well, her arrival here in about a fortnight may be looked for."

In order to help reduce such accidents among the numerous rocks and islands round the Japan coast, the government issued notification that lighthouses were to be fitted with permanent lighting systems. The superseding of wood fires was of the highest importance in pursuance of the axiom of lighthouse legislation that it was better to have no light than one liable to be extinguished. Wood fires were liable to extinction by violent storms of rain or wind and, too often, were but treacherous guides for coasting vessels.

Henry returned in good time, relieved to see that Mary Julia looked fit and happy, but he had resolved to leave nothing to chance. He arranged for a doctor to be on call and for a trained nurse to live in for the first post-natal week. Thus wrapped in personal affairs, he allowed himself yet further indulgence in a private corner of the shipyard. Here, nearing completion, was the racing yacht he had designed to commemorate Emily's birth. Most of the construction had been carried out by a few trusted craftsmen who had become used to their employer's arrival at unexpected times to match their skills.

It was still impossible to launch completed vessels into the Creek, a situation causing financial embarrassment to several neighbouring builders. Salvage and extensive repair commissions had provided a continuing source of income for Henry's own yard. For her launching, the *Emily* had to be manhandled to the western quay of the French *hatoba*, at the mouth of the Creek, where several enthusiasts kept their racing craft. Henry resisted the temptation to have baby Emily there as she was far too young to understand the honour he intended. On the following day, 6th July 1871, William Henry Cook was born and Henry prayed that no epidemic would be spawned in the Creek's black ooze to destroy their happiness during the remaining hot months of summer.

It had been an aesthetic whim to build a yacht to celebrate Emily's birth, but no such thought occurred relating to William, perhaps because sailors refer to ships as 'she'. After putting the *Emily* through a rigorous trial he had an urge to test her in racing conditions. A friend, Mr.Carst, owned a yacht of similar potential called the *Mermaid* and he willingly accepted a challenge arranged for the 12th July. Henry's varying activities had become newsworthy and the press and interested residents gathered to follow the dual between well-matched experts. The result was reported in the Yokohama papers, typically in "The Far East":

"On Saturday afternoon, the 12th instant, a race came off between Mr. Cook's yacht "Emily" and Mr. Carst's "Mermaid". The course was from the French hatoba, round the Lightship and the ships in the harbour. After a good race the "Emily", although having lost her gaff-topsail, came in the winner."

Was the masculine act of racing perhaps, in its turn, a subconscious celebration of William's birth? Such an idea would have been too subtle for Henry, but his wife accepted the triumph as a good omen for William. She had hoped that her son's name would not be shortened but all her friends, and workmen in the yard, affectionately called him "Willie". She had to agree that "Willie" did seem to suit the little chap.

The family survived the summer heat without illness, but not without damage to the house and works. In August, a second typhoon swept across the area. Its power was sustained for much longer than before and raindrops the size of hailstones pounded every resisting surface. It seemed that everyone suffered damage. A new hotel nearing completion had its whole facade swept away. Surely Nature had but few surprises left?

In December, just before Christmas, Henry's brother, John, arrived again without prior warning. Two years had passed since he began to work for the Pacific Mail steamers and he had made no attempt to contact Henry during that time, not even by letter. They talked about the family and life in Newport in a formal manner normally reserved for casual acquaintances. John displayed no sign of emotion until Henry showed him a recent letter from Bridget containing the sad news that their elder sister, Anne, had died in Cardiff on 11th June. The moment soon passed as he tried to impress Henry with his success in a business sideline much frowned upon by the steamship company. He was buying curios and souvenirs at various ports of call and selling them privately to any interested trader. Henry's suggestion, that he could complete his blacksmith apprenticeship by joining his brother Anthony on railway construction, was met with silence. John left to find a room for the night when he learned that Henry could offer nothing in the house.

When discussing the brief visit later that night, Mary Julia confessed she had heard nothing to change her first impressions of John. Henry confided his own doubts to her. He distrusted what might lie behind the hard veneer he had failed to penetrate except for the one fleeting moment. He felt obliged to offer help as an elder brother, but could only see a stranger with an alien temperament. John did not call again and loyalties were not to be tested in the near future.

Henry began to understand and feel a genuine concern for Anthony after visiting him at Shimbashi when on a business trip to Tokyo. Although earning good wages on the railway, he had failed to improve his social life and most of his free time was spent alone. Henry detected the weary look of a solitary drinker and had been moved to offer work and a place to live back at the shipyard. Anthony had declined the offer. After breaking the sad news about the death of their sister Anne, Henry told him about John's visits and the circumstances leading to his premature arrival in Japan. Anthony remembered John being spoilt at home; he was the baby of the family and had become rather headstrong and obstinate as a schoolboy. He guessed that John was an intelligent lad and assured Henry that he would be very happy to support any move to steer him back into gaining experience as a smithy. Henry was grateful for Anthony's promise and as they shook hands each looked honestly at the other and recognised a brotherly reconciliation to be relied upon for the future.

Unlike both his brothers, Henry was good company and a popular guest. He was the product of a receptive nature exposed to countless experiences. Consequently he had a fund of stories and reminiscences with an Irishman's gift for delivery. Mary Julia could always rely on him to cheer her up with some amusing anecdote whenever she was feeling low. The more recent demands for his services aboard Japanese naval and merchant vessels had increased his repertoire considerably. One of these was overheard by a journalist who persuaded Henry to let him use it in an October issue of "The Far East":

"Mr. COOK, the shipwright, tells a good story of his reception on board one of the Japanese Men-of-war, a few days ago. He had occasion to go on board, about some repairs, and asked to see the Captain. He being in his cabin dressing, asked Mr. Cook to wait a little, and chat with the officers until he was ready. Turning to them, after a few minutes, one of them asked him his name. He told them; and then observed that they turned and spoke among themselves, and the result of the "aside" was, that one of them who spoke English, putting on "an air", said to him:-
"We do not wish to speak with the cook. On our ships the cook is a very small man."

Sometimes in Yokohama a sense of humour was of greater value than a sense of history!

25
Sea Voyage And Rescue

The year 1872 crept in ominously quiet and peaceful. Henry and his wife had enjoyed several happy evenings with friends during Christmas and New Year. To round off the celebrations, they spent a long-promised evening at the Gaiety Theatre on Main Street. Although the theatre had been opened just over a year previously, they had never before spared the time to attend. It was an imposing building with good acoustics and a large stage. Most productions were put on by the Amateur Dramatic Corps, who had built up a first class reputation with excellent scenery and props. Professional groups and individuals occasionally called into Yokohama when on tours of the Far East, but seeing their friends perform was always more popular with the residents.

As winter gave way to the early warmth of March, Mary Julia had to confide to Henry the news, recurring with never-decreasing regularity, that once again she was pregnant. Henry rarely turned down an opportunity for a celebration tipple but, on reaching for a new bottle of his favourite Hennessey, he paused and glared at the label. He had only that morning read a warning in "The Japan Weekly Mail" to: ..."beware of horrible abominations which were often sold under the brand of Hennessey & Martell and could kill those rash enough to taste them". The analysis of a typical bottle showed it was composed of alum, iron, sulphuric acid, essential oil of some kind, tannic acid, Guinea pepper, burnt sugar, lead and copper, with a basis of whisky.

Commodity frauds were continually being foisted on the evergrowing number of settlers. An apparently 'bona fide' brand of matches was in circulation giving half the expected quantity of matches per box. Two matches cunningly placed diagonally supported a perfectly even top layer. The custom of wiring stacked coins together into even amounts led to a solid rod of metal being tooled and wired in perfect simulation.

However, the need to celebrate overcame Henry's hesitation. As he sipped, his mind drifted back to Newport. He remembered how the house was never large enough to accommodate new babies and maturing brothers and sisters. The same situation was happening to him in Yokohama, but this time he was sufficiently wealthy to do something about it. He would redesign the site to give room for a larger house. This could be done by concentrating the storage of materials under one roof with the forge and casting-workshops and by making greater use of the coastal site at No. 187 which he had still continued to use after splitting with Cameron. That site had been reserved for work required on ships too large to enter the Creek.

As plans were rationalised on paper, Mary Julia gave excited approval. She had longed for rooms which would give more space and air during the heat of summer and an office where a state of order could be fact and not solely in the mind. Her pleasure in anticipation of watching the transformation was to be shattered.

The promised opening of the Creek had been constantly delayed, partly because of the unsatisfactory manner in which the walls had been built. The outlook was much the same as the year before with mud and black ooze heaped everywhere. Public consternation over the delay, coupled with fears of summer epidemics of typhoid and cholera, was given front page editorial comment. Henry was facing a repeat dilemma. Mary Julia was pregnant and young Willie had not been well - nothing specific, but he seemed to lack the boisterous health of his sister Emily. A natural sailor, Henry had salt-water in his veins and when in trouble he instinctively turned to the sea for an answer. Last time, he had taken the family with him when working in the Bay, but this summer he must try to remain ashore more often to supervise the changes at 115. However, once again the sea did provide an answer, though a drastic one.

Damage to ships was often extensive and repairs could cost an amount far in excess of the owner's capacity to pay. Occasionally, in order to offset some of the debt, Henry was in a position to accept part-ownership of a vessel. This enabled him to share in the trading profits earned by the ship. One such sailing vessel, in which Henry had decided it safe to accept a majority share, was in harbour waiting for a cargo of engineered parts destined for Kobe, a developing port south of Yokohama. After Kobe, the captain was to seek trade freely for a period of three to four months, reporting back to Yokohama towards the end of August. The ship had passenger cabin space and Henry used his majority position to insist that his family be allowed to use it for the duration of the voyage. The captain was not pleased to be burdened with the extra responsibility but had to agree that it was an inspired solution to a worrying problem.

Mary Julia was horrified at the idea; not the least of her objections was to be at sea during the middle months of her pregnancy. Henry would not be convinced by any alternative. Arrangements were completed and Henry saw his family comfortably installed in their cabins by the first week in May. Mary Julia felt less apprehensive when she knew that the children's Japanese nurse and a trusted servant would be with them for the whole voyage. Henry smiled to himself when later he learned from the captain that Mary Julia soon recovered her assertive nature and reorganised parts of his ship as though she owned it, which in part, of course, through Henry she did!

New building and reconstruction at 115 began immediately and at a pace to be expected where Japanese craftsmen were employed. Henry was very conscious of the need to design the buildings to minimise the ever-present risk of fire. Just before his wife and family left, there had been a terrible fire in Tokyo where two square miles were laid waste. Ten thousand houses were burned down, over three hundred people were killed and thirty thousand were rendered homeless.

Mary Julia had been very distressed when she saw hundreds of *jinrikishas* coming into Yokohama bringing the suffering refugees, each of whom was clutching some small valued household article. The government had stepped in to prevent the instinctive urge to rebuild, sometimes even before the ashes were completely cold, causing new fires to break out. Such devastation would give an opportunity to plan for greater safety in the area, as in Yokohama.

The house at 115 Creekside

Henry's new home was built in Japanese style but with European solid interior walls and stone fireplace and chimney construction. The tiled roof had a deep overhang extending beyond the first-floor wooden balcony which surrounded the house on three sides. This balcony was supported from roof to ground by stout wooden columns and its floor gave external shelter for the kitchen and servants' quarters on the lower floor. It was planned to use the first floor for the family with a children's nursery and playroom and a communicating room for their Japanese nurse. A diamond lattice of natural pine decorated the external walls of the first storey relieving the severity of simple design.

By a stroke of good fortune, plot No. 120, which adjoined the rear of 115, became vacant and Henry was able to purchase it. It gave him the space to build a superb machine workshop equipped for every type of work in metal. He was looking ahead to the increasing demand for steamship construction and repair. To one side of these new premises he built a second house, smaller than his own, in the hope that Anthony would eventually be tempted by the new facilities and perhaps agree to manage that side of the business.

With the exception of the nurse, the family had found their sea-legs fairly quickly. Young Willie had a good colour and seemed to have overcome his winter sickness. The crew enjoyed making a fuss of the children and insisted on being called 'uncles'. The captain declared his ship had become a floating nursery, but found he could relax his formal discipline without losing the alertness of his crew. Mary Julia was as well as could be expected although she had suffered some distressing nausea during periods of moderately rough weather. She felt at ease with the captain once he had overcome a wary resistance to her forthright manner. It took him almost two weeks to realise that the positive nature of her suggestions and instructions was not a quest for power. She came to decisions quite naturally through her clarity of intellectual reasoning, which perfectly complemented Henry's instinctive gut reactions. That she was often correct gave her no feeling of superiority but could antagonise strangers until they understood her true value.

The trading voyage had been successful and the captain was anxious to convert his satisfaction into wages for himself and his crew. He set course for Yokohama, feeling very pleased to have avoided ballast by securing a compact cargo of building timber. The ship was heading into the Pacific Ocean from Hakodate where the captain hoped to pick up a favourable wind to sweep him back towards the east coast of Japan.

The house and works at 115 Creekside

While still sailing into the Pacific, the man on watch called the captain's attention to smoke on the horizon. It was dismissed fairly casually as steam-assisted ships were now common in the area and betrayed their presence by belching black smoke. A while later the smoke was still on the port side, to north of them, but as the first officer was observing it through the glass he noticed that the smoke was not coming from the narrow neck of a stack but was broadly-based and now very low to the water. He took his observation to the captain for confirmation. The captain had little doubt that it was the last stage of a ship which had been burning for many hours. They discussed the possibility of reaching it to give assistance, but its position was against their arriving in time. They would have to make way against the wind to satisfy a somewhat forlorn hope.

Mary Julia overheard their discussion and was furious at such negative thinking. Her own experience of shipwreck was still vivid in her memory but could never compare with the horror of a fire at sea. She was aware that a sailing ship could gradually make way upwind by tacking on a reach. It would take time, but what did time matter when concerned with saving life? She confronted the captain with the possible consequences of his attitude and insisted that it was his duty to search the area however remote he considered the chances of success. The captain was shamed by the moral logic of her anger and knew she would pursue it further if he failed to take action.

After manoeuvring for several hours, they approached the location of the wreck from a downwind direction but there was little to see. The ship had burned and sunk. A few blackened timbers wallowed heavily in the sea, some still steaming as they cooled. Small pieces of wreckage had drifted over a wide area and every eye on board was alert for survivors. Sails were lowered and some of the crew began a systematic search using the ship's dinghy. They failed even to establish the name of the stricken vessel.

It was while returning to their ship from the final extremity of their search that they found her, a young girl, almost certainly dead. She had been tied to some timber, obviously in a great hurry, with a rope hawser far too massive for her tiny body. The timber and heavy rope were sodden with water and had lost their buoyancy allowing the sea to wash over the captive child. One of the crew had to jump into the sea to help release the tension of the swollen rope and direct the rigid little corpse to the eager hands reaching down from the dinghy. As they rowed back to the ship, one of the men wept without shame and hugged the child close as though she were his own. They were within hailing distance when he realised that she had lost that unnatural stiffness and responded to his cradling warmth. She was still alive! A hint of miracle silenced their excitement but oars were never pulled more strongly.

The little girl was rushed to Mary Julia's cabin and wrapped in a warm blanket as soon as her wet clothes had been removed. Her breathing was shallow and sometimes hesitant but that was the only sign of life. The nurse massaged her through the blanket, willing the child to acknowledge the life still there. As the limbs began to move and eyes struggled with the light, Mary Julia watched life evolve from death and prayed her thanks.

The girl was about eight or nine years of age with black hair, dark eyes and a slightly sallow complexion. Her eyes asked no questions prompted by memory or concern. She offered no recognition when Mary Julia spoke to her in English or French. A plea for linguists among the crew produced a smattering of Spanish, Italian and German. The one who could recall something akin to Spanish was justifiably proud when he elicited her name, Rosa. He was unable to establish anything else; whether she was from Spain or South America, the name of the ship, not even her family name. She seemed to be in some sort of shock that eliminated fear, distress or puzzlement.

After a day or two, Rosa's strength returned and she could enjoy playing with Emily and Willie. Emily was a three-year-old chatterbox seemingly unconcerned at the lack of verbal response where instinct and gesture sufficed. Sometimes Rosa chatted at length but whether to herself or to them Mary Julia could never be sure. A few simple words and phrases were deduced from situations and could be shared, but the information they needed to know remained locked in a secret corner of her mind. They cared for her as one of the family and she became 'Rosie' to everyone on board.

The captain was ill at ease with his conscience and waited patiently for Mary Julia to confront him with the success of her interference but that was not her nature. The correct action had been taken and that was all that mattered.

26
New Home - New Enterprise

As soon as Henry received news of the ship's return, he hurried down to the harbour to be reunited with his family. He was greeted with exuberant hugs, and Rosie. Old habits die hard and, after hearing the story from his wife, he asked to see the captain's log and questioned the crew who had found her. He was impressed by their skill and with the decision to search. When later the Japanese servant confided what he knew of the story, Henry kept the knowledge to himself, respecting his wife's attitude. The captain agreed that Mary Julia should continue to care for Rosie until some official arrangement could be made.

The new house met with general approval although the interior was incomplete and clearly in need of a woman's touch. Henry notified the British Legation of the circumstances of Rosie's rescue and enlisted their help in tracing the missing ship. He also contacted a doctor who promised to come to the house, together with someone who could speak Spanish fluently, and give Rosie a careful examination. The result brought a mixture of thankfulness and disappointment. Rosie had recovered from her ordeal with all the resilience of youth and with careful nursing. She was physically fit and the traces of deep bruising left by the swollen ropes would soon disappear without leaving any scars, but her memory would reveal nothing. Yes, her name was Rosa and her language indicated an origin in southern Spain. For any other information perhaps nature had the kindest remedy. Her mind had built an impenetrable barrier against her memory. The doctor was certain that her almost casual disclaimer of all that had happened could not be the subterfuge of a child. She could recall nothing previous to waking in Mary Julia's cabin, not even her parents or her home.

The doctor feared for the child's sanity if she were pressed too hard to break through the barrier separating her from terror and pain. He left strict instructions that all such attempts must be avoided, but any little subconscious revelations should be noted in writing. It seemed reasonable to assume that

Rosie had had a Catholic upbringing and it was hoped that taking her to Mass might coax a distant memory. The Abbé had already heard about the addition to Henry's family and expressed his concern that Rosie had no regular use of her own language at a time when she should be at school. He invited Mary Julia into the sacristy where he offered a sensible solution to the whole problem.

For several years the Abbé had recognised the need for a good Catholic convent school capable of providing education for the multi-national residents of Yokohama. Perhaps the most experienced in that field were the 'Dames de St. Maur' whose mother house in Paris he knew well. The official name of the Order was the Congregation of the Holy Child Jesus. In answer to his plea, a small group of nuns had been sent to Yokohama and were beginning to establish a centre for girls and young boys. Plans were in hand for a purpose-built convent and boarding school on a site in the residential part of the Bluff. Their ability to teach in most of the major national languages made them the obvious choice to care for Rosie and to pursue the search for her origin.

Back at the house Mary Julia put the idea to Henry. Apart from the common sense of the proposal, he recognised the relief it would bring to his wife who would soon be nursing a young baby. They both agreed that Rosie should still be treated as one of the family and Henry would pay the nuns for her keep and education until she could be suitably employed or, better still, returned to her own family. Fortunately Henry could not know that his generosity to Rosie would be repaid with avaricious spite at a time when he was in deep trouble of his own making.

Conditions along Creekside were improving all the time and Mary Julia was particularly pleased that the unhealthy stench had disappeared. On 11th October 1872 she gave birth to her second daughter, Beatrice Marion. Emily was delighted with her new living doll and spent many extra hours in the nursery where her bilingual chatter greatly amused the nurse. Mary Julia teased her husband that he had no immediate plans to 'give birth' to a new vessel in honour of his second daughter. Henry countered by revealing that plans were well ahead for a hunting vessel of special design that he intended to name the "Beatrice", but outside contracts were too numerous to contemplate such private work for many months.

Just three days after Beatrice was born, the State opening took place of the completed railway from Yokohama to the Tokyo terminus. The total length of the line was eighteen miles. Henry failed to persuade Anthony to quit the railway after its completion as there was still plenty of maintenance work available and new lines to be constructed. The new railway was certain to be a huge success with the travelling public who had to use the road or coastal ferry. The *jinrikisha* men were not so happy. They could expect a loss of very lucrative business and announced their intention to compete against the railway by covering the nineteen mile road distance in 1 hr. 40 min. for a fare of 12½ *sen*. But what a rough journey compared with the train which covered its eighteen mile journey in 55 min. for 18½ *sen*!

Western manners and customs were slowly being introduced to the Japanese, some enforced by their own government. The *jinrikisha* men were no longer allowed to run naked except for a brief loincloth, but must be properly clothed to avoid offence to European women. One particularly strange order by the government concerned Henry as he employed over a hundred Japanese workmen. Official notices were posted on all municipal notice boards to decree, in Japanese, that:

> "The 'Mage' of every male who has not, on or before the 25th January 1873, adopted the European manner of wearing the hair, will be cut off by the policeman at the time and place of apprehending such offenders, for which purpose said policemen will be provided with scissors."

Some of his men had already changed to western style, some others had their heads totally shaved. A few still retained the traditional *mage* which was a hairstyle imposed at a coming-of-age ceremony when the hair was gathered up at the back, well oiled and waxed and then tied up into a queue. The queue was further oiled and waxed before being bent forward over the shaven crown. This strange custom led to the use of the wooden neck pillow to avoid daily renewal of the elaborate and lengthy routine. Henry had a couple of ex-sailors in his employ who were used to giving haircuts to fellow crew members. He let it be known that a corner of the new workshop would be set aside temporarily as a barber's shop for any Japanese needing to be westernised.

To celebrate the first Christmas in their new home, Henry and his wife organised several parties to renew friendships disrupted by all the alterations and Mary Julia's sea voyage. Taking advantage of the extra space, they arranged for Rosie to stay for the holiday and share the nursery accommodation. Much to Henry's surprise, Anthony allowed himself to be persuaded to leave his bachelor habits and join them. As the house was full with extra visitors

JAPANESE CARPENTERS, typical of the hundred
employed by Henry Cook, showing typical hairstyle.

he was pleased to accept Henry's suggestion that he could use the new house,
just completed at 120, and have the assistance of one of the servants. Was it
Henry's experience of human nature that prompted the suggestion or just a
lucky coincidence? Anthony was so taken with the house and with the scale
of the workshop equipment, now that he had seen it for himself, that he
changed his mind and agreed to leave the railway after finishing his contract
in November 1873.

Plans were made to register the workshops as a subsidiary company using Anthony's name and anglicized spelling, "Carroll & Company". Although Anthony would have a degree of autonomy to trade freely, it was understood that priority must be given to Henry's shipyard requirements. Anthony would be responsible for the high quality of workmanship on which Henry had built his reputation.

Henry wished he had been able to secure Anthony's help much earlier when, on the afternoon of 8th February 1873, the British barque *Parmenio* was towed into Yokohama harbour. It had left Marseilles the previous August with a full cargo. Nearing the end of its voyage it had suffered terrible damage when hit by a storm as it passed the point where the Emperor's yacht had been stranded. The main mast and rigging were lost, the head of the mizzen mast had broken at the cross-trees losing the top mast and all the gear. The rails and bulwarks were washed away and all the boats were smashed. Many of the timbers had sprung.

Henry was called in to survey the damage and give a preliminary estimation of repair costs. After a long conference with Captain Cochrane, master of the vessel, it became clear that the sale of cargo would not cover the cost of repairs and Henry could see that once again he might have to consider taking on a part-ownership. Following a common practice in those days of regular disasters at sea, Captain Cochrane was requested by his fellow shareholders to sell both the cargo and the vessel and not to enter any negotiations for repairs.

The *Parmenio* was a ship of 369 tons and could open up the possibility of worldwide trade, so Henry considered making an offer though unwilling to shoulder the entire burden of purchase. The decision was taken out of his hands when Captain R.H. Abbott of No. 217 The Bluff, a man Henry had known for many years, bought the vessel valued at $16,000. He commissioned Henry to proceed with repairs and made the almost inevitable suggestion that he might like to become joint shareholder. Henry was tempted. Had he been gifted with foresight it might have been the one transaction in his life that he would have resisted, but he was never one to refuse a challenge.

Just at this time, when Henry was ready to employ more Japanese labour, the native quarter in Yokohama was ravaged by the worst fire since that of 1866. No less than 1,509 houses were burned, covering nearly 44 acres, and more than five and half thousand Japanese were rendered homeless, including many of Henry's workmen. Native labour was preoccupied with salvaging and rebuilding their houses, which put an extra strain on his security arrangements. His ample stocks of timber were at risk, especially at night, from enterprising employees anxious to help themselves and their friends.

Work on the *Parmenio* was obviously going to continue well into the autumn and would use up a considerable amount of Henry's working capital. Since Beatrice was born he had insisted that Mary Julia should spend much less time looking after the finances of his business so that the children could benefit from her care and training. He was far less punctilious over detail; accounts were not always kept by office staff and there was no regular supervision. Bearing in mind his intention to buy shares in the *Parmenio* and to offset the drain on capital, Henry began to call in a few outstanding debts. One American partnership, T.S. Stevens & C. Nye, were particularly resistant to his requests for the final payment due on a vessel built for them many months earlier. His claim against them for the sum of $1,354 principal and interest was heard in the U.S. Consular Court on 11th December 1873. The amount was hurriedly paid into the Court by the defendants before the Court sat; this satisfied Henry sufficiently to agree with the Consul's decision that costs incurred should be shared equally. Diplomatic circles later commented on the frequency that Yokohama merchants resorted to the law for the settlement of their differences, and Henry was certainly no exception!

Henry's secret ambition to enter the fur-hunting trade with his own vessel never wavered and the intention was always renewed when repairing such ships or hearing news of their activities. In August, four sailors on the American hunting schooner *Otsego* had some disagreement with the captain, who put them ashore on the island of Itoropu. They returned to Yokohama in a junk; Henry learned with some envy that the *Otsego* had on board a cargo of three hundred otter skins, worth some $45,000 in the London market. It was enough to keep the ambition alive.

In spite of some labour difficulties, repairs to the *Parmenio* were completed by the middle of September. Henry agreed to buy in shares to cover the cost of his work and also managed to persuade a Mr. F.E. White to become a small investor. Mr. White was a merchant of varied experience with a useful knowledge of business practice and the law. Henry had been grateful for his advice on more than one occasion during their friendship. It was agreed that the three joint owners would share an open account between them, with Captain Abbott holding 36/64 shares, Henry 20/64, and Mr. White 8/64. They also agreed that Captain Abbott should be registered as the *Parmenio's* new master.

It was with cheers from the men who had been working on her that the *Parmenio* left Yokohama in ballast on 29th September, bound for Hakodate. Captain Abbott returned with his first successful cargo on 28th October and the ship looked all set to reap substantial profits for its new owners.

27
Rabbits Don't Commit Suicide

Anthony kept his promise. In early December he left the railway and moved into the new house at 120 ready to become manager of Carroll & Co. Henry's servants were kept busy during the Christmas period of 1873 right into the New Year with a constant flurry of visitors. Their reassuring smiles never wavered, concealing private resentments if any existed.

It was decided that Emily and William were old enough to maintain the motionless posture required for having a photograph taken. Mary Julia rehearsed them until they were almost perfect. For a special Christmas treat they were dressed in their best clothes and Henry took them to S. Suzuki, a popular Japanese photographer in Honchodori. It was an afternoon of magic, sitting in front of a huge

Henry Cook with Emily and William
Photograph by Suzuki
169

backcloth depicting Mount Fuji, but their excitement was dutifully suppressed when instructed by the photographer. The photographs, showing Emily standing and Father seated next to her with Willie on his knee, were given a place of honour when they were delivered two days later.

Henry's brother John also came for the festivities and this time he had the courtesy to give fair warning. He stayed with Anthony at 120 which gave them ample opportunity to reminisce about the family and Newport. John was nearly twenty-two and had matured sufficiently to admit that he should have completed his blacksmith's apprenticeship. He even accepted Anthony's offer to intercede on his behalf with Mr. Holtham, who was principal engineer on the railway, with the aim of starting employment early in the new year. Rosie, who was home from the Convent for Christmas, seemed to enjoy John's less serious, casual manner. Perhaps flattered by her attention he played up to her stumbling attempts to speak English and marvelled when he heard about the rescue of this precocious eleven-year-old.

The house was crowded but, as past differences with Henry's brothers resolved themselves, Mary Julia felt relaxed and enjoyed reading an accumulation of local newspapers. While scanning a copy of the "Japan Gazette" of the previous Wednesday evening, she was intrigued by a comment:

"We hear that two Court Milliners from Swan and Edgar's, London, are coming out to Japan to make European millinery, dresses, etc. for the Empress and the Princesses."

Her first reaction, as a very fashion conscious European, was of excited approval but after discussing it with Henry later that evening she was not so sure. He had noticed that Japanese men appeared at a disadvantage in western dress even though it was more conveniently suited to an active life. A Japanese gentleman could move with grace and dignity in his own national dress and derive from it an air of self-respect. It also covered defects often seen in the limbs of adults which probably arose from the restricted diet and possibly from the habit of sitting cross-legged from childhood. Mary Julia agreed that, as well as being very picturesque, the clothes worn by Japanese women suited their stature and carriage admirably. There were many stories in current gossip about those who had ventured into European fashion wearing corsets back-to-front, waistlines in strange places and ungainly attempts to walk in western shoes. She deplored that any woman should suffer such indignity in public in the name of fashion. Perhaps professional advice would save the Imperial Household from such mistakes but very few Japanese women would be able to afford to follow their example.

Their discussion finished on a lighter note when Henry mused over a reverse trend. The Police of many districts who had for some time been clothed in uniform of European style were returning to the use of the ordinary native costume!

To the relief of Henry and Anthony, John began his employment on the railway on 23rd February 1874 and appeared keen to complete his training and gain experience as a blacksmith. The workshop at 120 had no doubt inspired him and perhaps he visualised opportunities there for the future.

Emily started school in the September. She joined Rosie at the Convent but it was arranged that she would spend every weekend at home. Just after her first week at school she was allowed home for a special occasion. Henry had been building a new steam launch for the Yokohama Custom House and it was to be delivered and go on public display with demonstration trips round the harbour. The engine and boiler had been fitted by Messrs. Whitfield and Dowson, a most reliable firm that Henry had come to rely on for that type of installation. Emily and young Willie felt most important when ushered on board for their trip.

Although when Henry had agreed to be one of the founders of the O'Tentosama Lodge he was not interested in seeking high office or playing any great part in Masonic affairs, he had nevertheless become very concerned when membership and regular attendance started to fall off. After careful and detailed investigation it became fairly clear that the problem lay in the constant movement of members in a busy port area. Businesses were kept viable only through a constant search for new avenues of trade. At last a steady increase in membership was leading to the expected degree of success. He was pleased to see the double-column report of this healthy change in the "Japan Herald Mail Summary" of 3rd August. Mary Julia had attended the traditional annual 'Ladies Nights' with her husband and never failed to tease him, scarcely veiling a sting of truth, that the reply to the toast to the ladies was always made by a man, on their behalf! She was sure she could perform the function equally well although, as she agreed, the man usually made all the correct responses. These evenings were very happy social occasions for the community.

The *Parmenio* was beginning to show some profit but maintenance on the vessel was expensive. Before leaving for Takao, Melbourne and Sydney on 8th January 1875, Captain Abbott had to remain in Yokohama while Henry and Anthony carried out extensive repairs and coppering. Henry's bill was for $2,285 while Anthony's for copper and metal repairs also came to over $2,000 - a useful order for Carroll & Co. Joint ownership of the *Parmenio* was successful in spite of Henry's typically informal methods. No disputes had arisen although no statement of accounts had been offered. It was a situation that Mary Julia could see was fraught with danger, but her husband's methods seemed to suit his business. Before setting sail Abbott joined Henry and his family for a farewell meal.

After free trading along the route Captain Abbott finally arrived at Sydney where he purchased 600 tons of top quality coal on the ship's account. The *Parmenio* returned to Yokohama exactly eight months to the day after leaving in January. The coal was valued at $11 per ton. 324 tons were sold to two Russian men-of-war at $12, but $97^{3}/_{4}$ tons were sold to the U.S. man-of-war *Saco* at $12.50. In actual fact, 100 tons were sent but $2^{1}/_{4}$ tons were returned as she had no room for it. This was loaded into Henry's yard together with the balance of 176 tons. Abbott received the payment from *Saco* for himself.

When Mary Julia started to leave the accounts in Henry's care, using the babies as an excuse at his suggestion, perhaps she knew she could never change his ways. Her intuition would have been confirmed had she accompanied him during the sale of the coal. Robert Beattie, a British subject living at 121 and employed by Henry in the office, was with him at the time. As they went from ship to ship Henry put the cash payments into a black canvas bag. It was all in dollars. He asked Beattie for his necktie which he then used to secure the neck of the bag. The next day he went out to the *Parmenio* in a Japanese boat; in one hand he held the black bag, still tied up with Beattie's tie, and in the other was a roll of dollar bills. He shouted to Captain Abbott asking if he wanted any money, peeled off a $100 bill, gave it to him and left. It was all so casual, even if profitable, and not to the liking of the third co-owner, Mr. White. He asked to be bought out. His eight shares were divided equally giving Abbott a total of forty and Henry twenty-four.

While Henry was busy selling coal - "just like my father" - he was heard to say, Mary Julia was trying to interest young Willie in going to school. Emily was very happy there but Willie was more concerned about leaving his pet rabbit behind than joining his sister and Rosie. The rabbit originally had belonged to Emily and was bought during a national craze for buying them. The Japanese seemed to have a mania for collecting things according to a current fashion. One craze had been to own a pig and dealers flooded the market with pigs until quite suddenly the fashion switched to rabbits, leaving the dealers with thousands of piglets on their hands. Now, so many rabbits were being collected and bred that the government had put a tax per head on them. One man, unable to pay the tax demanded for his fifty rabbits, committed suicide. The most recent whim was the investment of large sums of money in choice roses, a new nightmare for dealers. Willie's rabbit had to suffer a surfeit of attention every weekend for several months, not having a tradition of suicide!

28
Danger Money

The two years 1876-77 were destined to confront Henry with almost every emotion experienced by man. Early one Sunday morning towards the end of January, a messenger hurried to the house to inform Henry that Mr.Mack, Chief Officer of the *Parmenio*, had been found dead in his cabin. He had not complained of any sickness or pain previously. Dr. Wheeler, well known in Yokohama, carried out a post-mortem examination and found the cause of death to be "the bursting of an aneurism of the abdominal aorta". Mr. Mack had been a first rate officer and a reliable friend. It seemed callous to hurry the search for an immediate replacement but *Parmenio* was due to be towed to Shinagawa on 26th to load with rice for San Francisco and be ready to sail by 8th February. The consignors, Messrs. Wilkin and Robison, would countenance no delay.

During April Henry received a letter from his sister Bridget. She continued to be his source of news from home which often left him unsettled and with a vague feeling of guilt. She had confided her distress when her baby son, Lyman James, died when only four months old, and again when her daughter, Sarah Ann, died a month before her third birthday, but this letter really hit him hard. The mother he had not seen for twenty-four years had died on 18th January and been buried in St. Woollas' cemetery in Newport. His mind was flooded with memories and regrets of neglected duties. He calculated she must have been seventy-two years old. His own maturity enabled him to recognise her stable strength in organising her family and her unselfish treatment when allowing him to flee from Newport. Mary Julia was able to restore some sense of proportion to his feelings of guilt but it left a wound that never quite healed.

It was providential that Henry had at last found the right opportunity to fulfil a private ambition, the building of a special schooner for himself. He had known it would be called the "Beatrice" ever since the birth of his daughter, but the design details were still locked in his mind. Committing the plans to paper was just the mental therapy needed to restore his natural high spirits.

The *Beatrice* was going to be a hunter. Henry had always found trading in the Far East tantalisingly profitable even when set against the high risks of natural hazards, feared by every sailor and experienced by himself when shipwrecked off Gutzlaff. Perhaps the most dangerous and, to Henry, the most fascinating commercial enterprise in those waters was the hunting of sea otter and fur seals in sufficient quantity to satisfy the insatiable demand for good quality pelts. London was the great attraction for this trade and in its wholesale market a single pelt from a sea otter commanded from £15 to £210 according to quality. These were the going rates in 1872 with every indication of continuing stability. Henry had been handling otter pelts as part of his general trading but was anxious to become more deeply involved in this lucrative form of hunting.

Extreme conditions could confront any vessel intruding into otter colonies and the *Beatrice* would be fully equipped to have all the speed, strength and manoeuvrability essential to such an enterprise. The most densely populated area for hunting was among the Kuril Islands. These islands stretched for 750 miles from the southern tip of Kamchatka in Russia to the eastern edge of Hokkaido. They formed a chain of thirty-six islands apart from innumerable rocky protrusions showing above the surface of the sea with as many hidden below.

Nature had given the Kurils a notorious reputation. Earthquakes, devastating tidal waves, volcanic eruptions, treacherous currents, blistering winter winds, impenetrable summer fogs, swarms of mosquitoes and malodorous masses of floating seaweed all combined to create an environment inhospitable to hunters. Possibly a poet could have revelled in the lush, more gentle aspect of hidden fiords, hot springs, wild bamboo, giant grasses and virgin forests of silver fir, but few crewmen aboard hunting schooners were poets!

The Kurils, located along one of the most volatile sections of the Pacific 'rim of fire', contained over a hundred volcanoes, thirty-nine of which were active. Underwater eruptions were a regular occurrence, some causing visible disturbance on the surface. At times boiling water was propelled upwards, spouting like lethal geysers.

In 1892 the British barque *Hesper*, having left Kobe, was fortunate to survive just such a volcanic upheaval when seventy-five miles off the Japanese coast. The captain stated that:-

"On the morning of October 30th a rumbling noise was heard and immediately afterwards the vessel was thrown on her beam ends. Immense waves came tumbling towards the ship and rushed over the deck, stern, bows and bulwarks. The water was boiling hot and the men were compelled to go into the rigging, where they remained for five hours. During this time great blasts of hot sulphurous gas escaped from the boiling ocean and almost suffocated the crew. The scalding water melted the pitch in the deck seams, and the rolling of the vessel was so great that the main topmast cross-tree was pitched into the sea, and the men momentarily expected the masts to go over the side. The phenomena disappeared at the end of eight hours but most of the crew were ill for several days after."

Although hostile to man, the Kuril environment suited the otter and seal population. There was abundant life in the sea to sustain them in considerable numbers. Starting in the eighteenth century and culminating in the 1850's, Russian, Japanese, American and English hunters swarmed to the Kurils in search of the prized pelts.

Dense masses of seaweed, mainly kelp, covered most of the area. The kelp main stalks reached over two hundred feet in length with branch shoots of fifty feet. It could cluster so thickly that boats encountered difficulty when trying to navigate through it. The otters were usually spotted napping in a tangle of this weed and, when suitably equipped, a schooner would lower three long-boats, each carrying five or six men. These formed a triangle round the otter. Bubbles from the otter's fur betrayed its underwater flight to open sea. When caught and killed, it was immediately skinned to prevent deterioration of a perfect pelt. Cleaned of all adhering fat, the skin was stretched and dried, then stored below decks.

Not all expeditions were so well equipped. Smaller vessels had to manage without the long-boats. Greed and rising adrenalin through the chase often led to indiscriminate slaughter. Wielding guns and clubs, hunters would risk damaging the very pelts they prized by shooting from boats or from the shore, even wading out into colonies of the frightened animals.

Henry had first-hand experience of the damage sustained by many of these hunting vessels in such hazardous working conditions. He had been responsible for extensive repairs and modifications to several craft. That knowledge would influence his own design. It would be a staunch little vessel of seventy to ninety tons, 65 feet in length with a beam of 19 feet and a hold of 7 ft.8ins. depth. Her cabin would accommodate eight men and be neatly panelled in polished wood. He pressed ahead with the plans so that construction could begin as soon as possible. His aim was to have the *Beatrice* fully operational by the following summer in time for the fur-hunting season. Unknown to him, this schedule was perfectly timed to profit from a fellow captain's tragedy.

The American otter-hunting schooner *Otsego*, well known to Henry and captained by Mr. B.W.Johnson, left San Francisco for the Kuril Islands on 18th March 1876. She made the island of Shiashkotan on 5th May and continued her hunting expedition along the coast until 9th September when she sailed for Sikotan. It was a successful voyage, securing 157 good quality skins. At top prices in the London market they could fetch over £32,000. Henry remembered that in 1873 this vessel actually secured 300 skins in one trip! The crew set about drying the skins. On the evening of 23rd September they set sail only to be hit by a violent storm two days later. Losing one boat, Captain Johnson anchored for shelter in Christmas Bay, a Japanese harbour on the south-east side of Shiashkotan.

At 1 a.m. on 26th September, an ominously heavy swell came rolling in, breaking across the entrance to the bay. By 1.30 a.m. the captain wisely got under way and attempted to tack the vessel into a better position. His efforts were thwarted by the huge swell. He let go the main anchor in five fathoms, lying about two ship's lengths from the rocks. A second anchor was prepared but the vessel was struck by a heavy sea which broke the main anchor chain. Under a pitch black sky, at 3 a.m. the centre board struck the rocks and in a short time the *Otsego* was driven so far up the beach that the sea left her almost dry at low water. The bottom was broken through amidships, the sternpost, rudder and keel were gone, the forecastle was full of water and some of the planks were damaged.

When the seas moderated, a boat was launched an an experienced crew was sent to S.E. Bay to ask for assistance in saving cargo and to make a survey of the ship. Two days were spent in removing stores and gear. Three vessels arrived on the 29th in response to Captain Johnson's plea for help; a pilot ship *Banner*, a Russian schooner *Lottie* and the German schooner *Jupiter*. At first they tried to heave the *Otsego* off its rocky prison but all their combined tackle failed to move her. The three captains then took on the responsibility of carrying out a survey of the extensive damage. Noting that the planks were now beginning to be breached, they decided that the vessel could not be made seaworthy. They recommended that the *Otsego* should be sold for the benefit of the owners and underwriters.

As was customary in these circumstances, Captain Johnson wasted no time and held an auction to dispose of the schooner and all other assets. Presumably the pelts were not included with the cargo and gear which only fetched $500, some items being left without a bid. A bid of $10 for the wreck was rejected by the captain. He and his crew divided themselves between the *Jupiter* and the *Caroline*, another vessel in the vicinity. They returned to Yokohama with all remaining stores.

News of troubles at sea travels fast in a port. Henry Cook made no secret of his professional interest and contacted the captains of the ill-fated *Otsego* and the *Jupiter* to glean as much first-hand information as possible. His interest deepened on learning that the wreck and some of its gear would be auctioned on 25th October. Damage to the *Otsego* was obviously severe but, having ascertained details of the vessel's construction, he felt confident that with his experience in this particular field he could repair and refloat her. Here was a coincidence he could not resist!

Back at the works he discussed plans with his wife, who volunteered to try to establish some coherent state of accounts and current orders to be cleared. Henry estimated that the *Beatrice* would be ready for her first voyage to the Kurils by the following July. She could be loaded with the equipment and workmen required for repairs to the *Otsego* plus a minimum spare crew to help him sail the refloated schooner back to Yokohama. After discharging Henry's rescue team, the *Beatrice* would continue with her first hunting season as planned. Following refitting at Creekside, the *Otsego* could be recommissioned and Henry would own another fur-hunting schooner.

Mary Julia found that it was not easy to gather all the relevant information she required as details were dispersed among various foremen, and figures seemed to be in people's heads rather than on paper. She finally assessed with reasonable confidence that priority contracts could be completed without leaving Henry short of the finance and skilled workmen he would require, so it was agreed to put his plan into action. She had rather enjoyed getting back into the business and offered to look after Henry's affairs during his absence, an offer welcomed with a grateful hug.

Naturally, Mary Julia was a little apprehensive that her husband would have to face possible danger and uncertain success in the venture. The children were very young and after seventeen years Yokohama still had many of the rough elements of a frontier town. The women often felt that the sense of security was only a fragile veneer. Rumours abounded, sometimes leading to panic, as occurred during a recent scare of a cholera epidemic. Some eight hundred people, suspecting infection, invaded the General Hospital where only mild colic was diagnosed. Women left alone in Yokohama had to call on great reserves of courage and self-confidence.

Such was Henry Cook's reputation that Yokohama soon learned how his final bid of $130 for the wreck had carried the day with very little opposition. Mary Julia regained some confidence and a little pride when she read the "Japan Daily Herald Mail's" report on this new enterprise. Commenting on the difficulties they concluded:

". . . . as that gentleman's skill in such matters is well known, the undertaking is considered quite practicable."

Could Henry live up to this sort of expectation? Certainly he now had more equipment and better-trained workmen than were available for his successful refloating of the emperor's yacht.

The building of the *Beatrice* progressed on schedule. It was completed and successfully launched in April 1877. Fitting out continued after launching and, when finally ready, she was registered as British with a tonnage of 96 tons. With the *Otsego* 48 tons and the *Jupiter* only 30 tons, the *Beatrice* should prove a better match for those desperate conditions in the Kurils. On 26th April the *Beatrice* made her trial trip in style. The Press continued to take interest and reported that:

". . . . considering she is not clipper-built, she made very good time indeed."

Wasting no time, and with too much on his mind to worry unduly about leaving Mary Julia to manage affairs at home, Henry set sail as planned in a fully-equipped *Beatrice* bound for Inturup in the Kuril Islands. From there he intended to begin work on the *Otsego*. He arrived on 11th May and found the wreck lying inside a formidable reef of rocks where the sea had driven her high and dry. Work started at once.

The repairs occupied thirty-seven days. Sections were remade and fitted, her sides and bottom had to be thoroughly caulked. Although they met with much opposition from the weather, which continued wet and misty with occasional gales, the ways were placed and, foot by foot,the *Otsego* was eased down over the rocks and finally into deep water. Two more days were spent in fitting up the rigging and other essential tackle and work was finished on 19th June.

The *Beatrice* was now despatched on her own adventure. Henry had commissioned Captain Jordan to be master of the *Beatrice* and it was with a strange mixture of wistfulness and exaltation that he watched her sail away with purposeful confidence.

Henry Cook captained the *Otsego* for her triumphant voyage to Yokohama where the Press were again waiting and eager to publish all the details. No doubt Mary Julia was given a more graphic account but the "Japan Daily Herald Mail" summed up the homeward voyage:

"... .after a disagreeable passage of twenty days, occupied in beating against fresh southerly winds and much foggy weather, Mr Cook had the satisfaction of anchoring his craft in port on 10th July. She is a fine sea boat and not much the worse for her accident."

A well earned tribute for transforming a 'total wreck'.

Just a few days later, on 29th June, Henry's father William Carrol died at Cardiff, aged 76, having survived his wife by only seventeen months. Henry could not know this for some time to come. William Carrol was buried with his wife Julia in a grave for two at St. Woollas' cemetery, Newport.

The *Otsego* remained in harbour for several months while Henry brought her fitments up to the standard he required. The new excitement would be the return of the *Beatrice*. Captain Jordan had sufficient experience in otter-hunting to shoulder the responsibility of testing the schooner in action. To his credit the *Beatrice* proved herself against every whim of otter and weather for almost three months. At the beginning of September, Captain Jordan set course for home. The weather was not good and by 15th September storms had whipped up a ferocious sea. Momentarily off guard, a Japanese member of the crew was caught by a determined wave that surged over the deck sweeping the poor man into the sea. Turning about was hazardous, and by the time it was achieved all sight of him was gone. His body was not recovered.

At last, on 19th September, the *Beatrice* made Yokohama without further incident and Captain Jordan and his crew had the privilege of bringing in a safe ship with a sizeable first cargo of furs.

Henry's enterprise had indeed lived up to public expectation.

29
Life's Fragile Thread

The public recognition of professional ability that Henry had achieved ensured a good continuity of business, but in no way eliminated the uncertainties common to ships and their encounters with the sea. As a prophet is often ignored in his own village, so Captain Abbott chose to reject Henry's considered opinion regarding the *Parmenio*. Profits from her trading had not been outstanding, particularly when set against the heavy cost of repairs required on a vessel of that size. Henry had decided that it would be imprudent to incur any further expense in maintaining her. A proposed bill of sale was drawn up between them on 10th February 1877 but on the 27th Captain Abbott had hurriedly set sail, without Henry's agreement, leaving behind a very angry partner.

Some people used Henry's reputation to falsify their own worth, in one case disastrously. Captain Johnson, master of the *Surprise*, an American ship sailing from New York, approached Yokohama harbour about 7 p.m. at the end of February. He sent up lights requesting a pilot. The captain was wary of the fact that pilots in that port could operate without certificates of efficiency, and he asked of the man who came aboard the length of his service in the harbour. David Shields, the pilot, claimed ten years' experience and added, quite falsely, that he was a partner of Mr. Cook and was using his boat. The captain knew Henry and felt confident that any partner of his must be a good pilot, so Shields was engaged.

In the subsequent enquiry following the total loss of the *Surprise*, Captain Johnson admitted that the pilot was sober and handled the ship remarkably well. He had accepted Shields' judgment, during approaching bad weather, when it went counter to his own. Leaving the anchorage in Mississippi Bay, the *Surprise* was holed when hitting a rock and had to be abandoned. This rock had been omitted from the corrected charts issued by the English Admiralty after its survey of 1869. When questioned at the enquiry, Shields denied saying he was a partner of Mr. Cook.

Mary Julia naturally enjoyed sharing the ever-growing prestige of her husband, which had undoubtedly been accelerated through her practical help and attention to detail. She had thoroughly enjoyed being back at the centre of affairs for the past year. One of her achievements was to persuade John to invest some of the savings she had been encouraging since he began work on the railway. In spite of Henry's scepticism John agreed to take up a quarter share in the *Otsego*, a move that reaped good profits for several years.

As usual, Mary Julia and Henry had been very happy when reunited after a forced separation, this time the three-month trip to the Kurils. Their joy resulted in an unexpected pregnancy for Mary Julia. She accepted the fact with mixed feelings of pleasure and some apprehension, bearing in mind that she would be forty next birthday and five years had elapsed since Beatrice was born. Henry could not disguise a certain masculine anticipation of an addition to his family which countenanced no such subtle doubts.

After the first weeks of occasional nausea, Mary Julia expected to regain her customary buoyant enthusiasm for her role in the family and the business. The reserves of energy on which she could always rely remained tantalisingly just beyond her reach. Henry slowly began to realise that the uncharacteristic listlessness was persisting far too long and he was relieved when she allowed him to arrange a consultation with a doctor. The prescribed tonic and diet for suspected anaemia restored some confidence but very little increase in her energy.

Early in November, defying a cool wind, Mary Julia felt the need to get out of the house for a while and have some gentle exercise. She slowly walked from one familiar construction site to another, enjoying the friendly greetings from the Japanese and European workmen. Immersed in a contented inner warmth fuelled by their genuine concern for her, she failed to notice a spar, still in its rough-hewn stage, left at an awkward angle across her path. She fell heavily with no time to cushion the impact with her arms and lost consciousness as her head struck the ground. The last group of workmen shouted a useless warning as they saw her fall.

They carried her back to the house and sent a messenger to the Custom House for Henry, while the Japanese nurse and servants laid her gently on the bed, whispering fearfully. When Henry arrived it was all over. The nurse was in tears as she told him that Mary Julia had lost the baby; she had taken the liberty of sending for the doctor who should arrive very soon. Henry thanked her for all she had done and went in to see his wife. She lay as though dead.

Her face was white and waxy smooth and a trace of blood had seeped through a pad on her left temple. To reassure himself he took her hand and spoke to her, eagerly watching her eyes, but they did not open to greet him. He recognised a little upward twitch at the corners of her mouth and knew she had intended a smile. He breathed a sigh of relief.

The doctor diagnosed the obvious, that she had been mildly concussed, but he was confident that she had suffered no lasting physical damage from her miscarriage. He had nothing but praise for the work done by the nurse, who bowed low and jerkily, emitting confused sounds of embarrassment.

Mary Julia needed careful nursing and Henry delegated work at the harbour so that he could remain at Creekside as often as possible. By Christmas she had regained some of her fresh Irish complexion and recovered much of her strength, but the old sparkle in her personality was forced or noticeably missing entirely. Christmas was a quiet affair and, although Rosie was the usual extrovert she had become, Henry noticed the other children often glancing at their mother, trying to understand. Emily was particularly affected. Her eight and a half years weighed heavily as though she understood something beyond the others, a feeling she would recall many years later.

After the sustained effort made during the festive season, Mary Julia found it more and more difficult to carry out her customary duties. Life was quieter with the children back at school and she was able to rest more, but her health continued to decline. The doctor was puzzled by the lack of symptoms - only a general debility shown by an underlying weakness which seemed to affect her muscles and even her strength of will. She did not leave the house and moved only slowly and with effort.

Mary Julia died in her sleep in the early hours of 18th February 1878, still only thirty-nine years of age. Henry tormented himself with regrets that he was not awake at that time. The Abbé, who had called to see her several times, assured Henry that she had been serenely untroubled at the thought of death. Her only concern had been for her children, doubting that Henry could manage the family without her. The cause of the gradual physical deterioration which had led to her final demise was a mystery to the doctor. It was as though she had lost the will to live but he could not reconcile that impression with his experience of her strong and positive personality. God alone could know the truth.

30
Reckless Anger

The nuns at the Convent advised Henry to have the children at home for a while so that they could see their mother for the last time and share their grief with him. Facing the reality of the situation would help them to adjust and eventually accept their loss more sensibly. A very resentful Rosie was not allowed to join them.

Mary Julia was buried in the Foreign Cemetery next to her baby son, whose grave she had visited for the past ten years. Henry arranged for a double grave so that he could join her when his own time came to die, so clinging to some irrational consolation. There were some minor earth tremors on the morning of the funeral which did little to lift his spirits. A few mornings later there were four shocks in three hours, the last one more prolonged than he had before experienced. He almost brushed aside the thoughts of ill omen, but not quite.

Fortunately most of Henry's projects were well in hand and competently managed. A new otter schooner, the *Diana*, was on the stocks with investors already designated. The *Otsego* was earning her keep, trading in the Bonin Islands and successfully hunting in the Kurils. The *Beatrice* still had to cover the cost of fitting-out, which had soared to over $9,000, but consignments to the Carolyne Islands and Guam were likely to be very profitable.

On returning from Guam, Captain Williams, master of the *Beatrice*, included a rather frightening experience in his report to Henry. He left Guam on 15th June and called in at Pulwat Island to deliver a small cargo. While unloading he was informed by some very scared traders that a boat containing twelve men had landed safely from their wrecked vessel at Namayonne Island, only to be murdered and afterwards eaten by the inhabitants. Natives from the neighbouring island of Piserrare then arrived, fought with the Namayonne men and took the boat from them.

Captain Williams had sailed to Piserrare hoping to find a clue to the ship's name or nationality but was informed, in a manner far from convincing, that the boat had been broken up. The master of a German schooner informed Captain Williams that he had seen a wreck on Namayonne some four days earlier but the islanders had warned him off when he tried to gain some details. The American barque *Sontag* was reported long overdue from the area and an American man-of-war was about to be despatched from Hong Kong to investigate.

As 1880 dawned, Henry felt lonely and isolated, even though few men in Yokohama could claim such a wide circle of friends. It had become clear to him how much he had come to rely on the honest opinions and clear-sighted judgment of his wife. How different the next six years might have been had she lived!

Towards the end of January, word reached Henry that the *Parmenio* had been wrecked off Formosa on the 15th. For a day or two his thoughts were clouded by rage and anxiety. The ship was not insured and had left on its last voyage without his consent. The agreed plan to sell the vessel had fallen apart and he knew only too well what action Captain Abbott would be forced to take.

Captain Abbott reported later that when within a day's sail of Taiwanfoo (Taichung), in thick rainy weather, a light had been seen after dark, about 9 p.m. The light must have been a lantern ashore for when he turned about the ship struck sand. He was fifty-six miles off course and had mistaken Steep Island (Kisan to) for the island of Fonio. The shore was not visible and he discharged cargo overboard throughout the night to lighten the *Parmenio* and get her nearer to the shore. She remained helpless for three or four days.

Eventually, Abbott was able to seek assistance from the British Consul at Tamsui. The remaining cargo was landed in native boats but all attempts to refloat the *Parmenio* were unsuccessful. He considered there was no alternative but to sell her, realising about $2,900. The cargo was stored for the intended purchaser.

As if to test Henry to the limit, a letter arrived from England containing more sad news. His very dear sister Bridget had died before Christmas on 14th December. Her husband, Lyman Durkee, had written the letter still using his favourite name for her, Sarah Bridget. She was only forty-seven years old and was buried at St. Woollas' cemetery in the same grave as her two children who had died many years before. With so many of his family laid to rest at St. Woollas, Henry felt a strong urge to visit them - but would he ever return to England?

No wonder that when John called in at Creekside, Henry's black mood lifted for a while, even though he had very little liking for his brother. John's visit was to let Henry know that he was thinking of leaving the railway if he could be found work at the shipyard. For the past few weeks he had been employed on the construction of the iron bridge at Kawasaki but his contract was due for renewal and he felt ready for a change. Henry gave careful thought to the idea; help was needed on the barque *Ophelia* which was slightly behind schedule, perhaps having more of his own flesh and blood nearby would be balm for his jaded nerves, also Anthony had lost some of his early fitness and seemed physically less able to manage a full day's work. So, sinking his doubts about John, he offered to employ him at $5 per day assisting Anthony. John was delighted and left the railway on 15th May.

Following the earth tremors experienced just after Mary Julia's funeral, yet another severe earthquake had shaken Yokohama on Sunday, 21st February. The Bluff suffered most, scarcely a house escaped without some damage. The Convent roof had been irremediably shaken, so its young boarders had to be sent home whilst urgent repairs were carried out. The children, including Rosie, had been at home for several weeks. John seemed to enjoy the opportunity to exercise his role as Uncle but Rosie was obviously his favourite. Although Emily was an attractive eleven-year-old, Rosie had already blossomed into young womanhood at sixteen and made no attempt to disguise the fact. Henry's attitude towards his brother softened considerably and he wondered if he had been unfair in his judgment of him in the past.

It was at the beginning of this more friendly relationship that a letter arrived from Amoy. In it Captain Abbott was demanding money to cover the cost of recoppering the ship at Amoy in September 1879, wages for the crew and himself, plus expenses incurred in trying to refloat the wrecked *Parmenio* - in all an expected sum of around $9,000! Henry read the letter several times with increasing disbelief and anger. The whole voyage had been against his expressed wishes let alone his refusal to allow any further repairs to be made to the ship. As to wages, they could be met from Abbott's own trading. His mind raced over years of casual finance, of debts between them, paid and unpaid. Without a doubt it was Abbott who owed money to him! He could probably raise $9,000 but why should he? He had three children and Rosie to care for. It was the undertone of threat in the letter that Henry really resented from a trusted partner.

Seething with Irish temper, he sought John and poured out his anger against Abbott, adding spitefully that if he owned nothing, Abbott could sing for his money and never get a penny even if he sued for it! The seed was sown. Within hours he had worked out a scheme to transfer all his assets to his brother until such time as any claims by Abbott had been dealt with either privately or through a legal settlement. John agreed to the fraudulent idea. He was only too willing to ingratiate himself with his brother and take advantage of his reckless mood.

The whole mad scheme was unworthy of a man of Henry's character and integrity. It must have grown out of his unbalanced state of mind at the time. Mary Julia would have scorned him into commonsense, but her influence was not there to counteract his hasty reaction.

31
Amateur Deceit

For the transfer to appear genuine it had to go through the full legal process. It suddenly became alarmingly clear to Henry that to have his estate returned to him, at a safe future date, would also entail going to law. John assured his brother that he fully understood the temporary nature of the transaction and Henry pushed aside the niggling distrust which persisted at the back of his mind.

Once again Henry sought the advice of his old friend, Frederick White, and explained his intention, giving financial embarrassment as the reason for the transfer. White knew Henry very well and was pretty sure that he was not really hard-up. There was some other motive behind it. He had no wish to offend Henry but he was not going to be party to any mad financial scheme. He declined to help but advised Henry to use William Walker to estimate a value on his property and to contact Mr Enslie at the Consulate for the legal work required. Henry had employed Walker several times in the past to draw up accounts for him and so approved the suggestion.

Mr Enslie drew up two deeds, one for transfer of the property and one for the goodwill, which were registered at the British Consulate. Walker could not fail to notice the rather distant relationship between the brothers and Henry felt obliged to take a chance and confided some of the reason for it, also his vague distrust of John. He hinted at the temporary nature of the transaction which could leave him rather vulnerable should anything happen to John. Henry had made sure that he had control of the deeds by locking them in his private safe but Walker suggested a further safeguard. He valued the goodwill of the business at roughly $4,500 and urged Henry to obtain from John a promissory note for that amount. John protested but Henry was adamant. Two promissory notes, one for $2,500 and the other for $2,000, were safely added to the deeds in his safe. At last Henry felt relaxed and well satisfied with his strategy.

Mr Enslie had counselled the brothers to continue the business under the well-known name of H. Cook. Henry had no intention of changing it and to demonstrate his determination he prepared a new advertisement to be included in the next year's "Japan Directory":

H. COOK,

SHIP-WRIGHT.

Repairs Neatly Executed. Masts, Boats, &c., Constantly on Hand. Iron-Work Fitted to Order.

No. 115, on the Creek, Yokohama.

A few of Henry's close friends had become concerned that he had been avoiding them and was looking far from happy. They plotted to coax him back into their regular company and chose the perfect occasion one Thursday morning, 24th June. The streets of the settlement echoed to an unusual sound, the fifes and drums of a British armed force. Some five hundred and fifty men were marching from the English *hatoba* up to an area of the reclaimed swamp. Henry offered no resistance when he was dragged from his work to join the procession, feeling more relaxed in the erroneous idea that he had put his affairs in order.

The contingent of seamen and marines were put through a series of manoeuvres carried out with a machine-like precision which delighted all the spectators, particularly the Japanese. After a short pause, the manual and platoon exercises were demonstrated with well rehearsed accuracy. Before marching back to the *hatoba* the order was given to 'pile arms' and the men broke ranks for a rest. As if by magic a number of Japanese itinerant refreshment stalls appeared and were soon doing a roaring trade as the blue-jackets and spectators surged round them. Henry had not enjoyed himself so much for weeks.

Before returning to work the friends had luncheon and a few drinks in the Grand Hotel and were soon swapping local yarns just like old times. It was just the tonic Henry needed. Trying to top all the other stories, one of the party read out a report from a Japanese journal which stated that a kitten had recently been born in Yokohama with four ears and two tails. The journal assured its readers that the animal was alive and would shortly be exhibited! Henry wagered five dollars that none of the group would ever see it. The wager was accepted and they all went their separate ways, still laughing.

Like most proverbs, the Japanese aphorism, "Happiness and misery are common to all times and places," was manifestly true. On 18th August 1880 trouble arrived in Yokohama in the guise of Captain Abbott. He called on Henry in a belligerent mood which was aggravated by Henry's refusal to meet his demands. The antagonism increased when he declared that, on the contrary, Abbott still owed him over $5,000. When Abbott replied that it would be a matter for the court to decide, Henry told him he would be wasting his time and money. He explained that he had neither cash nor business to his name. Abbott glared in disbelief and stormed out without another word.

Henry contacted John immediately for a long and serious discussion. It was time to make sure they each had the same story and rehearsed the details. During his meeting Henry suddenly realised the importance of the transfer having been made before the *Parmenio* was wrecked, if it were to withstand a possible charge of fraud. He had no idea what date would have been entered for registration of the transfer in the consul records. He sent John to the Consulate to view the register, which could be done for a small fee, where he found the date to be 14th June 1880 - much too recent! Quick thinking had not entirely deserted Henry and he rather favoured the idea of it being a clerical error. Of course, it should have been 14th January!

William Walker was called in once again to exercise his copperplate skills in compiling a statutory declaration correcting the 'error' which Henry signed before a named witness. He took the declaration to the Consulate where a clerk attached it to the entry in the register. Since Abbott's visit all guilt had been set aside. It had become a challenge to win, in or out of court. Confidence restored, Henry returned to the running of his business with all his usual energy.

32
A Local Tragedy

Later that month, about half past six in the morning, one of Henry's coolies fell from a spar into the Creek and was unable to pull himself out of the water. The poor man was nearly exhausted and sinking when an American, Thomas Seon, who luckily happened to be passing, jumped into the water and supported the drowning man until he was dragged out by some other people who were looking on. Mr Seon had a narrow escape himself as the coolie nearly dragged him under in his convulsive struggles.

Thomas Seon lived at No.61 and Henry called there to thank him for his courageous action. Mrs Seon was proud of her husband but horrified at this action as she was expecting a baby, due within a month. She gave birth to a daughter on 22nd August, which provided Henry with an excuse to call again with a small gift to show his appreciation. Sadly, the Japanese proverb about happiness and misery had its truth demonstrated yet again.

Mr Seon was an engineer, machinist and gunsmith with a reputation for being an industrious and skilful workman. On the 5th November he was working on a double-barrelled shotgun sent to him for repair. Being under the impression that the gun was not loaded, he placed the barrels into the forge for the purpose of loosening the breech when suddenly, as he was busy moving them about, there was a terrible explosion. Neighbours rushed in and as the smoke cleared away the poor fellow was found lying on the ground terribly mutilated. It appeared that both barrels had been loaded, with duck or some equally heavy shot, which had passed through his left loin and intestines and burst out on the other side. Medical aid was promptly summoned but he never spoke again and died within half an hour. Mrs Seon was now a widow with three young children, the baby not yet three months old, and home was the other side of the Pacific Ocean. Henry began a subscription list for the bereaved wife, which was liberally supported, but he missed Mary Julia who would have known how to console her in a more special way, if only she could have been there.

As summer came to a gentle close, it was time for the children to return to school. Now that Rosie had reached the age of sixteen she no longer attended school as a pupil. Henry had been paying her fees at the convent and for convenience she was known there as Rosa Cook until such time as her real identity could be established. The Reverend Mother remembered her promise to offer her full-time employment at the end of her school years and she was now kept busy helping in the classrooms and with general housework.

The St. Maur nuns were very conscious of the growing international requirements of education, nowhere more essential than in Yokohama, and had devised a unique programme for language tuition. The curriculum covered English, French and Japanese. A selected language was taught throughout the school for one hour to the appropriate ability of each age group. At the end of that hour, a bell was rung and the school would switch to another language for the next hour, changing again at the next bell. In this way communication in foreign languages became commonplace. Emily and Beatrice thrived on this unique discipline and within a few years of leaving school became competent in eight languages, including Russian and German. Having left the convent for a Jesuit college at the age of eight, William never achieved such a wide range of linguistic ability although his Japanese was excellent.

That concentration of language training perfectly matched the requirements of the Japanese as they desperately sought to understand foreign culture and technology. By then, in 1880, many areas in Japan had become accustomed to foreigners. There were about three thousand foreign residents spread throughout the country with large business communities centred in Yokohama, Kobe and Nagasaki, with Tokyo attracting most of the diplomatic set. British and American instructors and teachers were in great demand. Lectures at the Tokyo Imperial University were mostly in English but the Faculty of Medicine used German lecturers and doctors! The rapid growth of the Japanese printing industry brought contact with foreign ideas and literature to an ever-widening range of Japanese people.

Growing up in such an exciting cosmopolitan atmosphere and surrounded by the Japanese eagerness to learn, it was natural for an intelligent girl like Emily to set her heart, at a very early age, on becoming a teacher. Beatrice also liked the idea but was not so sure. Being younger she was perhaps content to follow her big sister, but neither had to make any such decision for a few years.

Yokohama was a regular port of call for the *Cilurnum,* a vessel built at

Jarrow back in 1874. This fine ship was hammered by a terrible storm on 8th November but managed to limp into the harbour some ten days later. Her masts, sails and rigging were mostly swept away and her superstructure was badly damaged. It was almost inevitable that Henry would be commissioned to carry out the repairs and refitment, such was his reputation in the handling of similar disasters.

Although the work presented few unexpected problems, the timing caused Henry to experience the first genuine feelings of guilt about his false position. It became virtually impossible to disguise the fact that he still owned and directed his business. John had neither the technical knowledge and experience nor the character and drive to manage. In fact, Henry had found him to be rather lazy and in need of careful supervision. Visiting customers and other workmen must have been aware of Henry's frequent orders, directions and even reprimands shouted at John. The lie would never be sustained by Henry if it endangered the integrity of the work, seamen's lives were at stake.

John had become more secretive with his money. He spent much of his spare time with Anthony who kept John's savings in a box beneath his bed. Regularly there would be up to $5,000 in gold, silver and notes, from which amounts were taken for payment of debts to Henry. Both had complete confidence in the honesty of Anthony's Japanese housekeeper, Waka Sen, who knew all about the money and that Anthony kept his small savings in a box in his chest of drawers. He had very little money left at the end of each month since having drifted back into his old habit of drinking heavily. Henry was not sure whether drink was causing Anthony's ill health or used as a means of coping with it. He never interfered or offered advice.

The year ended with an official notification that Abbott had carried out his threat and an action against Henry was to be heard before Judge R.T. Rennie on Thursday, 17th February 1881. It gave Henry about five weeks to organise his defence.

33
The Court Decides

Henry secured the services of Mr Lowder to act as counsel during the court hearing. He was an experienced barrister on the official list for Yokohama. The lack of consistent and careful book-keeping gave him many a headache while trying to plan Henry's counter-claim against Abbott. He was further exasperated by the fact that very few agreements between the two men had been committed to paper.

All too quickly Thursday, 17th February 1881 arrived. Mr Hill, appearing for Abbott, opened the proceedings in front of Judge Rennie and only five jurymen. He claimed that Abbott's action was for wages due from 27th September 1873 to 17th May 1880, at the rate of $200 a month, and disbursements in connection with the working and repairing of the *Parmenio*. Mr Lowder immediately countered with a cross action claiming a balance of accounts in Henry's favour of $5,625. On the surface the lines of battle seemed clear, but how would the court sift out truth from falsehood and conjecture with so little documentation to guide it?

Mr Hill then outlined the points at issue, as he saw them, before calling Abbott to give his evidence. Abbott gave a lengthy account with carefully selected details of the ship's forty-two voyages. He claimed that from the beginning of the partnership there had been a verbal agreement that he should receive $200 per month for wages as master of the ship. Abbott continued with a history of cargo sales, some detailed, others estimated. He was interrupted when a promissory note for $2,017 was shown to him, which he agreed he had received from Henry in January 1875 for "wages to date and a few other items".

Abbott ended his evidence with an admission that he had been fifty-six miles off course when the *Parmenio* ran aground and he explained how the ship was sold for "about $2,900" when the British Consul at Tamsui had refused to advance any more money to save her. Although not insured, the vessel had been valued at $15,000 before her loss.

Henry had not thought of accusing his partner of poor seamanship. There was a mutual professional respect for each other's experience at sea. The quarrel had only arisen through casual and imprecise business management aggravated by the extended voyage, which was made in the first place without Henry's permission.

On Friday morning Mr Lowder began the difficult cross-examination of Abbott with creditable skill. Abbott admitted that he had given no accounts of any kind to Henry, even though it was his duty so to do upon request. He denied that there was an agreement that he should have returned from the voyage to Amoy in 1877 so that the *Parmenio* could be sold. Mr Lowder produced a proposed bill of sale dated 10th February 1877 to support Henry's claim that Abbott had taken the *Parmenio* on its final extended voyage without permission. Robert Beattie, a clerk employed by Henry, confirmed on oath that he had heard the two men agree that the ship was to be sold as soon as possible. When questioned by a juror, he stated that Henry and Abbott seemed to trust each other implicitly. Under pressure, Abbott revealed that the promissory note for $2,017 had been given to him by Henry and his wife who thought he might have need of it as he was about to put to sea "and no one knew what might happen", but he had declined to accept it. The court was adjourned until the Saturday morning.

Promptly at 9.30 a.m. Judge Rennie instructed the jury on three points he wished them to consider; After an absence of about twenty-five minutes, they returned and handed in the result of their deliberations.

1) Abbott did not forcibly take away the *Parmenio* as alleged.
2) Abbott was entitled to receive wages and at the rate of $200 per month.
3) There had been no settlement of accounts - the accounts still remained open.

Mr Enslie was then appointed referee and given the task of compiling an assessment of the claims of both parties. Each counsel could present arguments to the referee before the report was received by the court on 21st July 1881.

Henry was worried about Mr Enslie's appointment as referee as he was the Consulate lawyer who had supervised the transfer of Henry's business to his brother John. He dared make no mention of this to his counsel whose forbearance had probably been stretched to the limit. Henry rather naively calculated that if the court decided in his favour he would be able to resume ownership of his business with few people knowing that any switch had been arranged. Such musing dragged a reluctant feeling of guilt from his subconscious to confront him with the seriousness of the deceit he planned to use should events require it. A shallow confidence in winning was all he could cling to.

There was nothing Henry could do for the next five months of waiting, while Mr Lowder argued his case with the referee, except work in the shipyard. He was surprised and rather embarrassed at the public interest being voiced throughout the Yokohama community. The "Japan Weekly Mail" was giving full coverage, almost verbatim, to each session of the court hearing. His friends and business acquaintances were very supportive. They had learned to trust their interests to Henry's casual handling of finance and his past successes in the courts had always been well reported in the press.

Henry resisted all overtures from John to discuss the proceedings. In fact he was disturbed by the hint of arrogance and swagger that had returned to his brother's attitude. He was sometimes slow to act on instructions until driven by the force of Henry's anger, made fiercer by a growing suspicion that John would not keep secret his temporary ownership of the business.

At last, Thursday 21st July arrived and the court sat to hear the result of the referee's deliberations. As Mr Hill raised objection after objection to decisions made by Mr Enslie which were not adequately explained, Henry's optimism grew. Mr Enslie clarified the position by saying that, "as the books of both parties were unreliable all the sums he took up were from evidence given and not, as it may seem, from the accounts". Mr Hill again complained that, "if this had been a common case of book-keeping between two merchants, it would have been different; but now it is a question of veracity between Cook and Abbott, but the referee seems to have taken the part of Cook". Hearing this, Henry's confidence grew even stronger.

The judge adjourned the case until the following Tuesday to give the referee time to consider the comments of counsel, and to give reasons for his award. Henry's high hopes were somewhat dashed on Tuesday when, in front of Acting Judge Robertson, an award was ordered against him for $3,943.56. Although Abbott had lost most of his claim, Henry was furious and disappointed at having to pay anything, however small. His mood went from grey to black when, as the losing party, he was ordered to pay costs of the hearing and also to cover the referee's fee equally with Abbott.

Henry was an Irishman not given to accepting defeat without a fight. He instructed Mr Lowder to lodge an appeal immediately. As all appeals had to be referred to the Chief Justice of H.B.M's. Supreme Court for China and Japan in Shanghai, a final decision would not be known for many months.

34

In Very Deep Water

Although judgment was suspended pending the result of his appeal, Henry's instinct for survival led him to consider means of raising money towards the fees for his counsel and the referee whose decisions had been quite favourable. He still owned a quarter share in the *Otsego* which had recently returned from a disastrous hunting voyage securing only one otter skin! On the reputation of her past record with Captain Isaacs, her master and half-share owner, Henry managed to persuade a Captain Pearce to buy his quarter share for over $800. This move provided a boost to his cash balance without using funds from the business. His brother John retained his own quarter share.

Under Henry's renewed scrutiny, repairs to the *Cilurnum* progressed rapidly and restored some confidence and pride in himself, but his distrust of John grew at each encounter. Sometimes it affected his judgment as when Mr Hardy, a diver, placed an order for a small vessel to be built. On learning that Hardy was a close friend of John, Henry refused the order. He relented later and was persuaded to build the *Ada* during the winter of 1881/2.

On 20th May 1882 the result of Henry's appeal arrived from Shanghai. The Supreme Court upheld the judgment against him on eleven out of twelve points of objection raised by Mr Lowder. The Court dismissed a claim by Abbott for wages up to September 1875, amounting to $4,276, with a touch of dry, legalistic humour:

"By debiting the owners with this sum, the part-owner Abbott must be taken to have paid the master Abbott his wages up to that date. It was not necessary that he should take the dollars out of one pocket and put them into the other."

The humour was lost on Henry who now had the cost of the appeal added to his debt. The court's final decision failed to shake Henry's resolve not to give in to Abbott, even though his business could easily have withstood the payment of under $4,000. His unworthy plan of deception would have to be set in motion with a facade of truth sufficiently convincing to deceive the court at the next inevitable hearing.

Henry swallowed his pride and talked over the whole sorry situation with John. He had to agree that John's ownership of the business would have to be seen as a fact to the general public and, to enhance that appearance, Henry was to be put on the payroll as receiving $150 per month in wages. Part of the price he had to pay was the insufferable increase in John's arrogance towards him. People began to notice fierce arguments between the brothers. On several occasions Henry's temper reached breaking point and John was unceremoniously kicked out of the yard.

On Monday, 3rd July, Henry was summoned to show cause why he had not complied with the decree of the court ordering him to pay $3,943.56 to Abbott, the plaintiff. Henry, in the witness box, was close questioned by Mr Hill. The cross examination continued on the following Wednesday and Thursday. He gave some details of his early life but when asked to explain what he had done with various sums of money received during the past three or four years his replies were not at all precise. When the judge asked him to explain how he had disposed of the last instalment of $2,500 for his property, he rather lamely said, "it had gone in gambling and drinking".

By Wednesday the questioning by Mr Hill began to probe the validity of the transfer of Henry's property and he was uncomfortably close to the truth. Mr Enslie was questioned about the change of date noted in the official register. He assumed that if such an error existed it would have been made by the Registrar, not himself. Both Mr White and Mr Walker were called by Mr Hill to testify but affirmed their belief that the transfer was genuine.

For the first time John was issued with a subpoena to attend as witness. His opening statement when questioned was that "he believed he was brother to Mr Cook but had no recollection of him as a boy". Little wonder, as he was less than one year of age when Henry left home! He explained that all receipts signed by Henry for cash advances on his property were destroyed after transfer was completed. He said that Henry was paid $150 per month but with no written agreement and was liable to be discharged at any time. It was obvious to Mr Hill that Henry's case had no substance.

When the case was resumed on Tuesday, 11th July, Mr Hill was determined to expose the deception. Addressing court, his accusation was explicit. He said that:

> "Through certain facts that have come to my knowledge since the adjournment
> I could, given the opportunity of putting certain persons in the witness box, prove
> positively that the property said to have been disposed of by Cook has been simply

fraudulently transferred for the purpose of his escape from his liabilities. I intend to ask His Honour to grant execution against the property so transferred and, under certain circumstances, that Cook be committed to prison for the full term and utmost limit. I also . . ."

here Mr Lowder intervened and his objection was upheld by the judge.

In the cold light of this open accusation, the enormity of his folly was crystal clear and Henry experienced shame as never before. Mr Hill was not at first deterred by the judge and several times began the same theme until Mr Lowder complained successfully that, "Mr Cook was only before the court on the judgment summons and no charge of perjury could now be imported into the case." The judge agreed and Henry was saved.

The final judgment was that the decree must stand but should, in view of Henry's wage of $150, be paid at the rate of only $50 per month. The first payment was to be made on 1st August.

Now that John's ownership of the H.Cook business was public knowledge, he could no longer contain his sense of power over his brother. His bumptious manner arose from the knowledge that he was totally incapable of running Henry's business, whatever the public believed. His inexperience and shallow character surfaced at every stage of the work except in the details of forging metal. Deep down he knew that he could not use the prize in his grasp before returning it to Henry at a safe date in the future.

But, there was nothing to prevent him from using up the income while he remained the boss!

35

Face To Face With Reality

Emily, William and Beatrice were all home for the long summer holiday. Henry had forbidden them to come to the court. They had tried to follow the proceedings from the newspaper reports but much of the legal wrangling was beyond their understanding. Emily had only just had her thirteenth birthday. Henry had made up his mind to give them a guarded explanation without giving them any cause for worry. Halfway through his talk, young Willie blurted out that Uncle John had told them that be now owned Daddy's business. Henry had not believed that John would go that far and he tried to counter it by saying that Uncle John was looking after some of the business for a year or two. From that moment John became the new enemy to defeat and Henry felt almost friendly towards Abbott, who was an adversary only through an ill-considered battle of wits.

The family discussion was interrupted by tragedy far deeper than their own, which restored a spark of compassion into Henry's dark thoughts. Two of his coolies, both dripping wet, hammered on the door of his house. One of them cradled the body of a child in his arms. She was a little Japanese girl of about five years of age and the men happened to see her floating in the Creek just outside the shipyard. The poor girl was obviously quite dead but Henry's children instinctively rushed to get a blanket to restore some warmth to the cold wet body. The police discovered that she had been missing from a house in Ishikawa since Thursday, 13th July, only two days before. How did it happen? Henry could glean no details about parents in order to help them. Had the little child committed suicide? Was that possible for one so young?

The Creek was often used by Japanese wishing to commit suicide. One Tuesday midnight a policeman noticed a woman in the mud below the Nishinobashi, the bridge crossing the Creek near 115. He pulled her out and found her pockets to be full of stones. She too came from Ishikawa and confessed to trying to commit suicide after a quarrel with her husband, Sanada Kokichi. In the darkness she had not noticed that the tide was out!

The history of ritual suicide in Japan is well documented but the urge to 'save face' or resolve some private difficulty by suicide was quite usual among all classes. Men often resorted to drowning themselves but rarely cut their throats; women frequently favoured this mode of self-destruction. Suicide pacts were common among frustrated lovers who sought a watery grave bound together. A train driver reported how he was unable to stop when a young man and a remarkably beautiful girl lay down on the line holding hands as his train approached. A desperate mother had tied the hands of her children and was just prevented from plunging to death with them. Her husband spent all their money on drink.

More bizarre was the case of a farmer who had been infatuated with a girl from his village for a long time. She left and was very happily married, but the farmer never lost his intense jealousy. Finally he went to her home, forced his way in, beheaded her with his sword, caught the husband when he was trying to escape and stabbed him many times to his death. He then took the girl's head to his home, placed it on a table where he sat facing it, severely harangued it and finally cut his own throat. The Japanese press loved to report these incidents in great detail.

One or two cases had been reported of foreign residents committing suicide, usually because of extreme financial troubles, but never through love, jealousy or need to save face. That scenario was not for Henry. He was a fighter, even if he sometimes hit out blindly. Support from friends continued but they could not dispel his inner feeling of frustration and a deep sense of guilt whenever his thoughts turned to Mary Julia. It was after visiting her grave with the children that he felt compelled to go to the church and renew a practice neglected for many months. He unburdened himself to the priest and, as most penitents find, the priest merely revealed truths of which he was already acutely aware but needed strong help to face.

The path to forgiveness and peace of mind was uncompromising. He had to restore truth where he had lied and pay what was due to Abbott, in money and apology. Henry left the priest feeling clean, full of resolve and without fear of the path he had now chosen. His only worry was concern over the children. Would they forgive him? Could their love for him survive the publicity and the possibility of his being sent to prison? He decided to pay a long overdue visit to see Reverend Mother at the Convent before going home. She was pleased to see him and listened to his explanation of events with a grave but sympathetic silence. He expressed his concern for the children and warned that a situation could develop in which he would be without money for the school fees. Reverend Mother relieved him of that worry and added that, although Emily was still only thirteen, by the next year she would be able to give language tuition to young day pupils whose parents requested private coaching. The small fees could help. Henry was amazed and closed his eyes to hide the emotion he felt as he realised how little he knew his children, Mary Julia's children.

The road back was not going to be easy but his resolve was tested to the limit when Reverend Mother asked whether John had set the date for the wedding! Wedding? . . . She confided that John had been visiting the convent regularly to see Rosie. They had spent many hours together in the convent grounds and, only last week, John had asked permission for their marriage. She had given her consent, hoping it would give Rosie a chance to make a life for herself in the world as her true origins had never been established. Fury was coaxed into resignation as Henry could see married life might soften John's manner and occupy him away from the shipyard. Before leaving the convent Henry was able to see Rosie who, after all, was almost one of his family. He promised to give her away at the wedding and tried to disguise his reservations as to John's suitability.

Poor Henry could not resist confronting John with the sly secrecy surrounding his intentions towards Rosie. He realised his indiscretion as a satisfied smile crossed John's face, followed by a rejoinder that now he was a man of means he was quite independent from Henry. The wedding was celebrated quietly in low key with Henry, confessing later, "as a very reluctant witness". John soon demonstrated his determination to spend money. He and Rosie moved into No. 45c The Bluff, the better class residential area, and furnished the house at a cost of more than $2,300 with insurance cover for $2,000. It was soon noticed and remarked upon by callers that a considerable quantity of silver was displayed in the house of such an ordinary working man.

Henry had resolved to demand restoration of his business rights, as agreed at the time of the fraudulent transfer, but stayed his hand out of some minimal respect for the first weeks of John's marriage. Further postponement was forced on him by the not entirely unexpected death of Anthony.

Anthony's health had steadily deteriorated during the past three years through his weakness for strong drink. For six or seven months he had been unable to contribute any practical labour in the workshop but had continued as manager, with a strong reliance on Henry and John to oversee the work.

Finally the doctor, who had been visiting him at regular intervals, decided he needed special treatment and arranged for him to be admitted to the General Hospital. His devoted Japanese servant, Waka Sen, tearfully relinquished her charge. For thirteen years she had earned Anthony's complete trust and confidence and nursed him during his frequent bouts of illness. The doctors were not able to prolong Anthony's life and he died on 12th November. Waka Sen, showing the most distress, left to join her husband at No.33, Tsukiji, Tokyo, where he was cook and she became an *amah*. Anthony was buried in the Foreign Cemetery directly from the hospital.

Henry, John, Rosie and the children were joined at the graveside by some of the workmen. Anthony had encouraged very few friends. Even the children more readily warmed to John as an uncle, finding in him an appropriate response. At last, if only for a short time, Henry and John were united as brothers in a common purpose. Could Anthony heal their wounds through his death? Sadly it was a miracle he was unable to perform.

With Anthony's death the management of the Carroll & Co. workshops passed to John. Within a few weeks the brotherly bond was strained to breaking point. The haughty rudeness from John, following this added source of power, rekindled Henry's resolve to end it. He demanded that John should act upon the original agreement between them and relinquish all claims to Henry's property temporarily entrusted to him. John refused, arguing that the court had accepted him as the rightful owner. Henry approached Rosie, hoping to enlist some sort of filial concern for his position, but she hurt him deeply by pouring scorn on the idea that her husband was not the true owner. She had no intention of giving up the source of her newly-found freedom and wealth.

Henry's first lucky break did not come until the December of 1883. After the transfer in 1880 Henry kept all the deeds and promissory notes in his safe at 115 as there had been no question of its being a permanent change. Sometimes the deeds were deposited with a Captain Martin to raise a small loan required in running the business. During the trial of 1882, Mr Lowder had required the deeds in court as part of Henry's defence, with a promise to return them after the hearing. Unfortunately, John was able to procure them from Mr Lowder's chambers and had kept them locked away at his home on the Bluff. However, because of his extravagance, John needed to raise some money urgently. He took the deeds to Captain Martin and left them with a promissory note for $500. About a fortnight later, Henry received some overdue payment into the shipyard which he promptly used to redeem the deeds. Once again he had them securely locked away in his own safe! Possession brought confidence. It was the first stage in his fight to establish the truth.

36
Judge Hannen's Dilemma

Henry began to obstruct John's use of equipment in the shipyard. As John became more and more disagreeable, Henry refused him entry until John almost ceased work there for the whole of 1884. Henry took over management of the blacksmith's shop and gave extra responsibility to one of the foremen.

The next stage in his fight back to self-esteem and a quiet conscience was to make peace with Abbott. Although Abbott was working as a sail-maker and rigger at No.43 Yokohama, Henry thought it wiser to meet him in his home at No. 217 The Bluff. The first meeting began full of tension but, as Henry apologised for trying to win his case unfairly and promised to make restitution as soon as possible, the atmosphere became noticeably more relaxed. Henry explained that he would keep up the monthly payments but could only pay off the whole debt if he were finally able to wrestle his property back from John. Abbott warned Henry that he would have to admit to committing perjury if he wanted to achieve that end. Henry replied that he was ready to face the ordeal.

Abbott contributed his own apologies for his high-handed use of the *Parmenio* and its almost total loss. A silent handshake restored a mutual trust that should never have been broken. Whilst sharing a drink in celebration, Abbott took Henry back twenty-four years by reminding him how he had slaughtered the very first beef for food in 1860. He showed him a notice in the "Mail" that the number of bullocks killed for food, just in Osaka for one year, had reached 4,530. He laughingly accused Henry of being responsible for changing the Japanese diet! They continued to meet on a friendly basis and Henry gained an ally against John, a fact suspected in court during a later hearing.

A reasonable flow of work still came to the shipyard but Henry had to find extra money for his personal use which could not be taken out of the business at that time. He solved this problem by accepting occasional offers of work for wages with the Pacific Mail and Mitsu Bishi companies. Urged on by his wife, Rosie, John decided on a final bid to secure his bogus claim against

Henry by seeking the court's help to acquire the original deeds, keys and full access to the business, all still under Henry's control. The trial was to begin on Friday, 27th March 1885.

This time Mr Litchfield would appear for Henry and Mr Kirkwood for John. Henry confided the whole truth to his counsel of the deceit planned by himself and John, of John's present refusal to acknowledge it and of his own renewed association with Abbott. Mr Kirkwood opened for John and claimed that Henry's retention of the deeds and other documents was unlawful. He then gave a lengthy account of John's claim, already thoroughly aired in earlier stages of the saga, punctuated with legal references.

Mr Litchfield called John to the witness box and questioned him closely to show how unlikely it was that he would have had sufficient money saved to buy Henry's business from him in 1880. Would he really have been so careless as to allow Henry to keep the promissory notes, still in Henry's possession, if he had actually paid the cash amounts there promised? In addition, was it not strange that John had burned the receipts he claims to have had from Henry for those large sums of money? This line of questioning seemed to be succeeding until the judge intervened. He upheld the feasibility of John's plea that he had trusted his brother and had seen no need for taking such precautions. Was the judge going to show prejudice in favour of John? Henry remembered that the presiding judge was the same Judge Hannen who had rejected his first appeal to the Supreme Court in Shanghai.

It was at this point that Mr Litchfield began to introduce the concept of fraud into the case. He submitted that Henry was:

"a hard-working man led by the advice of others to commit an indiscretion, if not an act technically called by a more severe name, the consequences of which he had suffered for years, and for which he was finally brought to punishment by those with whose assistance he had committed the indiscretion. He was now aware of his indiscretion and craved only from the Court justice tempered with more mercy than had been tendered to him by the brother who had assisted him in his previous purpose. He could not for a moment defend the action of the man Cook in making the statements that he had previously made but his client's only wish was to save from the wreck some slight amount of the earnings of a hard-spent life for his family."

Mr Kirkwood rose angrily to complain that Mr Litchfield was trying to set the whole matter aside on the score of fraud. If it was fraud the sale was invalid.

The judge observed that the story now told was consistent with the defence. Mr Kirkwood retorted that a suggestion of fraud also cast a reflection on his client for which there was no ground. Judge Hannen confessed to a dilemma. He agreed that Henry's attempt to admit to fraud was not part of the original court hearing but, on the other hand, it would be wrong for the court not to give every opportunity for such a gross fraud to be exposed. It also posed another problem that, if the confession were true, he would be in danger of "putting the court in motion to force one fraudulent person to give up to another fraudulent person certain deeds and land." He therefore gave Mr Litchfield until the next day to consider what steps he should take.

Mr Litchfield, now sure that Henry's aim was to reimburse Abbott, decided on a very unusual approach. His reply to the court on the following day was that Henry was entitled to retain the deeds as the unpaid vendor of the property. If that plea proved unacceptable, the alternative was that the original transaction was planned to avoid legal process against the property. He submitted that Henry had the option of either course and the court could decide which of the two to follow. If the deeds were passed to John, then John would become the fraudulent possessor! Mr Kirkwood thought that such an application was without precedent in the records of any court. So Henry was unexpectedly involved in yet another "first"! After much complicated legal argument, Mr Litchfield decided to pursue the first option that his client was the unpaid vendor. The case was adjourned until Tuesday, 31st March.

When the case was resumed Henry tried, through his counsel, to plead for an amendment to his defence that John only held the property in trust for him. He explained to the court that:

> "It has come to my knowledge since the commencement of these proceedings that the plaintiff (John) has admitted to certain persons in Yokohama that he holds this property in trust for me."

Mr Kirkwood viewed the statement with grave suspicion, explaining that in all probability it was an untruth.

The judge also decided he could not allow the amendment as the statement was far too "freshly convenient". Mr Litchfield made no attempt to press the point and said that he would now accept the judgment of the court. The date for reconvening was left open pending the scrutiny of all accounts and papers. Mr Litchfield gave notice that he would file a petition on behalf of Henry's children.

37
The Emperor Remembers

With the case still unresolved, Captain Abbott thought it opportune to take advantage of the confusion. In consulting with Henry and Mr Litchfield, he suggested the possibility of suing Henry and John together for the balance of money owed to him. He reasoned that either one or the other, or both, owned the property against which he had a claim! Henry liked the idea and agreed to allow Mr Litchfield to act for Abbot if the law would condone such a switch. Mr Litchfield agreed to appear for Abbott and the new case was arranged to be heard on 13th October 1885. Mr Kirkwood understandably refused to act for Henry with his brother, but Henry was quite happy to conduct his own defence as he wished Abbot to win.

The ramifications of the proceedings intrigued the Yokohama community and provided a natural topic for conversation and debate as the detailed reports were read in the "Japan Weekly Mail". They began to take sides; most were backing Henry as they approved that the man they trusted was apparently trying to make restitution for a past indiscretion.

The next court session was six months away and Henry had to make provision for any outcome. He knew that eventually he would be given some form of punishment for his perjury, probably a term of imprisonment. The future of his children, servants and workers in the shipyard was a source of great anxiety to him. Quite unexpectedly the commendable Japanese family tradition of honouring obligations of goodwill shown to them, even generations later, came to his rescue. The Emperor was anxious that members of the Royal Household should be able to speak and understand the English language. He was advised that English women were very good teachers of the language and would be particularly suitable for instructing the Japanese women and children of the Household. The linguistic reputation of the St. Maur nuns was well known among cultured Japanese circles, so an emissary was sent to the Convent to seek their help.

Reverend Mother had kept her word and Emily had been given charge of the extra-curricular tuition of several backward pupils. By using young Beatrice to help her, Emily had achieved some very creditable results. Reverend Mother was shrewd enough to see a 'heaven sent' solution to the problems of both the Emperor and Henry, although their needs could not have been more diverse. She gave her honest opinion to the emissary that Emily and Beatrice could provide an excellent and discreet service to the Emperor but stressed that first their father must be consulted. A messenger was sent with an urgent request for Henry to return with him to the Convent to talk with an envoy from the Palace. Such a request could not lightly be refused!

Henry had a private interview with Reverend Mother and was given a detailed account of the Emperor's wish and her own response. He could see the obvious advantage in giving his consent, but he questioned the part Beatrice could play when not ready to leave school at only thirteen years of age. He was assured that Emily found Beatrice very helpful with young children and that a delay of a year or two would not spoil her education. On the contrary, the experience could be highly beneficial. Henry was persuaded but he still had one serious reservation. The Emperor must not become associated in any way with what could become a criminal trial. He needed to obtain a rarely granted interview with His Majesty. The emissary looked very doubtful at the request but promised to act on Henry's next suggestion. He would remind the Emperor that he was the Henry Cook who had salvaged his yacht fifteen years earlier.

About a week later, Henry received a private invitation and went with the messenger to the Tokyo Palace, where he was carefully instructed in the intricate protocol required at such audiences. Henry felt stiff and ill at ease in his best western suit compared with the flowing, quiet movement displayed by the Court officials in their loose robes. As he approached, he was directed to a deep cushion placed in front of a low table. Behind it sat, not the Emperor, but a Court official, relaxed and smiling. While easing himself down into a squatting position, made awkward by his tight trousers, Henry saw in the centre of the table the carved model of a schooner which he had sent to the Emperor so many years before. The Emperor had not forgotten! It was a wise and considerate gesture by his Majesty to allow that simple model to bridge the vast difference between their backgrounds and experience.

Henry had little need of the interpreter and, encouraged by the Official's apparent willingness to listen, he gave an honest account of his predicament not excluding his fears for the future. It must have seemed strange to a

Japanese in high office that a man would seek the punishment of imprisonment to 'save face' but his expression betrayed no such thought.   After formally assuring the Official that he was pleased and honoured for his daughters to be of service in the Royal Household, Henry lapsed into the more natural role of an anxious father.   He explained that his wife had died and, lacking her help, he was most grateful that the girls would be looked after during his impending trial and possible period of imprisonment.   This left one other cause for worry, the safety of his son, As Henry spoke he had the distinct impression that the Official was already well informed and that his deliberations had been anticipated.   He was further convinced when the Official quickly suggested that William would be a beneficial western companion for the boys in the Household.   He beamed with pleasure as Henry's face recorded his amazement.   William's name had not previously been mentioned.   The Japanese system of acquiring information was second to none.   Henry lowered his head to conceal how close he was to tears of relief as he felt that major burden taken from him.

It was arranged that Henry would bring the children to the Palace in July, after Emily had finished her duties at the Convent and finally left school. Although not requested, Henry made a solemn promise that he would not reveal to anyone, not even to his brother or his counsel, that his children were being cared for at the Palace.   The Official nodded his approval and the interview was ended.   As he moved backwards towards the door, bowing at intervals, Henry hoped he had remembered the procedure correctly.

38

Judge Hannen Is Convinced

As Henry left the Palace, light-footed with the buoyancy of relief, he surveyed the intimate scenes of Tokyo with a renewed interest and pleasure. Something of his youthful flair for making simple clear-cut decisions had returned, no longer clouded by deceit and anxiety. His future course was clear and he was at peace with himself.

He returned to Yokohama by train and reflected with pride, thrusting bitterness aside, that his two brothers had given much of their lives to the construction of this railway. As the train crossed the iron bridge at Kawasaki, Henry could not fail to approve its sound construction, some of it supervised by John during his last four years as foreman blacksmith. What a strong team the three brothers would have made had they been blessed with a single mind and a common purpose!

Reverend Mother was openly delighted with Henry's good news and was sufficiently wordly-wise to recognise the need for absolute secrecy. She agreed to reveal nothing to the children concerning the exciting prospect planned for them. The Principal of William's college was not so pleased when Henry told him that his son would not be returning for the following school year. Perhaps that was due to the fact that Henry gave no explanation for his decision other than to plead change of circumstances.

When the children came home at the end of the school year, Henry allowed himself to enjoy their company for a few days before calling an historic family conference which would change the course of their lives, without exception. The children noticed the new light-hearted bearing of their father; they liked what they saw but were the more puzzled by his serious manner when he called them to a very formal meeting in the sitting room. After making sure the servants had left as instructed, Henry gave a full and frank account of all that had happened. He was shocked at the distress shown by Beatrice when he explained that he might have to serve some time in prison and at her resistance to his attempts to comfort her. Fortunately she was soon caught up in the general excitement as he told them about their immediate future in the Imperial Household. They would be safe and cared for. They each promised the secrecy demanded of them, not to reveal any hint to servants or friends, not even to Uncle John.

Just a few things were packed and, after the thrill of travelling to Tokyo by train, they were taken directly to the Palace. Henry was allowed into the Palace with them so that he could see where they would be living. Emily and Beatrice could not conceal their pleasure as they learned that they would live in traditional Japanese style, including native dress. William was no so sure. He was already wondering how to modify the male costume! Henry was given permission to visit them once each week until they had settled into a comfortable routine. The children had not seen tears in their father's eyes since the death of their mother and yet this time his face looked happy, not sad. Henry found cheap native lodgings in Tokyo and remained there for five weeks, at peace away from lawyers and content to see his children for a brief visit each week.

At last it was time for Henry to return and face the legal hurdles ahead, which he did with confidence. He could see the way forward quite clearly. Unfortunately he forgot that lawyers seemed suspicious of clear black and white solutions. Even before the hearing began, when Abbott was the plaintiff suing both Henry and John for a final settlement, Mr Kirkwood put in a request. Acting on John's behalf, he attempted to have Henry dropped as co-defendant for fear of John's implication in Henry's plea of fraud. Judge Hannen refused the request as Abbott was accusing the brothers of joint fraud.

The hearing began on Tuesday, 13th October 1885. Abbott's claim was quite straightforward. He had received $1,600 by monthly instalments. This slow recompense was due solely to the amendment made to the original judgment through false statements sworn by the brothers on oath. He now demanded that the amendment be cancelled and the remaining $2,343.65 be paid in full. Mr Litchfield, now acting for Abbott, explained that his client had decided to reopen his case to see if he could take advantage of the "falling out of these two brothers over their dishonest transaction". Mr Litchfield then informed the court that Henry had consented to his appearing for Abbott, in spite of leaving himself without counsel. He then explained that he had made this comment because "it might be attempted to be made out that the plaintiff Abbott and the defendant Cook were acting in collusion, but in reality Cook had nothing to gain by the success or failure of the action". The comment probably implanted the truth that there was indeed collusion!

As expected, when Mr Kirkwood took the floor he immediately tried to prove collusion and so, this time, to have John struck from the action. He claimed that Henry had either perjured himself in 1882 to avoid paying the debt all at once, or he was now perjuring himself to be rid of the entire debt. He then produced witnesses from the railway company to vouch for John's good character and his possible ability to have saved sufficient money to pay for the transaction legitimately.

Mr Litchfield read the evidence, taken by Commission at Shanghai, from William Walker who had helped in the original transfer by evaluating the stock and premises. After giving a clear account of his involvement, adding the usual complaint of inadequate book-keeping, Walker ended his statement by affirming that -

"... from various conversations between myself, Cook and John Carroll I became convinced that the sale by Cook to John Carroll was not a bona fide transaction, but was fictitious and made to defeat the claim of Abbott. In fact, on more than one occasion both Cook and Carroll stated or implied that such was the fact in an unmistakable manner."

John Carroll was then called to the witness stand by his own counsel, Mr Kirkwood. A very poorly-worded admission, made just before standing down, turned the Yokohama community irrevocably against John as the truth of his action became clear. Henry had gradually closed down his business and let it be known that he could accept no new orders. This also affected the flow of work into the blacksmith's workshop in 120 and John was becoming very short of money. After selling much of his furniture and silver, he resorted to a more desperate course of action. During Henry's five week stay in Tokyo, an absence which John could not fathom, the office was only casually attended. Taking advantage of easy access, John was able to gain possession of the much disputed deeds.

Ever since he had realised Henry's determination to make them both suffer for the perjury they had committed, fear had replaced greed as the prime motivator. With the approval of his wife, Rosie, it was decided to raise as much money as possible and leave Japan before the beginning of the trial. To use the stolen deeds in a public sale of 115 and 120 Creekside would have been far too risky and involve use of legal processes from which he was hoping to escape. He succeeded in raising a lesser sum by lodging them as security against a loan, a resource with which he was all too familiar.

With cash in hand, the way seemed clear and John booked a passage for himself and his wife on the *Catherine Sudden* with the expectation of sailing just one day before the opening of the trial. John was out of luck. His passage was recorded in the official sailing lists and was noticed by a sharp-eyed member of the British Consulate staff. The Consul informed Mr Kirkwood of his intention and together they persuaded John to cancel his trip. They argued that to leave would be seen as an admission of guilt, that he should stay and attempt to save his good name. However, his good name was to be lost for ever as he revealed in court to the public:

"I asked to get a passage by the "Catherine Sudden" and it was granted, but I saw the Consul and Mr Kirkwood and saw the position I was in."

Mr Litchfield considered that his rush to leave the country was "one of the straws that showed the direction of the wind" and most of Yokohama voiced agreement.

When the court resumed sitting on 19th October, Mr Lowder, who was concerned that Henry had no counsel, tried to speak on his behalf and to recall Mr White as a witness. Judge Hannen was reluctant to allow this deviation and asked what defence Mr Cook wished to present. Mr Lowder explained that his defence was an admission of everything stated in the petition but wished to bring more evidence to support it. The Judge disallowed the intervention and said that Mr Cook must prove his defence through questions asked by Mr Abbott and his counsel.

There followed a very lengthy summing-up by both counsel detailing points raised during the past three and half years' litigation. Mr Litchfield ended by contrasting John's attempt to leave the country and the evidence of Henry -

"who now wished to make reparation for the error he had committed, certainly reparation he had been driven to make, but still he wished to do it."

Judgment was reserved for four days until 24th October, giving the public plenty of time to speculate and a climax to anticipate. Henry's friends continued to support him in his courageous efforts to regain a reputation for honesty and straight dealing. Since returning from Tokyo Henry had been staying with Mr Thomas Rose at No.116, from which address he continued to tie up loose ends of business. The support of such a staunch friend was invaluable during the final weeks of legal battle.

On 24th October Judge Hannen delivered his judgment to a full court. He gave a clear explanation of his deliberations in such a balanced manner that must have confirmed public confidence in its judiciary:-

"In this case, I reserved judgment because of the importance of the case to some, if not all, of the parties and to the public. When gentlemen on a jury have to consider their verdict, if upon turning round it appears that they are unanimous it is not necessary for them to deliberate further. If five men at once come to the same conclusion it may be safely assumed that it is warranted by the evidence. But the case is different with a single judge. It is sometimes just and necessary that he should carefully go through the evidence to see that he has not gathered a wrong impression from it, and has not overlooked anything which makes in favour of the side which at the conclusion of the trial he is inclined to condemn. I have done so in this case. I have carefully perused and considered the evidence and the very accurate report in the JAPAN MAIL of the addresses of the Counsel. I ought not to pass these by without saying that they were both able and exhaustive. Notwithstanding the very strenuous defence and ability of Mr. Kirkwood, I do not believe his client's story. Taking the whole case into consideration, moreover, I think the plaintiff has made out his allegations. I have convinced myself from Carroll's own statements that he had not and could not have paid over to Cook $9,190 by February 1879, and as he has repeatedly sworn that he has, his whole testimony is discredited. I find for the plaintiff, and grant the first three prayers of his petition."

The second prayer of Abbott's petition was that the deeds of assignment or conveyances of 14th June 1880 be declared void and reconveyed to Henry Cook so that the sum of money due may be made against those properties. Judge Hannen had made his own opinion clear to the court. Assistant Judge Robertson then proceeded to charge each of the brothers separately with perjury.

39
Judgement Versus Logic

Judge Robertson charged each of the brothers in turn, beginning with John. He was charged with having committed perjury in the testimony he gave on 14th October 1885. In answer he denied the charge and said he was telling nothing but the truth. He was told he must remain in custody until 2nd November unless he could obtain bail. John replied that he would have to see his wife before saying anything, that he did not know anyone to ask for bail and had only his clothing to give as security. This was the first time that John's remarks hinted that his wife was probably the driving force behind his actions against Henry.

Henry was charged with having committed perjury in the hearing of the judgment summons on 5th July 1882. He pleaded guilty. The Judge required two sureties in his case of $500 each. Henry said he thought Mr Rose would be one and he should be able to find another. Neither brother was charged with the fraud implied by their perjury.

Resuming after a few hours adjournment, Mr Lowder for Henry said "he was prepared with five good solid British subjects who would go bail for his client, and he could produce more if necessary". The Judge said he would be satisfied with two. Mr Rose and Captain Hardy were entered for Henry. Mr Kirkwood finally managed to secure Mr Aldrich and Mr Brown for John.

Both brothers surrendered to their bail on 2nd November. In the morning, during the hearing against John, Mr White was called as witness and revealed that, knowing he was friendly towards Henry, Mr Kirkwood had asked him to try to persuade Henry to settle and not to appear in court during the Abbott v. Cook and Carroll hearing. In return John would pay half the monthly instalment to Abbott and Mr Kirkwood would tell Henry what to say in court. Apparently Henry had answered in typical fashion, "I will see him damned first!" John was further remanded until 10th November when he was finally committed for trial.

In the afternoon Henry was formally accused and without hesitation he pleaded guilty to the charge. His Honour then committed him for trial. The same bail as before would be satisfactory for both brothers.

On 1st December 1885 Henry faced his judge and jury and was charged with the crime of perjury by Mr Litchfield acting as Crown Prosecutor. The long indictment ended with a colourful description of his crime,

"... it was charged against the said Henry Cook that on the 3rd and 5th days of July 1882, he did of his own act and consent, and of his own wicked and corrupt mind, in manner and form aforesaid falsely, wickedly, wilfully and corruptly, commit wilful and corrupt perjury."

Henry did not think of his indiscretion in quite those terms but he nevertheless pleaded guilty. In reply he merely reiterated how the deeds were transferred. Judge Hannen was not in sympathetic mood with this case which had occupied Yokohama gossip for so many years. He concluded:

"What you are saying now is not only no reason why sentence should not be passed upon you, but if you went on with it would probably rather be to your detriment that anything else. What you are accused of, and what you have pleaded guilty to, is having committed perjury upon a certain occasion. What you did before and by whose advice you did it cannot excuse that. You have pleaded to a charge of perjury - of perjury which you committed three years ago - by which the court was deceived and your creditor defrauded. You do not seem to have repented of your perjury and fraud until there was no longer anything to be gained by them. I trust you have been actuated by some good motive, but your conduct has not been such as to induce the Court to take a light view of your offence. May your example deter others from entering upon such a course as yours. The sentence of the Court is that you be imprisoned and be kept at hard labour for eighteen months from this day."

His Honour then dismissed the jurymen who had been summoned, and the Court rose.

Facilities for administering such sentences were very limited for the British in Yokohama. For Henry the 'hard labour' was more a lack of the hard work he always found so therapeutic. He was given his own suite of rooms and was allowed visitors on a fairly regular basis, many of whom still sought his professional advice. Permission was given for the family cook, first employed by Mary Julia, to join him in his exile from public life. The traditionally-worded sentence given by the judge bore no resemblance to the real punishment which was self-imposed by Henry, the public admission of his dishonesty.

John was still a free man but was his freedom more to be envied than Henry's imprisonment? After the Judge found in favour of Abbott, John had to spend every last dollar to redeem the deeds of 115 and 120 so that they could be lodged with the court. His wife, Rosie, was furious at the turn of events as she saw her plans for a comfortable life crumbling irretrievably.

John's trial for perjury began on 14th January 1886 with Mr Litchfield again acting as Crown Prosecutor. Mr Kirkwood, still representing John, promptly objected to two members of the jury who had interests in the case and they were replaced. Henry was brought from prison as a witness for the Crown. When questioned about his children he kept his promise to the Emperor and declared, "I do not know where my children are living." As the trial developed, it became clear that John's innocence or guilt hinged on the delicate balance between common sense and the restrictions and safeguards imposed by legal practice.

For the prosecution, Mr Litchfield failed to produce witnesses who could positively affirm their knowledge of the fraudulent transaction. He explained that the best witness, Mr Walker, could not be brought from Shanghai at Crown expense and his firm statement so effective in determining Henry's perjury could not be used in the present trial, nor could any previous evidence. He suggested that the jury might like to consider the common sense view that as John had confirmed in 1882 the statements for which Henry had been found guilty, then John must be equally guilty.

Mr Kirkwood quickly reminded the jury that they must be influenced only by what was said in the present court hearing. He made great play of the Crown's poor witnesses and produced some very effective character witnesses for John from his past employers on the railway. He also questioned the validity of Henry's evidence for the Crown, pointing out that he was already serving a prison sentence for making untrue statements and was known to dislike his brother. Any statement by Henry must therefore be substantiated by two or more witnesses, or one witness supported by very convincing evidence. Mr Enslie was a very influential witness against any suggestion of fraud. He had been promoted to the post of Consul for Nagasaki and had arrived only the previous day on the *Nagoya Maru* at his own expense. He was the one man from whom the brothers had kept all hint of fraud, so that his transfer of the property could not be other than perfect in support of John's claim but which, if allowed, must surely mean that Henry's statements in 1882 were not lies!

When John's turn came to make a statement, he was about to read from a paper proposed by his counsel but Judge Hannen intervened and insisted he should speak for himself. The resulting plea was most humiliating in its confusion. He even complained that his wife was not allowed to speak for him! Mr Kirkwood turned to the jury seeking sympathy for the painful position of his client and seemed to get it.

After each counsel had made his final appeal to the jury, Judge Hannen gave his own summing-up of the evidence in his usual very fair manner. Once again he praised the excellent reporting in the "Japan Mail" and advised the jury that they could use it to remind themselves of what had been said. He criticised Mr Kirkwood's exaggerated comments on the conduct of the case by the Crown. He acknowledged that the non-appearance of Mr Walker was a blow to the Crown prosecution. He made clear the various points charged against John and added that it was strange that he had waited passively for five years before bringing action against Henry, yet was supposed to have put all his savings into the transaction. He thought it was in favour of the Crown that, in all that time, John had assumed the position of a workman and not that of a proprietor. He had even complained to a witness that he should have been paid overtime but had not been paid. The Judge also commented on John's claim that he took over the business to safeguard it for Henry's children against their father's drinking and gambling. He could not reconcile this apparent generosity with evidence from most of John's witnesses who claimed him to be a "mean and saving man".

In favour of John, Judge Hannen questioned the credibility of Henry as a true witness and reminded the jury that revenge could have been an additional motive for Henry's statements. He thought it strange that the brothers should have gone into the witness box and perjured themselves for $3,900 when they had property valued at $15,000. He also noted that the date Mr Enslie gave for changing the deeds raised doubts to suggest they were changed to defeat Abbott after receiving Abbott's letter posted in Amoy only fourteen days earlier. Mr Enslie claimed that he usually required at least three weeks to complete such a transaction. Finally he mentioned the excellent character given to John by his witnesses.

The jury then retired and, after an absence of exactly one hour, returned with a verdict of "Not Guilty". The foreman stated that "there is not sufficient evidence to convict the accused". The Judge concluded, "John Carroll, you are discharged."

As the crowded court rose, a buzz of conversation increased in emphasis as people surged into the street. They were puzzled. How could only one person be guilty in a crime where two people had to be guilty if the crime were in fact committed? The process of law had brought about an illogical situation. If John were truly innocent, then Henry must also be innocent. If Henry were guilty, then John had to be guilty in equal measure. Avid collectors of the "Japan Mail" reports were quick to point out that the same Judge Hannen had declared in his Judgment of 24th October:-

"I have convinced myself from Carroll's own statements that he had not and could not have paid over to Cook $9,190 by February 1879, and as he has repeatedly sworn that he has, his whole testimony is discredited."

The public were inclined to believe Henry's guilt and resented John's freedom.

40
Hounded Out

Henry had become an established favourite among a host of friends and business acquaintances during the twenty-six years of his residence in Yokohama. His imprisonment was something they found hard to accept even though they were resigned to his guilt. No doubt most of them could recall incidents of a shady nature forced on them by a tenuous footing in early Yokohama. Now other news could claim attention for discussion over drinks and tiffin, such as the use or misuse of the Japanese language. Particularly in Japan, good knowledge of the language was essential to intelligent intercourse with its people. As Henry and his family found, residence among the Japanese assumed an entirely different complexion when they were able to exchange ideas with inhabitants in the native tongue. In January 1886 a conference was being called to try to establish a universal system of phonetic Japanese and the local paper used the occasion to criticise lazy attitudes of the settlers:

> "The residents of the treaty ports appear to have made up their minds that the execrable pidgin which now serves to obscure their meaning and burlesque their ideas is sufficient for all purposes, whether of business or society."

Also in January came the sad news of the loss of the *Cilurnum* repaired so carefully by Henry's workforce less than five years earlier. Her cargo of coal, coke, pig-iron, bricks, etc. had been correctly stowed and the coal was thoroughly cleaned and shipped in dry weather. In spite of every precaution, the coal caught fire and exploded. Most of the boats were launched before she went down, stern first.

Friends were soon back in action when news was published on 13th February that a compromise had been reached between Abbott, Cook and Carroll. This meant that no appeal in the case would have to go to Shanghai. The court had to order the sale of much of the property still in John's name to finance the settlement with Abbott. A group of Henry's close friends had agreed to purchase such property as became available against his release from

222

prison. They were able to secure some items from No.120, but John retained the house at No.115, having sold his own house on the Bluff when about to flee the country.

There developed among the residents a strong movement to appeal against the length of the sentence to be suffered by Henry. Their petition was reported in the "Japan Mail" on 3rd April:

"We understand that a petition is being signed in Yokohama which it is intended to present to the Hon. Sir F.R. Plunkett, H.B.M. Minister, craving for a reduction of the period of imprisonment to which Henry Cook was sentenced. Cook, it will be remembered, pleaded guilty to perjury before Mr. Justice Hannen on 1st December last, and was adjudged to suffer eighteen months' imprisonment, of which term nearly four months have elapsed. The petition is being very generally and influentially signed."

The proprietors of the "Mail" must have felt something of the futility of having organised such complicated in-depth reporting of the Abbot v. Cook case for over four years and seeing it end with a simple compromise which should have been made in the beginning and passed unnoticed. A hint of this attitude creeps into their reporting of the Minister's reply one week later:

"The Honourable Sir Francis Plunkett has expressed his inability to comply with the request recently addressed to him by a number of the residents of Yokohama, on behalf of the man Cook, who is at present undergoing imprisonment for the crime of perjury. In order to return a favourable answer to such a petition the concurrence of the Judge of H.B.M.'s Court at Kanagawa is necessary, and Mr. Justice Hannen, we believe, declared himself unable to discover any reason for mitigating Cook's sentence. We confess that this decision does not surprise us. So far as we can perceive, Cook's only claim to pity is that his confession of perjury failed to accomplish its vindictive purpose, and it is evident that great differences of opinion may exist as to the value of such a claim."

Perhaps the long stint of faithful reporting seemed more justified when it was announced that in consequence of favourable comments made in court about "the fine reporting by the MAIL of Henry Cook's trial, but with inevitable inaccuracies", changes had now been made to the court room layout. In future, reporters should no longer experience the sound and visual difficulties which had interfered with the accurate recording of cases in the past.

During August, prison visits were stopped because of a severe outbreak of cholera. During the height of the epidemic all public places were closed.

Temperatures reached an uncomfortable 90 degrees in the shade. The prevalence of cholera in Tokyo led the War Office to decide to place all troops in the capital on a meat diet, but no scientific reason was given for the action. There was an official statement issued giving assurance that the practice of dumping cholera excreta in the sea had been discontinued. This was to allay fears that the bacteria might survive in the water and spread the infection. In Yokohama, 2,154 new cases were reported in just five weeks and 1,389 of them died. Towards the end of August there were signs that the epidemic was slowing down when in the last week only 81 cases were reported and 65 deaths.

The public resentment towards John and the misery of friendless isolation felt by both Rosie and himself finally brought to an end all efforts to enjoy their ill-gotten gains in Yokohama. They were both shunned on social occasions and John failed to find employment or contracts for any blacksmith's work; ready cash was dwindling at an alarming rate. Even Rosie's spirit was broken and she persuaded John that it was time to leave. Henry later commented that they were "hounded out of Yokohama" and he could be forgiven for a satisfied sense of justice.

The house and works at No.115 were put up for sale and Henry's friends were at last able to secure these for him. Their generosity could not run to purchasing the remaining stock and machinery. Flush with money from the sale, John and Rosie booked a passage to Hong Kong on the French steamer "Menzaleh" due to leave on 25th September 1886, carrying eighty-six bales of silk for France.

John never had the mental toughness of the true pioneer. Following little success in Hong Kong, he tried his luck working a plantation in Borneo with predictable results. Rosie drifted out of the family without trace, having drifted into the family tied to floating timber when only nine years old. The strain of life proved too much for John and he became mentally unstable. He retired to a quiet village in Ireland where his outbursts earned him the reputation of being "the wild man from Borneo".

41
Reunion And Readjustment

There was no fanfare when Henry was released from prison in 1887. The community had exhausted its arguments and speculation and accepted his return as day follows night. After opening up the house at No. 115, he spent a few days visiting his many loyal friends to thank them and to gain confidence from their reassuring company. While sharing a few drinks with an old family friend, George Alcock, Henry admitted that he had learned a hard lesson through his casual approach in business matters and was hoping to find a reliable accountant to keep his books in order. George drew his attention to a man who was drinking alone at the far end of the bar counter. The man's name was George Warnecke, a German accountant with the reputation of being "a wizard with figures". Apparently Warnecke was a little too fond of his drink, but Alcock assured Henry that "Warnecke drunk was worth ten men sober" when it came to book-keeping. On this recommendation Henry enlisted Warnecke's help for the future business. It was a decision to be regretted within a few years.

In prison Henry had been sheltered from the day-to-day responsibilities of running a business and was suffering a temporary loss of some of his natural self-confidence. Although relaxed in the company of George Alcock and his wife Mary, Henry was faced with an obvious question from them - "Where were his children?" Reminiscence about the old days when Mary Julia was alive had choked him with sadness and regret, and the whole story flowed from him with a rush of relief. George and Mary stared at him with disbelief until the logic of the situation brought appreciative smiles and congratulations. Henry explained that he had arranged to bring the children home but was anxious about meeting them after such a long absence and prison sentence. Mary offered to go with him to Tokyo, suggesting she could help the girls with anything they might need. Henry nodded his gratitude, unable to speak.

In her quiet way, Mary steered the family away from confrontation and embarrassment. Henry had imagined the reunion many times but nothing like the reality. The girls were no longer girls. They were young women, with hair coiffured in the latest style and dressed in sophisticated western clothes made by the Court Dressmaker. He could not hug them as he had dreamed, but stood awkwardly, uncertain and shy. Mary saved the situation with excited chatter and approving observations about their clothes. Henry was more at ease with William but even as they shook hands he sensed something different in his son's bearing, a remote self-assurance. During the train journey home, all three kept glancing at their father as if trying to inspect him without it being noticed. Did he look as though he had been in prison? How would old friends treat them, the girls from school and the boys at college?

HENRY COOK - Photography by Suzuki

Even greater changes were revealed in the girls when they arrived home. They began to organise rooms and furniture without reference to their father and to give instructions to the servants only recently employed by him. Henry was sad but could understand why they kept a distance from him and avoided the spontaneous hugs he used to enjoy. As he quietly stepped aside and allowed things to develop without interfering, it dawned on him why he was not angry or anxious. He was being comfortably lulled by familiar shades of Mary Julia. Life and responsibility within the Royal Household had encouraged the breeding and authority inherited from their mother to surface prematurely and it was being exercised quite naturally.

Henry Cook's two daughters, Emily on right, and Beatrice - home from duty at the Imperial Palace, 1887.

An understanding of what had happened matured Henry's love for the girls and he felt so proud of them that he insisted that they should be photographed together as a present to himself. Although Henry had previously used the studio of S. Suzuki, Emily preferred to try the studio recently opened by A. Farsari at No. 16 The Bund. This had replaced his premises at No 17 Yokohama, destroyed by fire the year before. The photographic business was flourishing in Japan, accelerated by the desire of the Japanese to adopt western costume and the absolute necessity of then being photographed in it! It was part of social experience to have a studio portrait taken, but elaborate staging and the use of slow speed negative plates, requiring the subject to remain quite motionless, introduced apprehension into an otherwise happy occasion. This probably led clients to return for future portraits to the studio where a degree of confidence had already been gained. Beatrice certainly followed this pattern, returning to Farsari as late as 1895.

Not all photographic experiences were happy ones. It was reported that one young Japanese boy was approached in the street by a stranger and asked if he would like to have his photograph taken. Wide-eyed and excited he agreed and was taken to a studio. His benefactor suggested to the photographer that the boy was an ideal subject for a 'nature' photograph and the boy's clothes were removed. On going to get dressed after the session, the boy found that this patron and his clothes had vanished.

The photographs of Emily and Beatrice were successful and captured the change Henry had recognised in them. Supported by Emily's reassurance, Henry concluded that William and Beatrice need not return to school. There had been opportunities for study with the private tutors employed at the Palace and their education had progressed on a much broader base than achieved in the normal way. Most unusual for people not of the Royal Household and surely unique among members of western culture, the children had learned to converse in Court Japanese (*Kyūchū Kotoba*). This was a form of Japanese used only by the nobility and never taught outside that circle. Even the Japanese population could understand very little of it. Emily's complete grasp of the language was later to be usefully employed by the U.S. government in a most unexpected manner.

Whilst at the Palace William had become very friendly with Prince Yoshihito, then only seven and a half years of age and not very robust. Under strict supervision William had been allowed to take his young charge for very short sailing trips on inland waters using a tiny single-sailed dinghy.

Henry's fears for the immediate future of his children were resolved in a variety of ways. William had inherited much of his father's intuitive practical ability, so it was easy to plan a future for him. Before leaving prison, the manager of the Yokohama Engine and Iron works of No.69 Creekside had invited Henry to take charge of the shipwright and carpentry side of their production as soon as he was released. Henry had agreed and realised he could find employment for William in the yard but, looking to the future, he knew that shipbuilding would progress further away from timber construction towards the use of metal and engine power. With this in mind, he enlisted the help of his new employers to secure a place for William in an international school for marine engineering. Helped by practical experience with his father, William became an extremely well-qualified marine engineer. His friendship with Prince Yoshihito grew after accepting a request to teach him to sail. Young Yoshihito was nominated Crown Prince in 1889 and ascended to the throne in 1912, still a young man but in better health.

Henry was soon made Managing Director of the Company and one of his first tasks was to design and build a schooner of 130 tons for the Guam trade to replace the *Beatrice* which, at about 60 tons, her captain found too small for the purpose. The new schooner was named *Esmeralda*. As managing director, Henry was required to meet clients from many countries and was responsible for entertaining them. This was difficult for a man without a wife, but for a man with two very able and presentable daughters it became a pleasure.

Emily and Beatrice agreed to act as hostesses for their father and entered into the spirit of entertainment with serious efficiency. The cook and servants were carefully instructed and furnishings rearranged to accommodate the extra guests. Clients and Henry's friends were flattered when the girls, who finally mastered eight languages, including Russian, answered each in his own tongue. They admired the smooth courteous manner of the servants and the detailed attention to their comfort, never realising that the girls were putting into practice what they had experienced in the Palace. Several guests let Henry know that they found the girls attractive and asked permission to pursue the possibility of marriage, but Beatrice was too young and Emily already had ideas of her own.

Henry's position in the Company required meticulous attention to financial accountability. To ensure this, he employed George Warnecke as the firm's accountant on a half-time basis. Emily often met him at the works and as a guest at the house. She enjoyed his easy company, he was a convincing flatterer, and she was fascinated by his mental agility with figures and mathematics, a subject she had found difficult to master. Conversation with him in German was just one more attraction in a whirlwind romance. Within a month they were seeking Henry's permission to marry. He was not entirely happy with the idea. Emily was only eighteen and, although he could not fault Warnecke from experience and had seen no recent signs of drinking to excess, he did not feel he knew enough about the man. Finally, Emily pestered her father into submission and he agreed to their engagement. She promised to continue to help Beatrice at the house whenever possible, even after the wedding. In fact, loyalty between the sisters never wavered throughout their lives.

On 31st August 1877, Emily married George Warnecke at the German Consulate in Yokohama.

The Japan Weekly Mail.

" FAIS CE QUE DOIS: ADVIENNE QUE POURRA !"

YOKOHAMA: SATURDAY, SEPTEMBER 3RD, 1887.

MARRIAGE.

On 31st August, at the German Consulate, Yokohama, G. H. W., youngest son of Detrich Warnecke, Province of Hanover, to EMILY J. V., eldest daughter of Henry Cook, of Yokohama.

42

Beatrice Rebels

Beatrice,who was to become my grandmother, could not overcome the underlying shame she felt because her father had been in prison. Although she remained loyal in her service to him, she tried by every means to keep the scandal from future generations of the family - and almost succeeded. Why was it that Japanese and foreign residents of Yokohama did not share her sentiments? They continued to respect him and valued his friendship in spite of his public disgrace. Even Abbott still sought Henry's company after four years of stupid, legal wrangling. They seemed to have decided that Henry must have been driven to act out of character.

In 1888 there surfaced a possible clue to the mystery. It hinted that deep within himself, and reflected in his attitude to others, Henry valued the dignity and endeavours of people regardless of their race and position, and readily gave of his experience to help them. They were simple values, but to have exercised them in the amoral atmosphere of early Yokohama perhaps reveals Henry Cook to have been quite a remarkable man.

It began back in 1884 and early '85 when Henry occasionally worked for the Mitsubishi Company to supplement his meagre income. The company's main work was the repair of ships. He became aware of a young thirteen-old Japanese boy and was struck by his serious and strenuous attitude to the work. Henry made a point of showing him easier methods of doing the work and giving him instruction as seemed appropriate. Henry was impressed by the boy's eagerness to learn and ability to act on advice. The boy was Takejiro Yamada, adopted son of Shusuke Yamada. The art of iron shipbuilding was still in its infancy in Japan and there was no college to teach the subject. He was trying to gain the skills and knowledge through an apprenticeship at Mitsubishi but the training was far from adequate. While still only sixteen years of age, Takejiro's adopted father died leaving the family dependent on him.

By chance, Henry was talking to a client from Mitsubishi and asked after

Takejiro. On being told of the boy's predicament, Henry arranged for him to join the Iron Works and personally supervised his tuition. In a surprisingly short time, Henry put this young man in charge of an important section of the factory. Takejiro contributed to the improvement in iron quality and craftsmanship and went on to found his own company, the Iron and Shipbuilding Company at 3559 Banchi, Aokicho, which he ran like one big family. Even fifty years after Henry's death, several Japanese families continued to express their obligation to Henry Cook's generosity. It would seem that Yokohama's verdict was probably correct.

Experience gives no guarantee of immunity from mishap. Henry's last major construction for the Engine and Iron Works before his retirement was a whaling schooner which had been built on a piece of ground, adjoining the Pacific Mail's coal wharf, considerably above high water level. The vessel could be safely launched only by cutting a gap in a wall on the seaward side and excavating a channel to provide sufficient depth of water at high tide. On 25th April 1891, when the tide was right, Miss May Wheeler, watched by her parents Dr. and Mrs Wheeler, broke a bottle of wine on the vessel's bows and named her the "Narwhal". The ship slid towards the sea but after moving nearly a length, it came to a sudden halt. The channel had not been made sufficiently deep! Henry was in charge of the launch and his wide experience in salvage had to compensate for his earlier miscalculation.

The *Narwhal* was shored up until the next day's high tide, by which time the channel had been adequately excavated. The Wheeler family very sportingly turned up to witness the final launch. Two tugs were brought in to supplement the effort but as they took up the strain, Henry was struck in the face by a tautening rope. Dr. Wheeler rushed over to him but, although he was suffering from a cut forehead and some degree of shock, Henry's injuries were not considered serious. The *Narwhal* slid safely into deep water followed by cheers of relief.

After near tragedy came comedy! The *Narwhal* was towed out to a buoy in the harbour and a watchman left on board. During the night a wind blew up, the pin of the shackle dropped out and the *Narwhal* began a voyage of exploration and discovery about the harbour. The watch on board the *Monocacy* was surprised to see a mastless vessel slip alongside quite sociably and, seeing no-one on board, they made a rope fast to her. In the morning, the future captain of the *Narwhal* saw her attached to the *Monocacy* and went to investigate. There being nobody on deck, he went below and there found the watchman asleep. He had slumbered 'watchfully' through it all! On 4th April 1892 tragedy returned when that same captain was washed overboard in bad weather and his body was never recovered.

Now that iron was beginning to supersede his beloved timber for shipbuilding, Henry seriously considered retiring from the mainstream of trade to go into business in a more leisurely manner constructing small boats for sport and pleasure. The deaths of several contemporary settlers had perhaps encouraged this idea. His old business partner, adversary and friend, Captain Abbott, died in May 1892. Early in the previous year Mr. Henry Harding died. He was one of Inspector Peter Peacock's company of Legation Police who escorted Sir Harry Parkes at the time of the assassination attempt. Peter Peacock was still alive and a regular visitor to Henry's house. Peter was one of the very few western men officially to marry a Japanese woman at that time. He and his wife, Sato, had a daughter and a son, Charles. Born in 1886 in Tokyo, baby Charles had become a chubby six-year old and Beatrice had become quite fond of him and his quaint manners. He became a link in the nostalgia that she hoped to recapture when, many years later, she tried to arrange for her own daughter to marry him.

Henry retired in the summer of 1892 and Beatrice could see that it was a good time to follow her sister's example and get married now that her father had less need of her. She was twenty years old and had set her heart on a French diplomat's son who was successfully trading in silk between France and Japan. He was equally devoted to Beatrice. Full of excitement she sought her father's consent, but he would have none of it. George Warnecke had become an unhappy choice for Emily as he drifted back into his old drinking habits and spent too much time away from home. Henry was adamant and did not bother to choose his words carefully - one damned foreigner was enough in the family and he had no intention of allowing another. Beatrice was terribly hurt and could never forgive him. She could not see that he was tactless in his worry for her. Her French suitor had to return to France and could not remain to fight his case. Before leaving he promised to make arrangements for her to follow him.

A few weeks later, word came to Beatrice from the young man's father that a passage had been secured for her if she could take advantage of it. She confided in Emily and enlisted her help in a conspiracy to leave. Henry's suspicions must have been aroused by his daughter's tense manner and the extra activity in her own room. The sisters were sure they had left for the harbour unobserved but Henry was waiting ahead of them and thwarted the escape at the quayside. He was an old hand at running away!

Beatrice, who had become accustomed to being obeyed without question, felt compelled to act out of frustration and spite against her father. There had been several potential suitors mentally rejected in past months in favour of her French boy. She placed all their names in a hat and picked one at random to be her husband. It was a recipe for bitterness which remained close to the surface for the rest of her life. The unsuspecting substitute candidate was Alexander McWhannell Wright, a thirty-eight year old chief engineer sailing with the P. & O. S.N. Company. He was a Scotsman from Perthshire. Already a widower and almost twice the age of Beatrice, he had never expected to succeed against more eligible rivals. In fact, he was a little in awe of her confident, aristocratic manner, a feeling which did not prevent him from acting on the broad hint he received from her.

When approached by Alexander, Henry was taken aback by his daughter's sudden change of heart, but he was relieved that she had 'come to her senses'. He gave his consent though not sure he was making the right decision. Emily was opposed to the idea but agreed to support her sister when she recognised a stubborn determination. The marriage took place on 5th July 1893, with Emily and her husband as chief witnesses.

The Japan Weekly Mail.

YOKOHAMA: SATURDAY, JULY 8TH, 1893.

MARRIAGE.

On the 5th inst., at the Roman Catholic Church, before Rev. Alfred Pettier, and afterwards at Christ Church, before Rev. E. Champneys Irwine, M.A., BEATRICE MARION, youngest daughter of Henry Cook, of Yokohama, to ALEXANDER WRIGHT, of Perthshire, Scotland. No cards.

From the start Beatrice knew that she had made a grave mistake but the same stubborn pride made her honour that decision, though her family had to suffer in consequence. From the first night of marriage she was tempted to run away in disgust. In an attempt to make himself appear more eligible, Alexander had given the impression that his father was a wealthy gentleman farmer. After all, Scotland was a long way off! When circumstances led Beatrice to Scotland some years later, she discovered that her father-in-law and relatives were humble crofters. This so outraged her self-engendered sense of dignity and social position that poor Alexander suffered her scorn and resentment for the remainder of his long life.

43
Joy And Sorrow In Retirement

Henry retired to a shipbuilding yard that he had often used in the past at No.187 Honmoku, situated across the Creek, close to the harbour and open sea. Here he extended a small residence on the site and employed a few skilled carpenters. He recaptured his love of timber by constructing some highly successful rowing craft, including racing boats for rowing clubs of the Tokyo and Yokohama schools. He signed over his old premises at No.115 Creekside, including the house, to Emily and her husband. George Warnecke had been made redundant by Henry's retirement and Henry had felt obliged to help them.

George had no technical experience in the repairing of ships, so he went into partnership with a Captain Peterson who was qualified in the servicing of engines and boilers. They were short of capital and resorted to using a considerable number of young 'apprentices'. Inadequate supervision in their first months of business led to an incident which might have ended in a very large loss of life. A sampan containing an incredible forty to fifty boys was despatched to the steamer *Bellona* to carry out some work on the boilers. As the sampan came alongside, the boys, anxious to climb on board, rushed to the gunwales and capsized her. All were thrown into the water. A terrible struggle then ensued but fortunately ended with everyone accounted for except two, who were presumed drowned. It was a hard lesson but the business began to prosper, helped by the good housekeeping and public relations organised by Emily.

Two developments in the family brought great pleasure to Henry. His son William qualified so well as a marine engineer that he secured a position with the great Japanese shipping company, Nippon Yusen Kaisha. He became a chief engineer and one of the best known foreign employees of the company. William also continued his friendship with the Crown Prince and became adviser to him on maritime matters. The other joy was the birth of his first grandchild. Beatrice gave birth to a son on 13th November 1894 at their home

LATER DEVELOPMENT, SOUTH OF THE CANAL, YOKOHAMA. 1889.

268 The Bluff. He was baptised "Andrew John" and was registered under the British Consulate, Yokohama. He was destined to become my father.

Two years later Beatrice came near to death at the birth of a second son. There was difficulty with the delivery and she was attended by a German doctor who resorted to the use of instruments. The doctor omitted to take the precaution of sterilising his instruments so that, not only did he fail to save the baby, but he also left Beatrice with severe internal infection.

Beatrice's son, Andrew, with his nurse -
Photograph by Farsari, 1895

Emily helped to nurse her sister back to health with mixed feelings of love and impatience - impatience because it delayed plans of her own. Her husband had been spending more time away from home since his partnership with Peterson had prospered. He often returned in a drunken state, which sickened her, and his unwarranted abuse humiliated her in front of the servants. Her disgust peaked when she found, in one of his jacket pockets, a ticket from the main Yokohama brothel or *Yoshiwara*. Her decision to leave him had been postponed while nursing Beatrice. She confided her intention to Beatrice and to her father, neither of whom tried to change her mind. Biding her time, she made private arrangements with the captain of a merchant vessel leaving for San Francisco and, by this means, avoided detection through the official sailing lists.

When George Warnecke discovered what had happened, his anger drove him into further bouts of drinking and he became a liability to the business. A resulting period of illness brought him to his senses and to a strong desire to be reconciled with Emily. He set about trying to trace her without success and finally realised she must have left the country. It was by chance that he recognised her handwriting on a letter at the house of a mutual friend and saw that the postmark was "San Francisco". Determined to find his wife, he sold out to Peterson, who was delighted to be rid of him, and took passage for America. The business became known as the Peterson Engineering Company.

Persistent enquiry gradually led George to the area where Emily was living and finally to her actual address. On the morning he had decided to make his presence known to her, he went into a drugstore for early refreshment. While sipping a drink and rehearsing his next move, the strain of the past weeks and the anticipation of meeting Emily proved too much for a constitution weakened by years of dissipation. He suffered a major heart attack and died in the store. Emily came to know of her husband's presence and death only because her address was found in one of his pockets. Although she felt compassion for the sorry state in which she found him, she had no regrets for her action and went forward into a successful new life.

Back in Yokohama Beatrice, like most wives of seamen, had long periods when her husband was away from home. Young Andrew had been photographed with his Japanese nurse at the Farsari studio so that his father could have a copy in his cabin while at sea.

Beatrice also had a portrait taken which revealed what an attractive young woman she had become. She began to expand her interests in the community

Beatrice Marion Cook - Photograph by Farasari 1895.

and took part in many of the social occasions. Her friendship with Peter Peacock and his family had deepened since he had spent more time on Legation business in Yokohama, although still attached to the British Legation in Tokyo.

This safe routine of the social round was brought to an end by a war in a far away continent. Britain became involved in the second Boer War against the Transvaal and Orange Free State, beginning in 1899, and the British government commandeered vessels of the P. & O. Company for transportation of troops and supplies. This meant Alexander would be permanently away from Yokohama and in the future would be based in England. Beatrice had no option but to follow him; in effect to emigrate to a 'foreign' country with all the traumas that could involve. With Andrew then five years old and ready to begin school, it was probably better to make the move sooner rather than later.

Wives and children of P. & O. officers were allowed free passage in company vessels but were not allowed to travel on the same ship as the husband. On 24th July 1900, Henry accompanied his daughter and grandson to the harbour where they were to embark on the P. & O. ship *Rohilla* which was scheduled to sail for Hong Kong on the following day. From there Beatrice would join a different ship bound for England. She was terribly sad at leaving the country and the Japanese people she had come to love. Both she and Henry were in tears as they finally said "goodbye". They had faced many joys and sorrows together and, although she could not forgive the stigma of his time in prison, she loved him in a very special way.

As Henry turned to leave, he knew they would never meet again and a little more of his fighting spirit left him. Instead of going straight back to his home, he climbed the hill to the Bluff and the cemetery where he shared his sorrow with Mary Julia. The journey home tired him more than usual.

THE JAPAN WEEKLY MAIL. [July 28, 1900.

PASSENGERS.

DEPARTED.

Per British steamer *Rohilla*, for Hongkong via ports :—Mrs. A. Wright and son, Mr. J. S. Haines, Mrs. Ho, Mrs. Loo Lee Man, Mrs. Loo Yne She and two children, Mrs. Loo Wai Tong and two children, Mr. R. Masujima, and Mr. H. E. Reynell, in cabin ; 12 Chinese and 2 infants, in steerage.

Rohilla, British steamer, 2,216, C. H. S. Tocque, 25th July,—Hongkong via Kobe and Nagasaki, Mails and General.—P. & O. S.N. Co.

44
The Final Years

Failing health began to restrict Henry's activities, and friends began to notice that his conversation turned more frequently to reminiscences of the early days in Yokohama. Seriously concerned that such memories should not be lost, he was asked on several occasions to commit them to paper, but he always declined. Indeed, he probably lacked the ability to attempt such a task. A severe attack of potato blight throughout the Tokyo area took him back even further into early childhood memories. The crippling hardships experienced by the peasants of Ireland were not likely to be repeated in Japan where rice was the staple of the people. It certainly would not influence the direction of Henry's life a second time.

Far away in England, on 22nd January 1901, Queen Victoria died. The British residents in Yokohama organised various commemorative ceremonies in public and in the Christian churches. Henry attended several of these occasions, caught up in the patriotic euphoria of the British community, but his true feelings about the Queen were very vague. In contrast, the reality of the Emperor of Japan was crystal clear through personal contact; Japan would be Henry's home for the rest of his life.

One ceremony at which Henry could not be present because of ill health was on 24th March 1906 when his old friend, Peter Peacock, was decorated with the M.V.O. for his loyal service of over forty years with the Legation Police. It was presented to him by the visiting Prince Arthur of Connaught. Peter Peacock was liked and respected by all who knew him and not least by members of the British Consular Service in Japan. During the following May, Peter was in Yokohama on service matters and called in to see Henry. It was the last day of the month and Peter was returning on his bicycle to the station when he suddenly collapsed and died. He was taken to the General Hospital. Disregarding medical advice, Henry attended the funeral service at Christ Church and joined the procession which followed the hearse to the cemetery, now so familiar to him. It was a defiant gesture against his increasing weakness and reliance on others.

Four months later, on 27th September 1906, Henry died in his home at Honmoku, comforted by his son William and his Japanese servants. Yokohama's oldest foreign resident and colourful link with the first day of its opening to the western world had passed into memory and history. Henry was laid to rest with Mary Julia and their infant son, surrounded by a crowd of Japanese and western friends led by his son, William Henry Cook, who would continue his father's respect for the Japanese people.

APAN DAILY HERALD, FI

DEATH OF MR. HENRY COOK.

THE OLDEST FOREIGN RESIDENT IN JAPAN.

By the death of Mr. Henry Cook, which, as briefly announced in our last issue, occurred at his residence at No. 187, Honmoku, yesterday, at the age of 72, the oldest foreign resident in Japan has been removed. Mr. Cook was born in Ireland, and when a boy emigrated to the United States with the object of learning the trade of a shipwright. In the early fifties, however, he came to the East in a sailing ship, and, landing at Shanghai, was for several years engaged in the shipping trade on the China coast. In 1856 Mr. Cook arrived at Nagasaki, and from there was engaged in shipping business with Shanghai. Hearing that Yokohama had been thrown open to foreign trade, Mr. Cook proceeded northward, only to find when entering the bay that Mr. Harris, the first American Minister to Japan, was still negotiating with the Japanese for the opening of the port, and consequently he had to wait in the bay for three days before entering. Mr. Cook's ship was therefore the first foreign merchant vessel to enter the port of Yokohama. One trip was later made to Nagasaki, and then Mr. Cook settled in Yokohama, where he has resided permanently ever since. Shortly after his arrival Mr. Cook commenced business as a boat builder and shipwright and was very successful, the oldest yacht in Yokohama to day—the *Mosquito*—being built at Mr. Cook's yard some thirty years ago.

At one time Mr. Cook carried on an extensive business at No. 115, Creekside, the site now occupied by Petersen's ironworks. Mr. Cook was also very successful in the construction of rowing craft, and only last year he built several racing boats for the rowing clubs of the Tokyo schools and the Yokohama Commercial School. Of late years Mr. Cook has resided at Honmoku, where his shipbuilding yard was established. Some years ago he married an Irish lady, who was on a visit to Japan, by whom he had issue—one son and two daughters, the son being a chief engineer in the service of the Nippon Yusen Kaisha, while the two daughters are married and reside abroad.

The deceased, who survived his wife by several years, was a very old member of the Masonic Order, being a charter member of the Scotch Lodge and of Lodge "Otentosama." For several years he has been in indifferent health. Mr. Cook's reminiscences of the "early days" in Japan were naturally always of interest, and he would often entertain his friends with tales of the early period of foreign intercourse with this country. Unfortunately, however, he could never be persuaded to put them in writing. By his death the oldest foreign resident has been removed, and another link binding the stirring days of forty years ago with the present has been severed.

The funeral take places this afternoon.

The "Japan Daily Herald" reported Henry's death and gave a fairly accurate resumé of his life. This newspaper cutting was found in the Family Bible, once sent to Henry by his sister from Cardiff, and returned to Beatrice in England after William's death in 1937. It was curiosity about this solitary piece of evidence, supporting family tradition, that led to four years of exciting research and the writing of this book. We end with the cuttings which prompted the beginning.

THE JAPAN WEEKLY CHRONICLE.
October 4th, 1906.

DEATH OF MR. HENRY COOK.

AN OLD FOREIGN RESIDENT IN JAPAN.

By the death of Mr. Henry Cook, which occurred at his residence at No. 187, Honmoku, on the 27th ultimo, at the age of 72, one of the oldest foreign residents in Japan has been removed.

The funeral of Mr. Cook took place on Friday evening, the first portion of the service being held in the Catholic churh. Mr. W. H. Cook, son, was chief mourner, while among the old residents who followed immediately in rear of the coffin were Captain Eckstrand, Captain Carst and Messrs. Julius Helm and E. H. Mudgett. Many floral wreaths were sent by friends, testifying to the respect in which deceased was held by foreigners and Japanese alike.

MAY HE REST IN PEACE

THE ORIGINAL GRAVE OF HENRY AND MARY JULIA before its destruction in the earthquake of 1923.

An exact replica was erected later at the request of his elder daughter, Emily, who was living in San Francisco.

THE PRESENT GRAVE OF HENRY AND MARY JULIA after its re-erection by S. OKAMOTO in 1957.

The replica of the original tombstone was totally obliterated in a bombing raid during the Second World War.

Postscript

Henry William COOK. 3rd April 1836 - 27th Sept. 1906

The great earthquake of 1923 destroyed the family grave in the Foreign Cemetery at Yokohama. Emily financed the erection of an exact replica made possible by early photographs of the original. The second grave was totally obliterated by American bombing towards the end of the Second World War. A Japanese family, who still wished to honour a debt of gratitude to Henry, erected a very substantial stone tomb of different design but with identical inscriptions. It is sited in a different part of the cemetery and the Japanese family has made a permanent link with Henry by adding - "ERECTED RENEW BY S. OKAMOTO 12 1957"
Henry was featured as the first shipwright in an exhibition of "YOKOHAMA FIRSTS" researched and arranged by the Yokohama Archives of History (Yokohama Kaikō Shiryōkan). Several of their publications refer to him. We have had a most rewarding visit and a mutual exchange of information and photographs concerning Henry Cook's life in Yokohama.

Mary Julia BUTLER COOK. 1839 - 18th Feb. 1878.

She was disinherited by her family when she married in 1867 and all contact was lost. Her early death at the age of 39 when Beatrice was only five years old resulted in a paucity of detail about her early life in Ireland.

Emily Julia COOK WARNECKE later AUSTIN. 2nd July 1869 -
13th Feb. 1948.

After the death of her first husband, Emily married a wealthy timber merchant by the name of "Austin" and continued to live in San Francisco. Her linguistic ability helped her to secure employment with the U.S. Immigration Authority at Angel Island, San Francisco. She became one of their chief officers with special responsibility for Japanese immigrants. All foreigners wishing to enter the United States via San Francisco had first to report to Angel Island, where their papers and suitability were scrutinised. Only those Japanese from aristocratic families were accepted for high-class positions in the country. The lower classes were allowed to enter if considered suitable for manual work.

When interviewing the first-class passengers from ships, it became her practice to speak to them in Court Japanese to verify claims of nobility. False claimants would not have understood her questions or conversation. This was her personal seal:-

Emily continued to wear Japanese costume at home whenever possible. Unlike her sister, she was willing to talk about her life in Yokohama to Beatrice's daughter, Mary, who stayed with her in San Francisco for a short time in 1930. Mary's memory of these conversations initiated several fruitful lines of research. Emily died while visiting friends in Auburn, New York. Her body was returned to California and buried at Holy Cross Cemetery in the county of San Mateo.

William Henry COOK. 6th July 1871 - 19th Jan. 1937.

Trained as a marine engineer, William was Chief Engineer with Nippon Yusen Kaisha until retirement at 45. He then joined Nickel & Lyons as manager of Shinzaike Yard, near Kobe. He always had a keen interest in yachting and built small sailing boats and dinghies for the Kobe Sailing Club's fleet and the yacht *Thetis*. He took Japanese citizenship and married but had no children. He was buried at the Kasugano Cemetery, Kobe. His gold watch and chain, inherited from his father Henry Cook, was sent to England to his nephew (my father), Andrew Wright, under the terms of his Will and was received in November 1939 before the entry of Japan into the War. My grandmother also received some documents and records, handwritten on vellum, which we suspect were Court transcripts of the trial. They were put on a bonfire at Ross and lost for ever!

Beatrice Marion COOK WRIGHT. 11th Oct. 1872 - 9th Feb. 1958.

After leaving Japan, Beatrice and Andrew, aged six, went to Scotland to visit her husband's family. A house had been prepared for her at the Crook of Devon, Kinross, Perthshire, but she was shocked by the lowly social standing of the crofters, having anticipated that her father-in-law was a gentleman farmer. The anti-Catholic bigotry of the Scots in that area also contributed to her decision to leave and go to Ireland.

The Butler family, on the other hand, were wealthy and she felt unable to keep up with their way of life in Ireland, so she finally decided to make her home in England. The P. & O. ships docked at Tilbury, so Ilford in Essex was a convenient base. She took an active part in church work and gave instruction to those wishing to embrace the Catholic faith. They spent many years in Ilford, even after her husband's retirement, and then moved to Ross-on-Wye in Herefordshire some years before the Second World War. Alexander died there at the ripe old age of 93. Beatrice continued to live at Ross until she moved into convent Homes at Cinderford and Letchworth. Finally she resided at Swanage in a Red Cross Home. She died at the age of 85 and was buried there.

Andrew John WRIGHT. 13th Nov. 1894 - 20th Feb.1941.

Andrew went to a boarding school at Dumfries and later qualified as a marine engineer with the P. & O. S.N. Co. like his father. One of the candidates for instruction in the Catholic faith by his mother was Helen Merckel; an introduction was arranged which led to their marriage on Aug.5th 1919. Two daughters were born to them, Joan Margaret on Sept.18th 1920, and Veronica Mary on 14th April 1922. When serving as Chief Engineer in India, Andrew was invalided home in 1938 and underwent treatment for a tumour behind the eye. After a long and difficult period of illness in 1940-41, he died at the early age of 46, before the wedding of his daughter Veronica in October of that year.

Beatrice Mary WRIGHT, HAMER, PEACOCK, now HAMER.
(Born 2nd Jan.) 1907 - Still living.

Beatrice Marion's daughter was always known as "Mary" to avoid confusion. She was twelve years younger than her brother, who was away at school or college during her childhood. She spent some time at boarding school in Southwark, but most of her education was with the Ursuline nuns at Forest Gate, E.London. She became governess to the children of several well-known families and finally to the Duff Gordons at Credenhill in Hereford. She met and married Joshua Hamer in 1941 and lived in Credenhill until after his death in 1958. Charles Peacock, son of the family friends in Japan, wrote to Mary after his death and a friendship was established, as her mother had always wanted. They married in Hereford on 4th July 1959.

Charles Francis Xavier PEACOCK. 4th Feb. 1886 - 6th March 1972.

Son of Inspector Peacock, M.V.O., of the Legation Police in Japan, Charles had come to England with his Japanese mother after his father's death. He had an aunt living in Ilford and it was natural that Beatrice and Charles would keep in touch. He always carried a photograph of Mary and, with the encouragement of her mother, had nurtured a forlorn hope of eventual marriage. When Mary was widowed in 1958, he saw an opportunity to end the lone existence since his mother's death at the age of 99 two years earlier. A bachelor for seventy-three years and brought up in a very different culture by his Japanese mother, it was predictable that Mary and Charles would prove to be incompatible. Eventually, Charles became subject to fits of violence and had to be removed to hospital. He died in Hereford at the age of 87.

After his death, Mary changed her name by Deed Poll from Beatrice Mary Peacock back to "Hamer". All items belonging to the Peacock family, such as the MVO and citation, silver serviette rings from Sir Harry Parkes, deed box, etc. were unfortunately disposed of by Mary to remove unhappy memories.

GENEALOGY - 1825 to 1941

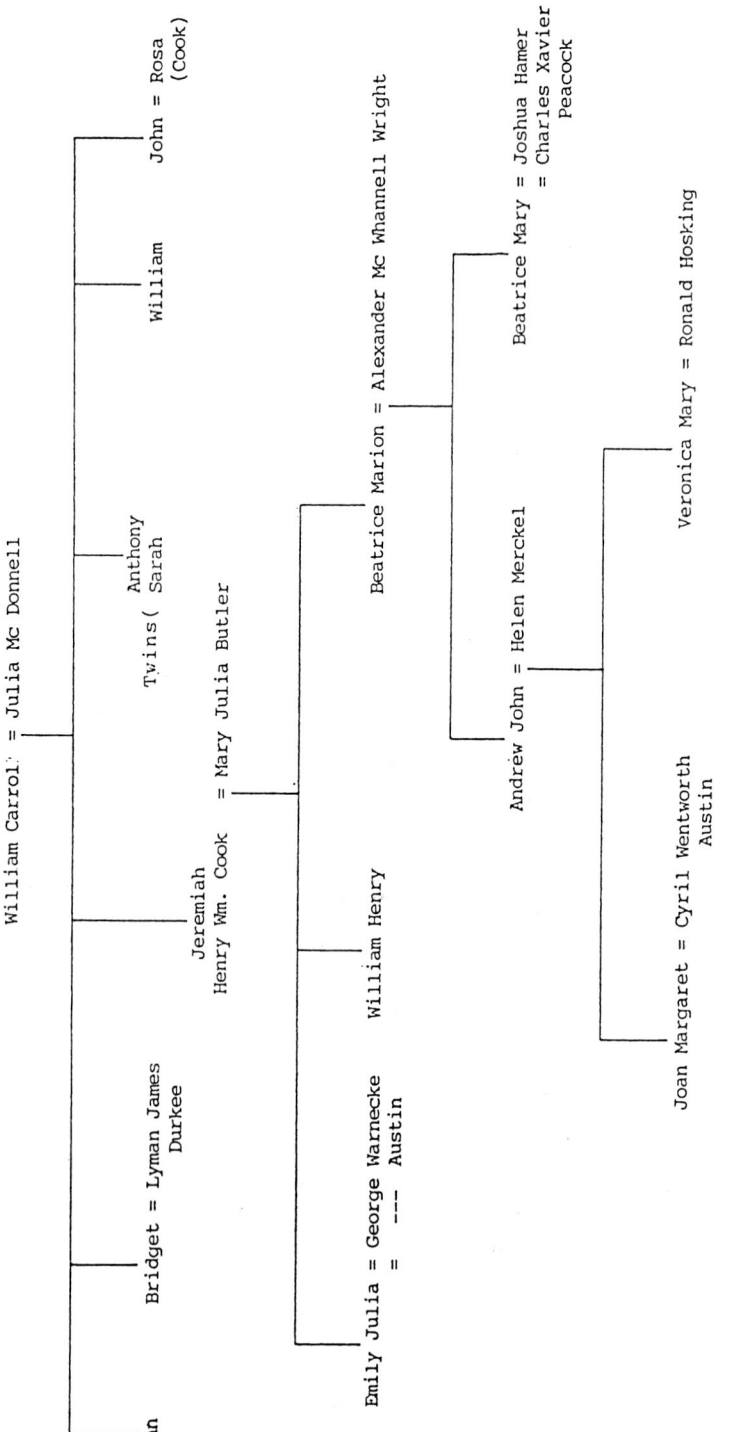

Bibliography

NEWSPAPERS.

THE NAGASAKI SHIPPING LIST AND ADVERTISER.
THE JAPAN HERALD.
THE JAPAN DAILY HERALD MAIL SUMMARY.
THE JAPAN WEEKLY MAIL.
THE JAPAN FORTNIGHTLY MAIL.
THE JAPAN WEEKLY CHRONICLE.
THE FAR EAST.
THE JAPAN TIMES.

BOOKS.

BLACK John R.: "YOUNG JAPAN". London, 1880 -81. Reprint, Oxford University Press 1968.

HAFFNER Christopher: "THE CRAFT IN THE EAST". District Grand Lodge of Hong Kong and the Far East. Hong Kong, 1977.

HAWKS Francis L. (Compiler): "THE EXPEDITION OF AN AMERICAN SQUADRON TO THE CHINA SEAS AND JAPAN. COMMODORE M.C.PERRY". Beverly Tucker, Washington, 1856.

LEONARD Jonathan Norton, and the Editors of Time-Life Books: "EARLY JAPAN". Time-Life International, British Edition, 1976.

PINEAU Roger (Editor): "THE PERSONAL JOURNAL OF COMMODORE MATTHEW C. PERRY. THE JAPAN EXPEDITION 1852-1854". Smithsonian Institution Press, Washington, 1968.

SATOW Sir Ernest: "A DIPLOMAT IN JAPAN". Seeley, London, 1921. Reprint 1968.

STEPHAN John J.: "THE KURIL ISLANDS". Clarendon Press, Oxford, 1974.

STORRY Richard: "A HISTORY OF MODERN JAPAN". Penguin Books, 1968.

WOODHAM-SMITH Cecil: "THE GREAT HUNGER". Hamish Hamilton, London, 1980.

A manual - "CHINA SEA PILOT" Vol.III. 1982.